melv, 17182023

A SUDDEN FRENZY

A Sudden Frenzy

*Improvisation, Orality, and Power
in Renaissance Italy*

JAMES K. COLEMAN

UNIVERSITY OF TORONTO PRESS
Toronto Buffalo London

ISBN 978-1-4875-6344-8 (cloth)
ISBN 978-1-4875-6346-2 (EPUB)
ISBN 978-1-4875-6345-5 (PDF)

Toronto Italian Studies

Library and Archives Canada Cataloguing in Publication

Title: A sudden frenzy : improvisation, orality, and power in Renaissance Italy /
James K. Coleman.
Names: Coleman, James K., 1981– author.
Series: Toronto Italian studies.
Description: Series statement: Toronto Italian studies |
Includes bibliographical references and index.
Identifiers: Canadiana (print) 20210360097 |
Canadiana (ebook) 20210360143 | ISBN 9781487563448 (cloth) |
ISBN 9781487563462 (EPUB) | ISBN 9781487563455 (PDF)
Subjects: LCSH: Vocal music – Italy – 15th century – History and criticism. |
LCSH: Folk poetry, Italian – History and criticism. |
LCSH: Performance poetry – Italy – History and criticism. |
LCSH: Italian poetry – 15th century – History and criticism. |
LCSH: Improvisation (Music) – History – 15th century. |
LCSH: Humanism – Italy. | LCSH: Renaissance – Italy. |
LCSH: Italy – Civilization – 1268–1559.
Classification: LCC ML1433.2 .C65 2022 | DDC 782.4/3094509024 – dc23

We wish to acknowledge the land on which the University of Toronto Press operates. This land is the traditional territory of the Wendat, the Anishnaabeg, the Haudenosaunee, the Métis, and the Mississaugas of the Credit First Nation.

University of Toronto Press acknowledges the financial support of the Government of Canada, the Canada Council for the Arts, and the Ontario Arts Council, an agency of the Government of Ontario, for its publishing activities.

Canada Council   Conseil des Arts
for the Arts   du Canada

ONTARIO ARTS COUNCIL
CONSEIL DES ARTS DE L'ONTARIO
an Ontario government agency
un organisme du gouvernement de l'Ontario

Funded by the   Financé par le
Government   gouvernement
of Canada   du Canada

Canada

Contents

Illustrations

Acknowledgments

It gives me great pleasure to reflect, at the conclusion of this project, on the many people who have helped to make it possible.

I begin by thanking Giuseppe Mazzotta, who was my PhD advisor at Yale, and whose brilliant scholarship, teaching, and mentorship have been invaluable to me. I am also very grateful to Millicent Marcus, David Quint, Kristen Phillips-Court, Olivia Holmes, Angela Capodivacca, David Lummus, and Risa Sodi, all of whom enriched my time at Yale. I also wish to thank Michael Allen and Arielle Saiber for the generous mentorship they provided while I was completing my graduate studies, and subsequently.

I warmly thank my colleagues in the Department of French and Italian at the University of Pittsburgh: Renate Blumenfeld-Kosinski, Lorraine Denman, Chloé Hogg, Lina Insana, Giuseppina Mecchia, David Pettersen, Todd Reeser, Francesca Savoia, John Walsh, and Brett Wells. I count myself truly fortunate to work in such a collegial department. I owe a special thanks to our departmental administrator, Monika Losagio. Other Pitt colleagues whose perspectives I have particularly benefited from include Drew Armstrong, Jacques Bromberg, Shirin Fozi, Ryan McDermott, Christopher Nygren, Pernille Røge, Adam Shear, Jennifer Waldron, and Molly Warsh.

My interest in Florence's *canterini* was first sparked by Alessandro Duranti and Marco Villoresi of the University of Florence, and I remain very grateful to both. Numerous subsequent research trips to Florence have made this book possible, and I am grateful to the colleagues and friends who have provided guidance, support, and camaraderie during my time in Florence, including Maria Checchi, Gian Paolo Pazzi, Mary Doyno, Michael Howerton, Stefano Baldassarri, Jason Houston, and Stefano Zamponi.

My work has benefited greatly from conversations with many other colleagues, among whom I wish to thank in particular Albert Ascoli,

Laura Benedetti, Paul Richard Blum, Stephen Campbell, Jo Ann Cavallo, Christopher Celenza, James Hankins, Earle Havens, Timothy Kircher, Victoria Kirkham, Arthur Lesley, John McLucas, Leslie Morgan, Andrea Moudarres, April Oettinger, Alessandro Polcri, Valery Rees, Hollis Robbins, Marcello Simonetta, Walter Stephens, Jane Tylus, and Susan Weiss.

My work has been supported by a number of institutions. The University of Pittsburgh's Dietrich School of Arts and Sciences provided essential support in the form of a junior research leave semester in the spring of 2019, which gave me the precious time to finish writing the manuscript. I gratefully acknowledge the University of Pittsburgh European Study Center's financial support in the form of a faculty research grant. A recent fellowship at Villa I Tatti, the Harvard University Center for Italian Renaissance Studies in Florence, allowed me to embark on a new project in the 2019–20 academic year after finishing this book's manuscript; access to the I Tatti library then proved extremely helpful for me while completing revisions to this text in 2021. I especially thank I Tatti's director, Alina Payne, as well as Giovanni Pagliarulo, Michael Rocke, and all of the I Tatti librarians. I also thank the librarians of the Biblioteca Riccardiana, the Biblioteca Medicea Laurenziana, the Biblioteca Nazionale Centrale di Firenze, the Vatican Library, the Biblioteca Casanatense, and the libraries of Yale University (especially the Beinecke), Johns Hopkins University, and the University of Pittsburgh.

My editor, Suzanne Rancourt, has been extraordinarily helpful and a pleasure to work with; I thank her and everyone at University of Toronto Press who has contributed to this book's publication. I thank the two anonymous readers who reviewed the manuscript for their thoughtful feedback, from which the book has certainly benefited. I am grateful to Lisa Regan and TextFormations for their careful work on the book's index.

I thank my parents, siblings, and all my family for their love and support. It is poignant to write these words at a time when the COVID-19 pandemic has kept us apart for so long; may they emerge from the press in a time of renewed togetherness.

This book would not have been possible without the support of my wife, Elizabeth Archibald, who has patiently read and discussed my work in progress and, with her love and humour, has brought me more joy than I can say. My children, Eleanor and Samuel, have brightened every one of my days since their arrivals. I dedicate this book to you three, with my love.

A SUDDEN FRENZY

Introduction

Poggio Bracciolini's famous repository of Renaissance humour, the *Facetiae*, takes aim at a wide range of stereotypes that tempted the condescension of fifteenth-century humanists: daft peasants, oversexed women, corrupt clerics. One pair of tales, though, set their sights on a very particular cultural context: the oral performances of *canterini* who entertained popular audiences by singing about historical events and legends in verse. At one gathering of humanists described in the *Facetiae*, the topic of conversation turns, predictably, to the classical past – specifically, the decline and fall of the Roman Empire, which seems to cause acute personal distress to the humanist Ciriaco d'Ancona. As Poggio puts it, "Ciriaco d'Ancona, a verbose and overly talkative person ... seemed extremely troubled about this matter."[1] Ciriaco's emotional response to matters of the distant past – a "silly concern" (*stulta cura*) – prompts a taunt from Antonio Lusco, who laughs and responds: "This is just like the man from Milan who was listening on a feast day to one of the flock of singers who sing the deeds of heroes to the common people. When he heard the story of the death of Roland, killed in battle some seven hundred years earlier, he burst into tears."[2] In Lusco's account, the Milanese man returns home weeping and, when questioned by his wife about his tears, laments, "Alas, wife, I am done for! ... Do you not know what news I have heard today? ... Roland is dead, Roland, the lone protector of Christendom!" The Milanese woman has to talk her husband down from his "inane grief" (*insulsa moestitia*) before the couple can get on with dinner.

This anecdote, in turn, brings up another about a humanist's ridiculous Florentine neighbour, a "simple person" (*homo simplex*), who listens to a *canterino* performance that ends with an advertisement for the next day's material: *The Death of Hector*. Concerned for the well-being of the Trojan hero, the Florentine bribes the *canterino* to delay his performance of the episode for several days. Only when the spectator runs out of money does Hector finally meet his end – which the Florentine endures "with much pain and weeping."[3]

These anecdotes provide an illuminating glimpse of the attitudes held by Poggio and his circle of Latin humanists towards the oral poets of fifteenth-century Italy and their audiences. It is obvious from the Latin-language anecdotes that Poggio and his friends perceive the *canterini* as entertainers for a different social and intellectual group: these performers are defined, with mild contempt, as "the flock of singers who sing the deeds of heroes to the common people." However, the *canterini* themselves, while perhaps somewhat greedy, are not exactly the butt of the joke: the specific point of derision is the effect that these performances have on audiences of common people. It is the "inane grief," the weeping of the overcome listeners, that the anecdotes mock, and the point of the stories is to remind Ciriaco d'Ancona and his peers that his distress at the past is unbecoming for a humanist: the past is not the present, and the humanists are not the plebs. These jokes hinge on enforcing a dichotomy between cultural modes in fifteenth-century Italy. It is implicit that no serious comparison can be drawn between, on the one hand, the highly literate, Latinate, elite culture of Ciriaco, Poggio, and their rational humanist peers, and on the other, the oral, vernacular, popular culture of the *canterini* and their emotionally overwhelmed audiences.

The delineation of cultural categories carried out by Poggio and some of his contemporaries has held enduring influence. While scholars of Renaissance Italy have long been concerned with establishing the cultural contributions of the humanist movement led by Poggio and his peers, the latter cultural mode – the world of oral and improvised poetic performance – is a sector of Renaissance Italian cultural activity that has traditionally received far less scholarly attention. In the last decade, the oral poetry of early modern Italy has finally begun to attract more consideration from scholars. Recent work by scholars of Italian literature, including Marco Villoresi, Brian Richardson, and Luca Degl'Innocenti, has helped to reveal that the role of oral performance and improvisation in the vernacular literature of early modern Italy, especially in Florence and in the genre of chivalric literature, was more extensive than previously acknowledged.[4] Historians including James Hankins, Massimo Rospocher, and Rosa Salzberg have done important work situating the oral performers of Renaissance Italy in the contexts of intellectual and urban history.[5] Moreover, musicologists, particularly Blake Wilson, James Haar, Timothy McGee, and Philippe Canguilhem, have shed new light on improvised and unwritten varieties of musical performance in early modern Italy, connecting them with contemporaneous developments in written musical composition and with other cultural phenomena, from rhetoric to mnemotechnics.[6]

These recent studies have swept away the old paradigm that tended to see the oral and improvisational poetry of early modern Italy as a minor or marginal phenomenon; recognition is growing that oral and improvisational performers of poetry and music were a major cultural force in Renaissance Italy. Recent work has also helped clarify the status of Florence as one of the most vibrant Italian centres for this type of performance throughout the second half of the fifteenth century, when *canterino* performances regularly attracted large audiences of Florentines to the stage in Piazza San Martino dedicated to this genre of entertainment. While the prominence of the humanist movement in fifteenth-century Florence has long been recognized, it is now clear that the culture of oral poetic improvisation was a powerful presence in the same context: in fact, both can be said to have had their moment of greatest cultural impact and vitality in the fifteenth century and, while significant developments in both spheres took place in multiple centres across Italy, Florence was a particularly important centre of both activities.

There are distinct challenges inherent in studying the oral and improvisational poetry of the Renaissance. Surviving texts attributed to a poet who performed orally can offer at most a partial and incomplete picture of the performer's work. As contemporary accounts of such performances make clear, the impact of such performances depended on much more than the poetic text itself. Oral poets moved spectators with their performance skills: their aptitude as singers and instrumentalists, their ability to convey powerful emotions and stimulate an audience's imagination through voice, gesture, and bearing – extratextual aspects that are lost when we encounter such works as silent text on a page. The precocious humanist Michele Verino reflects on this problem in describing a performance by the acclaimed *canterino* Antonio di Guido that he witnessed in the 1480s, which he contrasts with the experience of reading the same poetry:

> Once in Piazza San Martino I heard a certain Antonio singing the wars of Orlando with such eloquence that I felt as if I were hearing Petrarch himself, and you would have thought you were participating in the battle, not merely hearing about it. Later I read his poems, and they were so rough that they seemed like different works.[7]

For the young Verino, Antonio di Guido is an illustration of the role that eloquence and rhetorical delivery play in the experience of the audience: in live performance, Antonio seems to rival the talent of Petrarch, but his words fall flat when read silently. But Verino's account also raises the important question of the relationship between written and oral versions of the poetry of the *canterini*: it is possible that the works that Verino later read actually *were* different works. Many, perhaps most, Renaissance *canterini* did not refer to any written notation (either musical or textual) during their performances, which could last for hours. Instead, they relied on a combination of their prodigious powers of memory and their training in extemporaneous composition.[8]

Capturing an oral performance in writing required special techniques, which are occasionally described or alluded to in surviving sources. Several scribes working together could alternate lines of verse and thus work quickly enough to record a relatively accurate version of a performed text. A team of scribes once transcribed a performance by Niccolò Cieco without his advance approval, provoking his ire about the unauthorized recording.[9] Another such team was tasked with recording the lengthy cycles of narrative poetry improvised by Cristoforo l'Altissimo.[10] Some Latin verses improvised by Aurelio Brandolini survive thanks to a transcription that a young Pietro Bembo made during the performance.[11] In these rare cases in which an explicit account of the circumstances of transcription survives, we can have some confidence that the surviving text reflects to a significant extent the text originally performed (although inaccuracies and later revisions could still complicate this picture). But in many other cases of written texts attributed to oral poets, it is impossible to determine to what degree, if at all, the surviving text reflects the original performance.

While extraordinary powers of memory were often attributed to *canterini*, the most renowned of these performers did not simply rely on verbatim memorization of poetry but composed their works on the spot in performances described by observers as "all'improvviso," "estemporaneo," and "ex tempore." To be sure, studies of the dynamics of improvisatory performance in other spheres (from the oral bards of the former Yugoslavia to present-day jazz musicians) alert us that improvisation is never simply a matter of pure, unstudied invention in the moment.[12] Rather, such techniques of composition-in-performance are made possible by the prior rehearsal and internalization of extensive sets of patterns and motifs that can be readily deployed and recombined, with potentially infinite variations, in the course of performance.

The degree to which oral poets of the Renaissance improvised the texts and the instrumental and vocal music they performed varied from one performer to another. Conventions also varied among different oral poetic genres: according to Blake Wilson, improvisation "was *de rigueur* for singers of epic verse (*cantari*)," while shorter oral poetic forms like the *strambotto*, although they could be improvised, were sometimes performed as fixed texts.[13] It is not always possible to say in the case of a given text, or the description of a given performance, whether (or to what extent) the work was improvised. The same oral performers engaged in both more and less spontaneous sorts of composition, as we see in the case of the poet Niccolò da Correggio, who reminisced about his career path in the dedication of one of his works to Isabella d'Este in 1491:

> I developed familiarity with the celebrated skill of playing the aforementioned lyre and, once I had adapted my language to the vernacular poetic style, I found myself, many times, the winner of poetic competitions. And having been crowned with garlands of laurel, as was the academic custom, I pressed on to loftier exercises. On one occasion, as a diversion, I was taking turns with others singing verses extemporaneously, each of us being assigned by the others a different topic to improvise on.[14]

In da Correggio's case, it is clear not only that he engaged in both spontaneous and more traditional styles of poetic composition, and performed in both modes, but also that he regarded the improvisation of verses as a particular challenge for a proficient oral performer.

Especially with the historical distance of many centuries, we might be tempted to wonder to what extent oral performers of poetry in early modern Italy who claimed to be improvising were actually composing extemporaneously. Of course it is possible – even likely, in some cases, as we will see – that performers amplified the extent to which they were composing extemporaneously in order to impress listeners (and readers) with the difficulty of their task. But to wonder whether it is genuinely possible to improvise verse and music successfully is to join a long lineage of doubters: improvisors in every era, including the fifteenth century, have faced the scepticism of audiences, and the relationship between improvisational performers and their wondering audiences is a central concern of this book. Like performers of improvisational comedy today, poetic improvisors in the Renaissance often attempted to prove their extemporaneity was genuine by soliciting suggestions of subject matter from those present, as in the game described by Niccolò da Correggio, or by opening a book at random for subject matter. And the fact that improvisation was often genuinely extemporaneous is also revealed by the fact that it sometimes fell flat. A description of the acclaimed improvisor Raffaele (also known as "Lippo") Brandolini serves to illustrate such pitfalls: on one occasion, Brandolini "was ordered by Leo X to compete with [Andrea] Marone in the festival of Cosmas and Damian celebrated by the Medici, but he came out defeated" when Marone "struck all the others (including Lippo) dumb, so to speak, as if they were tongueless."[15] Given that most descriptions of improvisational performance skew towards

breathless accounts of performative successes, the occasional reference
to an improvisor's off day reminds us that improvisation was something
of a high-wire act even for acclaimed professionals.

An amusing anecdote recounted by Lodovico Domenichi about an
improvisational performance by Niccolò Machiavelli gives a sense of the
risks involved. At the time, Machiavelli and company were playing an improvisational game: "In order that the topics not appear premeditated,
they opened books of ancient poetry at chance, such as Ovid's *Metamorphoses,* and according to the randomly encountered material, they sang
all'improviso."[16] It fell to Machiavelli to improvise the story of Venus and
Mars surprised in bed by Vulcan. Domenichi recounts the performance:

> Having briefly recounted in the first six verses how Vulcan, aware of the
> adultery of his wife, and wanting vengeance, constructed a thin net of iron,
> to catch both of the lovers with it while they were in the act, he ended in
> this way, saying:
>
> He threw the net, catching them tight
> Venus nude …
>
> And stopping there, he continued nevertheless to play the *lira,* as if he were
> thinking about finding the missing bit of the verse. One of the gentlewomen
> … spoke up: "Finish quickly, Messer Niccolò, because if you think about it
> so much, it won't be improvised." At which point Niccolò immediately and
> without further hesitation, taking up the end of the stanza from the begin-
> ning again, said:
>
> Vulcan threw the net and caught them tight
> Venus nude and Mars … upright.
>
> Blushing with embarrassment, the gentlewomen said, "Alas! What are
> you saying, M. Niccolò?" To which he responded, "This woman pressured
> me so much with her words that I didn't think about what was coming scan-
> dalously out of my mouth."[17]

According to this anecdote, even for a careful performer, true improvisation could have unpredictable and even scandalous results. It is also
worth noting the dynamics of the improvisational performance: when
Machiavelli attempts to fall back on instrumental music to buy some time
for his verse, spectators object on the grounds that he is breaking the
rules; the verse must be truly extemporaneous. And, while we cannot
know the precise relationship between this anecdote and historical fact,
it is worth observing that Machiavelli's second attempt at the couplet
presents a slightly different text than his first. All the details of this performance hint at the true spontaneity – and the difficulty – of such improvisational poetic performances.

Many of the poets and performers whose works are examined in this book – like Machiavelli – possessed not only skill and interest in oral and improvisatory poetic forms but also a high degree of literacy. For such poets, even in the case of works that might have originally featured improvisational elements, or that were performed orally, it would have been natural to revise the texts before or after committing them to writing. It is unwise to assume that the poetic texts we have access to consist of the unmediated product of extemporaneous composition or the exact transcript of an oral performance. This book, while assuming that such texts have been shaped by literate practices (of writing, revision, transmission, and so forth), aims to establish how they can be more fully understood when we consider their thematic and formal characteristics in light of an author's documented engagement with oral and improvisational performance traditions.

While a startlingly wide array of terms were used in fifteenth- and sixteenth-century Italy to designate practitioners of oral and improvisational poetic performance – *cantastorie, cantimpanca, dicitori, saltimbanchi* – this book will primarily use the term *canterino*, which was widely applied in the period to performers who sang narrative and lyric poetry, whether on the public stages set up for this purpose in the piazzas of many Italian cities or for private aristocratic gatherings.[18] It is thus a broader and more versatile term than some other related words (like *cantimpanca*, applicable only to those who performed on public stages). Skill in improvisation of text and music was widely cultivated among Italy's oral poets, and when discussing performers known for their improvisational abilities, the book will also use the Italian term *improvvisatore*.

The *canterini* specialized in particular poetic genres and metres, their most favoured being *ottava rima*.[19] Oral poets employed this metre for long narrative poems (known as *cantari*) and for shorter lyrical works (known as *strambotti* or *rispetti*).[20] *Terza rima* was also widely used by the *canterini*, both for long narrative *cantari* and for shorter works, sometimes called *capitoli*, which often dealt with moral or spiritual themes. Previous scholarship dealing with the influence of *canterino* poetry on humanist literary culture has mostly focused on the narrative chivalric *cantari* and their influence on the epic romances of humanist poets like Matteo Maria Boiardo and Ludovico Ariosto. But as this book will show, *canterino* performance traditions were a major cultural force whose influence on humanist literary culture extended far beyond the phenomenon of humanists authoring chivalric epic romances. The number of poets who experimented with the genre of epic romance was necessarily restricted by the scope of such an undertaking, since these narrative chivalric poems in *ottava rima* were traditionally monumental in length.

Shorter oral poetic forms with roots in *canterino* traditions – such as lyric *strambotti* in *ottava rima* and *capitoli* in *terza rima* – proved more accessible, and a wide range of humanist authors experimented with these forms.

In addition to techniques of improvisation, early modern Italian poet-performers relied on musical skill. Some were renowned for their beautiful singing voices, but oral performances of poetry did not always entail singing in the fullest sense of the term. Contemporary accounts sometimes use the word *cantare* ("to sing") to describe performances, but they also use *recitare* ("to recite"); the most common vocal style for these performers may have been to intone verses with melodic and rhythmic variations that produced something midway between song and speech.[21] Accompaniment frequently took the form of a single stringed instrument, usually played by the singer-poet but sometimes entrusted to another musician. In the late fifteenth century, the most common instrument for the purpose was what musicologists today refer to as the *lira da braccio*, a stringed instrument played with a bow. In the fifteenth century, *lira da braccio* was interchangeable with other terms: *viola* (or *viuola*), *cetra* (or *cithara*), and simply *lira* (or *lyra*) could all be used to designate this instrument.[22] Before the emergence of the *lira da braccio* in the late fifteenth century, Italian singer-poets favoured an earlier variety of bowed string instrument, a version of what is today called a vielle.[23] The terms *lyra* and *cithara* are broad and could designate instruments with either bowed or plucked strings; when used by early modern authors to describe contemporary performances, such terms, despite their classicizing forms, do not refer to reconstructions of ancient instruments. While most Italian *canterini* favoured instruments in the viol family (and, by the late fifteenth century, especially the *lira da braccio*), there are occasional references to *canterini* who performed on the lute instead.

The association between the singing of poetry and the playing of stringed instruments, especially the *lira da braccio*, became so commonplace in the late fifteenth and early sixteenth centuries that humanist authors from the period routinely use the Latin phrase "cantare ad lyram" as shorthand for the art form that combined the improvisation of poetry and music. The close link between these improvisational practices and the *lira* is evident in the description of Machiavelli's scandalous performance, where the instrument serves as a means of buying time for the improvisation of verse. Though they denoted the same instruments, the terms *viola*, *lira*, and *cetra* carried different connotations. Early modern writers who used the classicizing terms *lira* and *cetra* for the instruments of contemporary *canterini* often did so in order to emphasize a commonality or even continuity between the oral poets of the ancient world and contemporary performers. Cassio da Narni, in his popular romance *La*

Morte del Danese, offers a particularly classicizing description of one of the most famous *improvvisatori* of the early sixteenth century, Bernardo Accolti, known by the colourful toponymic "l'Unico Aretino" ("the Unique Aretine"), whose career will be discussed in chapter 5:

> You could then see the Unique Aretine, a new Orpheus, perform verses improvisationally with the *cetra* held under his chin, in a style so divine that for many years Apollo envied him.[24]

The instrument described as a "cetra" in this passage with antiquarian exuberance is clearly a *lira da braccio*; other sources confirm that Accolti customarily played that instrument, and the *lira da braccio* was the only instrument in this milieu that was held under the player's chin. Meanwhile, the description of Accolti as a "new Orpheus" exemplifies a common genre. In letters and poems, "New Orpheus" was a standard description for musicians, especially those whose genre of choice was the singing of verse to the accompaniment of the *lira*, and as the ancient figure of Orpheus took on new significance in the minds of Italian humanists, the concept of the New Orpheus did as well.[25] The role of improvisational performance in fifteenth-century culture was clearly both more prevalent and more complex than Poggio's dismissive attitude suggests, and two examples will serve here to illustrate the depth of the entanglements between improvisational practices and humanist culture.

Orpheus as *Canterino* and *Canterini* as Orpheus

Descriptions of performers like Accolti as modern-day versions or even reincarnations of Orpheus were supported, conversely, by a widespread tradition in visual art of the Quattrocento and early Cinquecento that sought to turn the ancient Orpheus into a contemporary *canterino*. When the Florentine painter Jacopo del Sellaio, sometime between 1480 and 1490, represented Orpheus on a series of three *spalliera* panels, he depicted the ancient poet with two sets of attributes that held particular resonance within his own late-Quattrocento Florentine milieu.[26] On the one hand, as scholars including Jerzy Miziolek have noted, Sellaio's Orpheus, with his beard, turban, coat, and tunic, seems to bear the iconographical attributes of a sage, prophet, or magus (see figure 1).[27]

These details probably reflect the influence of a new understanding of the Orpheus figure that was emerging in Florence. Thanks to the recent availability of "Orphic" texts translated by Marsilio Ficino, Orpheus came to be known not just as a renowned musician and protagonist of mythical stories but as a poet, hierophant, and conduit for divine poetic frenzy.

Figure 1. Jacopo del Sellaio, *Orpheus Charming Animals with His Music* (c. 1480–90). Kraków, Wawel Royal Castle National Art Collection. Photo credit: Alamy Limited.

Miziolek has argued that this new reputation of Orpheus is evident in the scene that appears in the upper right of the *spalliera*, where Orpheus is depicted fixing his gaze on the heavens, perhaps in a state of spiritual rapture (a possibility reinforced by his position just outside a small temple). States of divine frenzy, as we will see in chapter 2, were particularly associated with Orpheus in the writings of Marsilio Ficino, who was known to affect such states of rapture himself while performing Orphic hymns to the accompaniment of his *lyra*, according to contemporary accounts.[28]

On the other hand, Sellaio's Orpheus is not simply an ancient sage playing an ancient lyre. In the painting, Orpheus is depicted playing the *lira da braccio*, the instrument of the late-fifteenth-century *canterini*; when Orpheus performs surrounded by a crowd of charmed beasts, his stance evokes that of a contemporary *canterino* surrounded by his rapt audience. Similarly, in Antonio Tubini's 1500 Florentine edition of Angelo Poliziano's *Orfeo* and *Stanze*, we find a woodcut that depicts Orpheus charming wild animals with music played on what is unmistakably a *lira da braccio* (see figure 2).[29]

Within the printed text, this is a clear visual suggestion of convergence between the ancient Orpheus and contemporary *canterini*. However, it also creates an interesting extratextual allusion: as we will see in chapter 3, at the original performance of Poliziano's stage play *La Fabula di Orfeo*, whose text is contained in the volume, the role of Orpheus was played by the renowned improvisor Baccio Ugolini. Is this a depiction of Orpheus as a *canterino* or a *canterino* as Orpheus?

Given the degree of identification between Orpheus and contemporary improvisational practices, it is not surprising that Poliziano's stage

Figure 2. Angelo Poliziano, *Stanze, Orfeo* (Florence, 1500), woodcut. Metropolitan Museum of Art. Photo credit: Metropolitan Museum of Art/Art Resource, NY.

play was later adapted by an anonymous *canterino* for performance in the piazza. Thus Poliziano's drama took the new form of a narrative poem in *ottava rima*. A version of this orally performed *cantare* was then printed and sold, apparently to great enthusiasm, since it saw many editions. In this edition of *La historia de Orpheo*, printed between 1495 and 1500, we again find a woodcut of Orpheus playing the *lira da braccio* in typical *canterino* fashion (see figure 3).

Since the original oral performances of this *cantare* were probably executed by a *canterino* playing the *lira da braccio*, readers of these early printed editions would undoubtedly have connected the representation of Orpheus playing this instrument in the woodcut with contemporary *canterino* performers. The ambiguous blending of the visual representation of Orpheus and that of a contemporary *canterino* is even more pronounced in an edition of the same *cantare* from 1567 (see figure 4).

In the usual fashion, Orpheus performs for an enthralled crowd, but rather than the audience of exotic animals depicted in Sellaio's painting, here the audience is composed of two attentive dogs and a crowd of

Figure 3. *La historia de Orpheo* (Rome, c. 1500), frontispiece. Biblioteca Casanatense, Rome, Vol. Inc. 1612. Photo credit: Biblioteca Casanatense.

human admirers in contemporary dress. The scene as a whole is quite similar to contemporary representations of public performances by early modern *canterini*. Especially given the complicated mixed-media origins of the work – a drama performed by a *canterino*, turned into an oral performance by another *canterino*, turned into a printed book – the identification of the image is ambiguous. It is left to the viewer to decide whether the figure represented is the ancient singer-poet Orpheus or the early modern *canterino* who performed this *cantare*.

The ambiguity in these images of Orpheus as a Renaissance *canterino* (or Renaissance *canterini* as Orpheus) poses a challenge to the dominant paradigm in modern scholarship on Renaissance Italian cultural and intellectual preoccupations. Poggio's *Facetiae* clearly stakes out an opposition between the literate, Latinate culture of humanists and the oral, vernacular culture of the *canterini*, and this opposition has proven

Figure 4. *La historia et favola d'Orpheo* (Florence, 1567), frontispiece. Biblioteca Riccardiana, Florence, NAO 91; with the permission of the Ministero della Cultura.

persuasive to modern scholars in fundamental ways. For a long time, scholarship assumed that the sort of disdain towards vernacular oral poetic performers on display in Poggio's text was widely shared by Renaissance Italy's intellectual and cultural elite. Yet the reality of humanist responses to this oral and improvisatory tradition was far more complex. While some humanists nurtured the kind of supercilious and dismissive attitude towards popular *canterini* represented in Poggio's *Facetiae*, examining the larger landscape of the interactions between humanist thought and oral poetic practices in this time and place reveals a much richer and more nuanced picture. Fifteenth-century humanists, especially those based in Florence, were unquestionably preoccupied with the interpretation of written texts from the ancient past. However, their increasing aptitude for the study of these materials did not merely reinforce a boundary between humanist and "popular" culture, if such a boundary can be said to have existed: instead, it led humanists to a new appreciation for and interest in the phenomena of improvisation and oral poetic performance that surrounded them and led improvisors to adopt insights drawn from classical scholarship to reinforce their own

status and to generate new material. The visual elision of Orpheus with
the contemporary figure of the *canterino* in these examples, as well as
the obvious blending of modes (Latin and vernacular, written and oral,
humanist and "popular") around the literary figure of Orpheus, suggests
that improvisational performance was a dynamic site of cultural production in the fifteenth century.

The Voice and the Pen

A text from around the turn of the sixteenth century provides a second
counterpoint to Poggio's rather hostile anecdotes regarding the *canterini*.
The work, a poem in *ottava rima* by the Bolognese poet Giovanni Andrea
Garisendi (c. 1470–1525) that survives in two manuscripts, presents itself
as a debate between two characters, both improvising in verse. Relatively
little is known about Garisendi, but he was clearly integrated into the
culture of oral poetic performance; according to the text's modern editor, the poem may have originated as an improvised performance by Garisendi.[30] The poem's dedication to Lucrezia d'Este, half-sister to Isabella
d'Este, also hints at the significant but somewhat obscure role of women
as a constituency in the culture of poetic improvisation that took hold during the fifteenth and sixteenth centuries. While women did not perform
as *canterini* in the piazza, the humanist interest in improvisational verse,
combined with the active participation in poetic culture of high-profile
figures like Lucrezia Tornabuoni, opened the door to greater integration
of women in the culture of musical and poetic improvisation, especially
in the courts of the sixteenth century, as chapter 5 will discuss.

In the poem, the interlocutors turn to the subject of poetic improvisation itself, debating the value of improvised verse relative to that of
poetry written on a page. One interlocutor, Antiphylo, echoes the separation of cultural categories apparent in Poggio's *Facetiae*, observing that
"it seems that learned people do not have a high regard for things that
are said in improvised verses."[31] Antiphylo, too, subscribes to this position, arguing that "a well-thought-out verse, written out with a pen on
pristine pages" is superior to poetry improvised orally. He argues that,
while improvised verse disappears as soon as the poet finishes singing,
written poetry can endure and ensure the author's fame. The other interlocutor, Phylero, responds to Antiphylo's "false speech" by defending
the value of improvised poetry. For Phylero, "improvisational speech"
("l'improviso dir") is able to transcend "well-written ink" ("ben stillato
inchiostro") because of its greater power to move listeners.[32]

In this poetic debate we see articulated many of the questions discussed by commentators on the value of oral poetry in Quattrocento

Italy. Is oral poetry inferior because it is not written "with a pen on pristine pages"? Does oral poetry necessarily belong to illiterate culture? Does its ephemerality exclude it from the canonical literary tradition? Does improvised verse deserve the scorn of learned people? Or, on the other hand, does oral poetry have a particular value that "well-written ink" does not? And if so, what is that value? This particular poem – a debate between two improvisors, possibly originating as improvised verse – unsurprisingly comes to the defence of improvised poetry, but in doing so it also complicates the oppositional frameworks that underlie some of these questions. As evidence in favour of improvised verse, Phylero cites the power of Orpheus's singing: "The lover Orpheus with his song and with his *cetra* / took away the fury of every monster of the underworld."[33] These lines clearly illustrate that Garisendi (and presumably many among his readers) considers Orpheus an oral poet comparable to contemporary *improvvisatori* – a significant piece of Marsilio Ficino's intellectual platform regarding both Orpheus and oral poetry, and an important argument underpinning humanist valorization of improvised oral poetry as a cultural form. Phylero's argument also isolates the central fascination of improvised oral verse for fifteenth-century commentators: its evident power to move listeners, whether they be wild beasts, Poggio's "simple people," or humanists.

This argument in favour of the power of improvised oral verse reveals the instability of hierarchical frameworks valorizing classical models and "well-written ink." Like Phylero and Antiphylo, many thinkers in the fifteenth and sixteenth centuries examined the value and role of improvised verse, and their considerations took them down some surprising paths as they sought to understand the power of extemporaneity. Did the frenzy of improvisation completely transcend the value of traditional composition? Was extemporaneous verse more valuable if its practitioners were not traditionally learned, or indeed illiterate? Were women, in particular, to be considered as models of inspiration? Was improvisation a more effective means of emulating classical models?

These theoretical considerations, in all their forms, were never far removed from real-life models. In Garisendi's poem, Phylero cites as evidence in favour of oral poetry a number of contemporary *improvvisatori*, singling out two performers. One of these is "the Aretine Bernardo Accolti / who with his voice and with his pen baffles everyone / with non-premeditated rhymes; his inspiration is such / that Phoebus and every Muse admires him."[34] As we will see in chapter 5, Accolti's classicizing approach to improvisational verse represents a kind of fusion of humanist and popular traditions, and Garisendi's allusion to the use of both voice and pen hints at the extent to which an improvisor like

Accolti could excel by embracing both literate and oral traditions and modes; in the end, what matters is the wonder of his audience.

The second improvisor Phylero singles out is "that honoured, divine, and exceptional Lauro, / Glory of the Arno, and of all of Tuscany" – Lorenzo ("il Magnifico") de' Medici, in other words – who "with a lyre of ebony and a plectrum of gold, / often used to spark his muse in this very style."[35] While it may seem surprising to find Lorenzo singled out for praise in this particular context, there is abundant evidence (as we will see in chapters 1 and 4) that Lorenzo engaged deeply with improvisational practices and theories and eventually sought to present himself as an inspired poet along the lines sketched by Ficino. Having presented these exhibits in favour of improvised verse, Phylero concludes his defence: "And beyond this, it further strengthens our case / when the frenzy of Apollo works quickly."[36] Here the poem is clearly influenced, again, by contemporary currents of thought about improvisation inspired by the theories of Marsilio Ficino on the concept of poetic frenzy. The emphasis on Apollo and his frenzy as a means of defending the value of improvised verse reveals the breadth of humanist perspectives on contemporary oral poetry across the fifteenth century. In Poggio's *Facetiae*, dismissiveness towards *canterini* and their audiences hinges primarily on the issue of rationality: it is their irrationality and excessive sentimental involvement with the past that makes his targets' emotional responses to the past risible and stupid (*simplex, stulta, insulsa*). But what if irrationality and atemporality were the keys to poetic achievement and divine insight? As this question became a major preoccupation and motivating force for humanists and *canterini* alike in the fifteenth century, its repercussions were felt in a number of fields, from poetry to politics, and the answers to this question had far-reaching and long-lasting results.

Chapter One

The Uses of Oral Poetry
in Quattrocento Florence

In spring of 1459, Galeazzo Maria Sforza, the teenaged son of Francesco Sforza, Duke of Milan, travelled to Florence as a guest of the Medici family. It was an important diplomatic visit, a reaffirmation of the strategic alliance between the Sforza dynasty and the Medici regime that had played a crucial role in maintaining Florentine political stability under Medici dominance. Among the festivities arranged for his benefit, Galeazzo Maria Sforza seems to have been particularly impressed by one event: a performance by the Florentine *canterino* Antonio di Guido.[1] He reported on the proceedings in a rather breathless letter to his father:

> After the meal, when the rest of the company and I had withdrawn into another room, I heard Maestro Antonio sing to the accompaniment of the cithara. I believe that your Excellency must know him, or at least have heard his name. He began his narration with the first deeds that your Excellency accomplished, and continued through to the most recent ones ... He then continued with tributes to me, and he narrated everything with such dignity, and in such a style that the greatest poet or orator in the world, if called upon to do the same, would perhaps not win as much praise as he did with his performance, from every quarter. In truth his performance left everyone struck with wonder – especially the most learned members of the audience, because they recognized that, among the similes that he created (with such skill that I am not sure Lucan or Dante ever created something more beautiful), he also incorporated so many elements of ancient history, names of innumerable ancient Romans, fables, poets, and all the Muses.[2]

Galeazzo Maria Sforza was by no means the first to admire the art of Antonio di Guido. Among the *canterini* who took the stage regularly in Florence's Piazza San Martino, the most common venue for this sort of performance, Antonio was the most renowned at a time when Florence was widely considered the leading Italian centre of this cultural form.[3] The performance was clearly designed at least in part to impress the Milanese prince with Florentine preeminence in this art.

Antonio di Guido was renowned for his ability to improvise verse on any theme, and to praise Galeazzo Maria Sforza in poetry must indeed have required Antonio to draw on his considerable capacity for invention: the fifteen-year-old had few accomplishments of his own and by most accounts had a cruel and overbearing personality (which would ultimately contribute to his assassination in his early thirties at the hands of embittered courtiers). But in narrating the deeds of Galeazzo's father, Francesco Sforza, Antonio di Guido was drawing on material with which he had considerable experience. The military exploits of Francesco Sforza were a recurring subject of the poems performed by *canterini* in Piazza San Martino at the time, and Antonio di Guido was among the Florentine *canterini* known for his poems in praise of Sforza. In fact, when Sforza was elevated to the duchy of Milan in 1450, Antonio had been one of the *canterini* who performed poems acclaiming the new duke.[4]

This episode reveals a great deal about the cultural politics of the Medici regime during the lifetime of Cosimo il Vecchio. Cosimo and his faction were adept at tapping the talents of their city's *canterini* to impress, flatter, and influence powerful guests and allies like Francesco Sforza and his son. As Galeazzo relayed in the report to his father, Antonio's performance elicited positive reviews from "the most learned members of the audience," who appreciated his many literary allusions. And indeed, there is evidence that fifteenth-century humanists held Antonio in high regard. Angelo Poliziano composed a distich "concerning the Tuscan improvisatory poet Antonio" ("de Antonio tusco extemporali poeta"):

> The Tuscan Antonio differs from the Thracian Orpheus in this
>   respect, Fabiano:
> the former moves men, the latter beasts.[5]

These lines, which must be understood in the context of Poliziano's lifelong engagement with the myth of Orpheus and Orphic texts, as well as his fascination with theories and practices of improvisation, are not simply a generic tribute to Antonio di Guido's eloquence. They are meant to suggest more substantive analogies between the type of poetry practised by Antonio di Guido and his fellow Quattrocento *canterini* – fundamentally improvisatory, oral, and musical – and the poetry of Orpheus, the most celebrated bard of antiquity.

To impress Poliziano was undoubtedly an achievement. However, the more important political function of the *canterini* was the way in which their performances influenced the attitudes of another audience: the broader Florentine public. Antonio di Guido's poetic and musical gifts were frequently sought by the Medici, and he was also part of the social network of the Medici family, as a member of a devotional company to which Giuliano de' Medici also belonged.[6] But his fame did not rest exclusively or even primarily on the favour of Florence's elite: he was known above all as a popular entertainer. As we have seen, it was the plebeian character of the audiences who frequented the public performances of *canterini* that made this poetic form the object of condescending jibes on the part of some of the more supercilious members of the Quattrocento humanist literary elite, including Poggio Bracciolini. But the alliances that the Medici family forged with the *canterini* proved to be shrewd political relationships. Florentine citizens who frequented the performances in San Martino could hear the latest victories of Francesco Sforza described as heroic deeds comparable to those of other recurring characters in the narrative poetry of the *canterini*, like Orlando and Hector. In adopting present-day military conflicts and other current events into their repertoire of improvisational themes narrated from the stage of the piazza, *canterini* wielded significant power over public attitudes, and this fact did not escape the notice of the Medici family.[7]

The extent to which Medici power in the fifteenth century was bolstered by the activities of Florence's *canterini* has rarely been examined by scholars.[8] To some extent this is understandable. The banking magnates Cosimo and his son Piero – both gouty, infirm, and without an iota of training or prowess in combat – accomplished no martial deeds that the *canterini* could triumphantly narrate in *ottava rima*. Moreover, Piazza San Martino was a public performance space, and the Medici did not directly control the performances held there. But oral poetry could be a powerful tool for an emerging political regime in fifteenth-century Italy, and as it rose to power the Medici family embraced the political possibilities of this public-facing art form. Between the period of Cosimo de' Medici's ascendance and the early life of his grandson, Lorenzo il Magnifico, entanglements between the Medici family and Florence's *canterini* were numerous. *Canterini* bolstered strategic alliances by performing for Medici allies in private contexts and influenced political discourse by performing in public contexts, in their capacity as both official *araldi* and public performers in Piazza San Martino. Furthermore, as time passed and the Medici family cemented their role as de facto rulers of Florence, their engagement with the *canterini* and their art grew more robust and complex. A key shift in the family's relationship with the Florentine network of poetic performers came with the arrival of Lucrezia Tornabuoni, who began to play an important role in Medicean cultural politics and poetics after her marriage to Piero de' Medici in 1444. And in the years following the death of Cosimo de' Medici in 1464, Lorenzo de' Medici, too, engaged directly with the art of the *canterini* in a way that had not been contemplated by his father and grandfather, by fashioning himself as a *canterino*. In the hands of the young Lorenzo, an avid poet, the art of *canterino* poetry became a powerful tool for managing the informal social bonds among elite Florentine males, thereby cementing his own grip on power.

In tracing the development of the Medici family's engagement with the possibilities of *canterino* poetry, we begin with Cosimo de' Medici – despite the fact that he had neither a gift for poetry nor any real literary training. Two poems survive with attributions to Cosimo, though they have attracted little scholarly interest – perhaps because of the belief that Cosimo himself could not have produced them.[9] Nevertheless, the poems reflect Cosimo's engagement with the possibilities presented by Florentine poetic culture; they are likely the product of a collaboration of sorts, with a trained poet crafting the verses at Cosimo's behest. As such they are revealing examples of the ways in which Cosimo harnessed the vernacular poetic tradition of his city, especially as practised by the *canterini*, to further his political agenda.

The first of these two poems takes the form of a political message from Cosimo to Francesco Sforza. When he ascended to the ducal throne in 1450, Sforza reaffirmed his commitment to his alliance with Florence. Dale Kent has suggested that the composition of the poem in Cosimo's voice was prompted by the new duke's declaration of loyalty to his Florentine allies.[10] In the poem, Cosimo in turn declares that his loyalty to Sforza is unwavering and eternal. The bulk of the *terza rima* poem is a tour de force of the literary device known as adynaton, describing outlandish events which would be more likely than Cosimo's betraying Sforza. A few verses serve to illustrate the structure:

> Sooner would the sea become a field plowed and sown, and sooner would you see fish walking through the mountains, than I could ever break the bond which constrains me, which is to help you, noble figure, who bring peace or war to Lombardy. And nature would change her course ... before I would ever stop helping you, or promise to help another instead. Sooner would the shadows in every place become bright with light, and the sun dark, and all skills and talents would sooner be extinguished ... and everything would proceed backwards, sooner than I would ever stop loving Francesco Sforza, continuously and eternally, above all else.[11]

In its overt flattery and plainly articulated acknowledgment that Sforza has power to bring war or peace, this poem is a rather blunt effort to deploy contemporary poetic practice to further a political alliance. Its *terza rima* format also suggests a connection to the forms of contemporary Florentine *canterino* poetry.

The other poem attributed to Cosimo provides further evidence not of Cosimo's direct engagement with political poetry but of his cultivation of alliances with oral poets themselves. This poem, a *sonetto caudato*, addresses itself (in the voice of Cosimo, seemingly) to Michele del Giogante, perhaps the most influential promoter of *canterino* poetry in Florence at that time, asking him to deliver a message to "il nostro cavalier" ("our knight"). In the poem, Cosimo expresses concern that the "cavaliere" is unwell and offers support: "My intention can be clearly seen: that I want to reward him for such loyalty."[12] The identity of the "cavaliere" is made clear by the sonnet which answers it in the surviving manuscripts, by the *canterino* Antonio di Meglio. In the sonnet, Antonio replies that he is Cosimo's "faithful servant" ("fedel servo") and that Cosimo's recognition of this (and, one presumes, an accompanying monetary gift) "prolongs my life, which would have been short."[13]

The close connection between Antonio di Meglio and the Medici family is evident not only from his poetic dialogue with Cosimo but also from a lengthy epicedium that Antonio composed and performed in 1440 in honour of the recently deceased Lorenzo di Giovanni de' Medici, Cosimo's younger brother. As Suzanne Branciforte has noted, the remarks that accompany the text in the original manuscript claim that Antonio had been a "singular friend and servant" ("singulare amico et servitore") to the departed Lorenzo.[14] The epicedium comprises three *capitoli* in *terza rima*, preceded by an opening sonnet addressed to Cosimo de' Medici. At the opening of the second *capitolo*, the herald imagines the soul of the departed Lorenzo returning to speak with him and addressing Antonio as "friend, you who are as dear and as grateful to me as reciprocal love demands" ("Amico ad me sì grato et tanto caro, / quanto che amore reciproco richiede").[15]

These documents clearly suggest an alliance between Antonio di Meglio and the Medici family, but it was not merely a personal bond articulated through poetry: it was also political. Between 1412 and 1442 Antonio di Meglio was among the most institutionally empowered of Florence's *canterini* because of his position as *araldo* to the Signoria. In the Florentine Republic, the *araldo* was the official oral poet of the Signoria, tasked with producing poetry that served the political and cultural agenda of the Signoria. *Araldi* entertained the members of this executive council with poetic performances, particularly in the context of the *mensa*, the communal meals that the members of the Signoria took together twice a day.[16] A small number of these poems performed by the *araldi* have survived – presumably only a portion of the poems performed orally in this context. Some idea of the traditional subject matter of this sung poetry is indicated in the statement appointing Antonio di Piero di Friano to the position of *araldo* in 1393, which states that Antonio will be responsible for "reciting moral songs and similar things in the presence of the Lord Priors and the Standard-Bearer at table, as is customary."[17] The songs of the *araldi* also frequently dealt with current events, particularly in the military and political spheres. With the Medici party exerting de facto control over the Signoria itself from 1434 on, these *araldi* were also bound to carry out their poetic functions in a manner congenial to Medici power.

As Paola Ventrone has observed, improvisation and oral performance techniques were among the most important skills for Quattrocento Florentine *araldi*.[18] Thus the skills that the office of *araldo* demanded were also those that allowed *canterini* to achieve acclaim as popular performers in Piazza San Martino. According to Dale Kent, "during Antonio di Meglio's long tenure of the office of herald, there was little difference between the entertainment offered the Signoria in their palace, and that presented to the crowd in the piazza. Antonio sang frequently at San Martino, and the star performers there were often brought in to entertain the Priors."[19] Antonio therefore had considerable power to influence the attitudes of both the priors and the Florentine public through his oral poetry. His loyalty to the Medici family, cultivated through their financial support, shaped the subject matter of his poetry in ways extending beyond his appreciation for the personal virtues of Cosimo de' Medici and his brother. Given that the Florentine alliance with Francesco Sforza was a primary political concern of both Florence and the Medici family during these years, it is not surprising that the celebration of Francesco Sforza's triumphs was a recurring element in Antonio's oral poetry.[20]

Nor was Antonio di Meglio the only Florentine *araldo* in this period to deploy his poetic talents in service of the specific foreign policy goal of maintaining strategic harmony with Francesco Sforza. In 1440, the *araldo* and *canterino* Anselmo Calderoni composed a *capitolo* "in laude del magnifico conte Francesco" in honour of Sforza's victory in the war that he waged (with Florentine, Venetian, papal, and Angevin forces) against the army of Filippo Maria Visconti and his allies under the command of Niccolò Piccinino. In the poem, Calderoni offers the "right and true prophecy" ("giusta e vera profezia") that "Francesco Sforza, the illustrious Count, will subdue the false duke [Filippo Maria Visconti] in Lombardia" ("Francesco Sforza, illustro conte, in piega metterà il falso duca in Lombardia") and singles out Cosimo's distant cousin Bernardo de' Medici for mention.[21] Calderoni's verses are, he claims, the fruit of his power of "fantasia." For the most part, though, the account of events is rather matter-of-fact, though Calderoni does muster some creativity in disparaging the enemies of Florence, like the Count of Poppi, Francesco Guidi da Battifolle, with the polemical palette of the *canterini*, referring to him as an "Epicurean" and a "new Gano," in an allusion to Gano di Maganza, the traitorous villain of the Carolingian *cantari* that were the bread-and-butter of *canterini* in Calderoni's time (setting the stage for the character's further development in the poems of Pulci and Boiardo a few decades later).

These works suggest the ways in which foreign policy priorities of the Medici family could be promoted through the works of poets with whom they were connected, and there is evidence revealing how the network of connections between the Medici and the *canterini* was organized. Within the *sonetto caudato* attributed to Cosimo de' Medici, Michele del Giogante is cast as a kind of go-between, tasked with delivering Cosimo's message to Antonio di Meglio. An accountant by trade and a poet by vocation, Michele del Giogante was a neighbour of the Medici (residing at the Canto alla Macina, very close to the Medici palazzo) and became a client of the Medici following Cosimo's return from exile in 1434.[22] Michele's passion for the poetry of the *canterini* made him an important promoter and chronicler of their activities and, according to Blake Wilson, akin to "an impresario and manager of San Martino."[23]

Michele del Giogante was thus an important node in the network of connections between the Medici family and the *canterini*, often serving as a mediator between Medici power and *canterino* culture. Among those on whose behalf Michele appealed to the Medici for support was the blind *canterino* Niccolò Cieco.[24] Little is known with certainty about the early life of this performer; his place of birth may have been Arezzo or Florence. In the 1430s he gained fame for his performances in Piazza San Martino and ultimately became so famous across Italy that the influential Neapolitan humanist Gioviano Pontano noted the *canterino*'s renown in his dialogue *De fortitudine*:

> Good gods, what an audience Niccolò Cieco used to attract, when on feast days he would sing from the stage, in Tuscan verses, sacred histories or chronicles of ancient deeds! What a crowd would gather of the learned men who were then in Florence![25]

Pontano's account suggests that Niccolò's performances held particular fascination for Florence's humanist intellectual elite. One such intellectual, the humanist and Medici insider Alessandro Braccesi, composed a vernacular sonnet "In Praise of Niccolò Cieco" ("In laude di Niccolò

Cieco") years after Niccolò's death. The poem confirms the high reputation that the poet enjoyed among elite Florentines, presenting Niccolò as a poet who succeeds through the power of his inner talent (*ingegno*), transcending the challenges imposed by his blindness:

> That which an evil fate took away from his nature – his power of vision and the light of the outside world – now shines within the confines of his intellect, for it has been gathered all together with him. He is therefore not blind, as fate willed; but his talent [*ingegno*] produces such a great light that he was a leader to many through his poem.[26]

Turning to ancient accounts of oral poetry in order to praise the art of this *canterino*, Braccesi claims that Niccolò's musical poetry compares favourably with the lyre of Sappho, with Alcaeus of Mytilene, and with Pindar. Anselmo Calderoni, the *araldo* who narrated Francesco Sforza's military exploits of 1440 in a *capitolo*, also praised Niccolò in classicizing terms, calling him "a Cicero in the art of oratory, a new Livy in the loftiest histories."[27]

In the year 1435 Niccolò Cieco was residing in Michele del Giogante's home while giving frequent performances in Piazza San Martino. Francesco Sforza, who had recently taken over command of Florence's troops, passed through the city in February of that year, and on 22 February, Niccolò performed a *capitolo*, "Viva virilità, florido onore," in honour of the *condottiero*.[28] The previously mentioned *capitolo* by Antonio di Meglio dedicated to Sforza, "Viva viva oramai viva l'onore," seems to have been performed when Sforza returned to Florence again later that year; given that the two poems' first lines employed the same opening and closing words, they may reflect a poetic rivalry of the sort common to *canterino* culture.[29]

Playing his usual role of intercessor for the *canterini*, Michele wrote to Piero de' Medici about Niccolò's improvisational skill, claiming that the emotional power of Niccolò's song was so great that one of his performances moved hundreds of people to tears: "A little work that Maestro Niccolò Cieco once sang as a motet in San Martino, which with its tenderness caused hundreds of people there to weep" ("un' operetta che già Maestro Niccolò Cieco per mottetto cantò in S. Martino, che per propria tenerezza vi fecie piagnere centinaia di persone").[30] Given Niccolò's obvious celebrity and ability to move audiences, as well as his willingness to engage in politically oriented literary production, it is easy to understand why Michele would have thought that this performer's talents would be of interest to the Medici family.

Further evidence of Michele del Giogante's role as mediator between the Medici and the *canterini* is found in a letter that he wrote on 24 May 1454 to Piero de' Medici, then in Venice. Michele writes to advocate on behalf of a young performer named Simone di Grazia, whom Michele describes as "that boy whom some time ago I had set up singing as an improvisor on the stage in San Martino, who has a good talent [*ingiegno*] and imagination [*fantasia*], and is gifted by nature for that ability."[31] Michele reminds Piero of a dinner held in Piero's honour at the house of Lionardo Bartolini, where Michele had brought Simone to perform. He explains that Simone has been in Venice for several years, in the service of a Venetian captain, but that his aging parents back in Florence have now fallen on hard times – Michele has been using his own money to help save Simone's family from extreme destitution – and he requests that Piero bring Simone home with him upon his return to Florence.

These anecdotes reveal Michele del Giogante's role in mediating Medicean support, financial and otherwise, for Florentine *canterini* in the middle decades of the fifteenth century. Michele was clearly adept at identifying ways in which the activities of the *canterini* could benefit Medici interests, particularly for public relations purposes. Michele probably played a role in organizing the *canterino* performances held in San Martino on 8 March 1450, to celebrate Francesco Sforza's elevation as Duke of Milan. The poems performed on this occasion – including one by Antonio di Guido – present this momentous development as a triumph not only for Sforza but also for Florence.[32] Michele's account of the event notes that one of the poems celebrating Sforza was performed by "a young boy who had an agreeable style of enunciation" – perhaps referring to the young prodigy Simone di Grazia.[33]

The most compelling evidence of the political dynamics of *canterino* performance in the early years of Medici rule, though, is found in a manuscript anthology that Michele del Giogante prepared, in his own hand, as a gift for Piero de' Medici. This anthology demonstrates the political relevance of the *canterino* poetry that Michele helped to promote. The manuscript (today held at the Biblioteca Nazionale Centrale of Florence as MS Mgl. XXV. 676) was given by Michele to Piero as Piero was leaving Florence for Milan at the head of a delegation of Florentine citizens travelling to the court of Francesco Sforza in 1450, to congratulate him on his ascent as duke and to reaffirm the ongoing alliance between Florence and Sforza. In the dedicatory sonnet written to Piero at the beginning of the manuscript, Michele states that he has prepared this "little book" (*libricciuol*) for Piero "because, as you know, it is my dream and desire to serve you."[34] Michele filled the manuscript with texts that he thought would help Piero in his diplomatic dealings with Sforza, essentially compiling a dossier. The manuscript contains copies of letters from Sforza, including the letter Sforza addressed to the Florentine Signoria on the day he became duke (26 February 1450) pledging his continued support (military, financial, and otherwise) to his Florentine allies, as well as a letter that Sforza had written to Cosimo de' Medici on 26 June 1441. It is clear enough why Michele believed it would be useful for Piero to have these expressions of loyalty by Sforza fresh in his mind as he prepared to meet with the new duke; in fact, in the manuscript Michele wrote that he considered the former letter so important "that it should be eternally inscribed in the heart" of every Florentine.[35] More intriguing is Michele's choice to include in his anthology a number of poems about Sforza by Florentine poets, including the poems that had been recited by renowned *canterini* at the performance held in Piazza San Martino to celebrate Sforza on 8 March. Perhaps Michele intended for Piero to relay details about this celebratory event to Sforza in order to flatter him with the poetic praise that Florentine *canterini* lavished on him.

As we have seen, evidence for connections between the Medici family and the network of *canterini* and *araldi* is extensive, particularly with Michele del Giogante working to maintain these strategic bonds of patronage and personal loyalty. The letters and dossier sent by Michele del Giogante to Piero de' Medici make it clear that the alliance between the Florentine *canterini* and the Medici family was not limited to the personal relationships of Cosimo il Vecchio but was robust and intergenerational. And in Lucrezia Tornabuoni, whose role in this network was significant after her marriage to Piero de' Medici in 1444, we see a new kind of engagement between the Medici family and Florentine poetic culture. There is evidence of close connections between Lucrezia and the circles of the *canterini*, but furthermore, Lucrezia was able to engage with this art form more directly than could her husband and father-in-law, since she was an accomplished writer and poet herself.

In a letter to Lucrezia dated 18 July 1479, Angelo Poliziano praises Lucrezia's poetry, mentioning specifically her *laude, sonetti*, and *ternari*, copies of which the humanist had borrowed and which he was returning along with the complimentary letter. Poliziano's letter refers to a group of women (presumably members of the Medici family and their circle) who appreciated Lucrezia's poetic gifts and claims that Lucrezia's granddaughter (also named Lucrezia) had memorized many of these poems:

> My magnificent lady, I am sending back to you, via Tommaso, those *laude* and sonnets and *ternari* that you lent me when I was there. Those ladies took the greatest pleasure in them. And Lady Lucrezia – or, I should say, Lucrezia – had learned by heart nearly all [the poetry of] Lucrezia.[36]

Poliziano seems to have regarded Lucrezia as something of a confidante; on 18 December 1478, while Lorenzo was away during a period of great danger and tension following the Pazzi conspiracy, Poliziano sent a letter to Lucrezia confessing his anxieties and loneliness: "I remain alone, and when I am sick of my studies, my mind wanders between plagues and wars, grief about the past and fears for the future; and I have no one here with whom I might sift through these fantasies of mine. I do not find my Lady Lucrezia in her room, with whom I might vent my feelings; and I am dying of boredom."[37]

In later centuries, one of the most vocal admirers of Lucrezia's poetry was Giovanni Mario Crescimbeni (1663–1728), who, in his *Istoria della volgar poesia* (*History of Vernacular Poetry*) wrote, "This noble lady had a particular aptitude for vernacular poetry; and she advanced so far in this pursuit, thanks to her felicitous natural talent, that she certainly outdid most of the poets of her age, if not all of them."[38] Despite the enthusiastic assessments of Lucrezia's poetry by her own contemporaries and later authors like Crescimbeni, Lucrezia's works received only sporadic scholarly attention through the nineteenth and twentieth centuries.[39] The publication of Jane Tylus's English translations of Lucrezia's *Sacred Narratives* in 2001, some of which had never before been published in any language, helped to spark new interest in the author in the Anglo-American world.[40]

Among the findings emerging from this new interest in Lucrezia's poetic compositions are a series of intertextual connections discovered by Luca Mazzoni between two of Lucrezia's poems (her *Storia di Hester* and *Vita di Tubia*) and poems by Pulci (*Morgante*), Poliziano (*rispetti*), and Lorenzo (including his *Rappresentazione di San Giovanni e Paolo*, *Laudi*, and *Selve*).[41] Since precise dates of composition are not known for either Lucrezia's poems or many of Poliziano's *rispetti*, it cannot be determined whether these instances of intertextuality reveal Poliziano alluding to poetry by Lucrezia or vice versa. Given that Pulci catalogues works by Lucrezia in *Morgante* 28, and Poliziano refers in the aforementioned letter to reading Lucrezia's poetry, one might suspect it was a case of Lucrezia's fellow poets imitating her. In any case, many of the relevant works by Lorenzo date from after Lucrezia's death in 1482, so these instances of intertextuality serve to demonstrate the enduring influence of Lucrezia's poetry on that of her son; the echoes of Lucrezia's verses identified by Mazzoni in Lorenzo's *Selve* are particularly interesting. The other works by Lorenzo in question are, like Lucrezia's compositions, Christian religious poetry, so the influence of Lucrezia's poetry detectable in them is perhaps less surprising. Lorenzo's *Selve*, though, explore spirituality in an entirely different way, permeated with Neoplatonic thought and ancient Greek and Roman mythology. But as poems in the *strambotto* genre, they share with Lucrezia's poetry roots in the oral poetic traditions of the Florentine *canterini*. Thus, Lorenzo's allusions to his mother's poetry suggest that Lucrezia's works were influential not only in shaping Lorenzo's interest, late in life, in Christian religious verse but also in stimulating, more broadly, his experiments in adapting traditional oral poetic genres for the exploration of serious spiritual and philosophical issues; Lorenzo's *Selve* were among the most interesting and complex fruits of this experimentation, as we will see in chapter 4.

Lucrezia's literary works operated in dialogue with the *canterini* in important respects. Lucrezia's lengthiest poetic works are her *storie sacre* – narrative poems on religious subjects composed in *ottava rima* and *terza rima* which were among the poetic genres favoured by some of the most noted *canterini*. We have seen, for instance, that Pontano listed "sacred narratives" ("sacras historias") among the mainstays of Niccolò Cieco's repertoire. Jane Tylus has observed that Lucrezia's *storie sacre* exhibit a number of stylistic parallels with popular *cantari* that survive from Trecento and Quattrocento Florence and Siena.[42] The Florentine *cantari* in question were likely performed in Piazza San Martino, and Lucrezia may well have attended such performances.[43] And she evidently conceptualized her own *storie sacre* as works intended not just for silent reading but for oral performance as well: her poems include periodic calls for the attention of the audience, and her poem *La istoria della casta Susanna* addresses "whoever hears or reads this little work."[44]

In addition to her close relationships with Pulci and Poliziano, Lucrezia was also connected with the poet and improvisor Bernardo Bellincioni, whose reputation for excellence as an improvisor is documented in a poem addressed to him by a certain Valditara, which credits Bellincioni with "having won the crown, as I have heard, in reciting polished verses, especially improvised ones."[45] Bellincioni was one of the many *improvvisatori* whose skills (including singing and playing the viola) earned him comparisons with Orpheus and other ancient singer-poets.[46] Like Poliziano, Bellincioni wrote a letter to Lucrezia praising her poetry and describing the pleasure that he and others had taken in a book of her works that Lucrezia had apparently lent to Bellincioni.[47] Bellincioni customarily deployed his talent for spontaneous composition of verse to build social ties and especially to cement his relationship with Lorenzo de' Medici; he addressed numerous (often humorous) sonnets to Lorenzo, and Lorenzo sometimes responded with sonnets of his own deploying the same rhyme scheme. This type of poetic exchange was central to the relationship between Bellincioni and Lucrezia, too. In a sonnet addressed to Bellincioni, Lucrezia laments that, while travelling between Florence and the baths at Morba, she has misplaced a sonnet that Bellincioni had sent to her. Bellincioni promptly responded with another sonnet of his own, following the rhyme scheme used by Lucrezia.[48]

Lucrezia's influence on Florentine oral and improvisational poetic culture and its political possibilities also extended to her role as a patron of literature. Luigi Pulci's *Morgante* represents arguably the most ambitious attempt of an author in the Medicean circle to adapt the dominant chivalric material performed in the repertoire of Piazza San Martino to serve the goals of Medicean cultural politics, and according to Pulci, it was Lucrezia who commissioned the work. In the unforgettable *ottave* of book 18 in which Pulci's iconic antihero Margutte introduces himself, the roguish half-giant recounts the myriad professions he has practised over the course of his chaotic life, including that of musical performer:

> I learned to play the rebec as a child,
> for I was dreaming that I would someday
> Troy, Hector, and Achilles sing in rhyme,
> and, oh, not once but many a thousand times.[49]

As the details of his account make clear, Margutte was, among other things, a *canterino*. In fact, Paolo Orvieto has argued that Margutte is meant to reflect not just the general class of Florentine *canterini* but a specific performer, Antonio di Guido, the one who so impressed Galeazzo Maria Sforza upon his visit to Florence in 1459.[50] In addition to being one of the most sought-after of the *canterini*, Antonio di Guido also had a reputation for loose morals (of which Margutte's gleeful admission to seventy-seven mortal sins may be the hyperbolic reflection), and he operated a tavern – much as Margutte recounts having been an "ostiere." Antonio di Guido and Pulci were friends, and Marco Villoresi has suggested that Antonio di Guido may have helped to facilitate Pulci's work on the *Morgante* by lending him copies of texts such as the *Cantare d'Orlando*, the *Cantare di Rinaldo*, and the *Cantare del Danese* – all *cantari* which were part of the oral repertoire performed in Piazza San Martino and which furnished source material for the *Morgante*.[51] At the end of the *Morgante*, Pulci pays homage to Antonio di Guido, "per cui la nostra cetra è gloriosa, / del dolce verso materno aüsonio" ("who makes our lyre gloriously sound / with our Ausonian sweet native verse").[52] Antonio di Guido, perhaps thanks in part to the mediation of his friend Pulci, began to frequent the circle of the Medici and ultimately became a valued companion of Lorenzo de' Medici.

There is considerable uncertainty regarding the chronology of the composition of Lucrezia's poems. Fulvio Pezzarossa, in the introduction to his edition of poems by Lucrezia, observes that some of her works were circulating in manuscript form by 1479 but considers it likely that at least some of the poems, including the *Giuditta*, are considerably earlier, perhaps from around 1474.[53] Since Pulci credits Lucrezia with commissioning the *Morgante*, which he had begun by 1461, it appears that Lucrezia grasped, earlier and more fully than other members of the Medici family, the ways in which supporting and cultivating the literary genres traditionally associated with Florence's *canterini* could bolster the prestige and power of the Medici.

Among the elements of Lucrezia's oeuvre that illustrate how she applied techniques associated with the oral poetry of the *canterini* to her biblical subject matter are the first two *capitoli* of her *Story of Queen Esther*, in *terza rima*.[54] The *capitoli* describe the wealth of King Ahasuerus of Persia, who will go on to marry Esther, focusing in particular on the details of the king's garden and palace, and two extravagant banquets held there by the king. In the Latin Vulgate Bible, the corresponding description occupies six verses (Esther 1:3–8). Lucrezia, however, in her vernacular poem, expands this descriptive passage to occupy fully 156 lines of poetry. Lucrezia's decision to expand this passage so extensively can be easily understood once it is recognized that she is tapping a poetic genre – *canterino* poetry – in which the introduction of a royal palace, garden, or *padiglione* (pavilion) regularly provided an occasion for the poet to showcase powers of *fantasia* and verbal artistry by delivering an extended and detailed description of a hyperbolically opulent decorated space. Nor was Lucrezia the only one of the poets of the Medicean circle to pick up this precise technique from the *canterino* tradition. As Mario Martelli and Paolo Orvieto have noted, Lucrezia's description of Ahasuerus's palace and garden can be compared with Pulci's description of the *padiglione* of Luciana, to which he dedicates forty-three *ottave* in the *Morgante*.[55] With this description, Pulci is quite self-consciously situating his work in a tradition of *canterino* poems that feature descriptions of the *padiglioni* of royals and heroes; numerous examples of such descriptions can be found within surviving, mostly anonymous, *cantari*.[56]

As we have seen, the entanglements between members of the Medici family and *canterini* who performed in Piazza San Martino during the early years of Medici hegemony were many and varied. However, Lucrezia's active and accomplished engagement with the arts of the *canterini* in her capacity as poet, and not merely as patron, was an important milestone in this developing relationship, and it was her son Lorenzo de' Medici whose activities as ruler and poet achieved the greatest integration of the worlds of magnates and *canterini*. Although, as we will see in chapter 4, the mature ruler Lorenzo would deploy the political possibilities of improvisational poetic culture in a different way, the young Lorenzo was already deeply and actively engaged in the literary and improvisational cultures of Quattrocento Florence.

The literary associations between Lucrezia Tornabuoni and Luigi Pulci are complex, as we have seen, and Lorenzo, in his youth, was also strongly influenced by Luigi Pulci. Pulci was known for his improvisational talents and his comic flair, and both of these elements became hallmarks of Lorenzo's early poetry as well. The poetic work that has attracted the most scholarly attention as an example of Lorenzo's fruitful early poetic collaboration with Pulci is *La Nencia da Barberino*, along with its companion poem *La Beca da Dicomano* – both of which aim for comic effects by adopting the voice of a rustic oral poet singing to his beloved. The former poem has long been attributed to Lorenzo and the latter to Pulci – Benedetto Varchi, for instance, in *L'Ercolano* (published in 1570) expresses appreciation for the style of writing pastoral poems "in the burlesque mode, like Lorenzo de' Medici's *Nencia* and Luigi Pulci's *Beca*."[57] However, the existence of multiple redactions of the *Nencia*, varying widely one from the other, ignited a fierce philological debate, known as the "questione nenciale," over which redaction to regard as authoritative and whether Lorenzo was the author of the original text.[58]

Paolo Orvieto has argued that the tools of traditional philology are not the right instruments to bring to bear on these texts, which are likely the partial written records of poetic practices that were originally largely oral and improvisational – like the *cantari*, the *strambotti*, and other poetic forms widely cultivated by Florentine *improvvisatori* in this period: "The *Nencia* belongs to, or at least has all the features of a poem that belongs to, this type of production of improvised song."[59] In Orvieto's view, to argue about who authored the *Nencia* is misleading, because the practices of oral composition and improvisation that gave rise to the variants in the written tradition likely involved many different oral poets within Lorenzo's circle: "In all probability the singing of the *ottave* about Nencia (because these *ottave* were indeed recited and sung before they were written down) was an activity in which Lorenzo, Pulci and Poliziano all participated, taking turns indiscriminately, and – why not? – probably also Alessandro Braccesi, who produced two known sonnets dedicated to Nencia."[60]

While the *Nencia* has attracted considerable critical attention, far less work has been devoted to Lorenzo's *Uccellagione di starne* (*The Partridge Hunt*). Yet this poem, too, offers intriguing evidence of the interest in improvisational poetic forms that the young Lorenzo shared with Pulci. It is, moreover, an even richer source than the *Nencia* for exploring the politically expedient homosocial functions that collaboration and competition in improvisatory genres of poetry served within Lorenzo's youthful *brigata*. In the case of the *Uccellagione di starne*, as in the case of the *Nencia*, the existence of multiple versions of the text (two substantially different versions of the *Uccellagione di starne*) gave rise to debates calling into question the attribution of the text to Lorenzo, though his primary role in its composition is today widely accepted.[61] The existence of multiple versions of both of these texts probably reflects a similar process of composition at work in both cases: the *Uccellagione di starne*, like the *Nencia*, was probably not written by Lorenzo alone; rather, the surviving written texts are likely at least in part the products of a process of oral composition and improvisation that saw the participation not only of Lorenzo but also Pulci and perhaps other members of his circle.

A clue to the close connection between Pulci and the *Uccellagione di starne* (besides Pulci's appearance as a character within the poem) is found in a letter that Pulci addressed to Lorenzo on 27 July 1473, which shows unmistakable verbal connections with the final verses of the *Uccellagione di starne*. Lorenzo's poem concludes with these verses:

> That's how, my friend, we spent the day in pleasure,
> And sang a thousand sugared rhymes in measure.[62]

Pulci, in his letter, appears to echo these verses when he writes, "May the Muses and the viola and the *sdrucciolo* rhymes of our faithful friend prevail; and we will find a rhyme that is even beyond *zucchero* [sugar]" ("Vagliano le muse e lla vihuola e lle rime sdrucciole del compare nostro tutto fedele; e troverremo poi rima più là che zucchero").[63] Lorenzo's poem is addressed to an unnamed "friend" ("compare"), and Pulci's letter appears to refer to this same individual, a mutual friend of Pulci's and Lorenzo's that Pulci's letter appears to characterize as an *improvvisatore* – devoted to the Muses, to the playing of the viola, and to inventing difficult rhymes. "Rime sdrucciole" – in which the accent of the rhyme word falls on the antepenultimate syllable – were considered a particularly difficult type of verse to improvise. Finding a word to rhyme with "zucchero" would be challenging indeed for an improvisational poet, and Pulci's letter, which can serve as a gloss for the obscure final verse of the *Uccellagione di starne* that it echoes, seem to present this type of improvisational challenge as a favourite pastime among the members of Lorenzo's *brigata*. In other words, when Lorenzo refers to the "mille rime a zucchero" with which he and his companions pass the time pleasurably, this may refer not simply to sweet-sounding rhymes, but to *difficult* rhymes, of the sort that improvisational poets would deploy to challenge and impress one another.

The term *compare* can mean "friend" or "comrade," but in musical contexts in this period it can also signify "accompanist" – someone who plays an instrument to accompany the singing of verses. The "compare" that both Lorenzo and Pulci refer to is evidently a friend of both men, and

Pulci's reference to his "vihuola" makes clear that he is also an instrumentalist. Paolo Orvieto has argued that the references to the "compare" found in these two texts, and in other texts by members of Lorenzo's circle in this period, are to Angelo Poliziano.[64]

Scholars have noted that Lorenzo's *Uccellagione di starne* draws inspiration from an earlier hunting poem in *ottava rima* entitled *La Caccia di Belfiore*, a very popular poem in late fifteenth-century Florence, judging from the number of copies that survive.[65] The identity of the author of the *Caccia di Belfiore* has long been uncertain (it was for a time attributed erroneously to Agostino Staccoli di Urbino), but Mario Martelli has advanced convincing arguments that it is the work of Antonio Bonciani, one of the *canterini* who performed in Piazza San Martino in the mid-fifteenth century. A rivalry between Bonciani and the more famous *canterino* Antonio di Guido gave rise (as was customary among oral poets) to verbal sparring via an exchange of insulting sonnets; one *sonetto caudato* by Bonciani against Antonio di Guido has survived. Bonciani pulls no punches in the sonnet, drawing on the most offensive language he can muster to accuse his rival of all manner of vices and excesses in his sex life, eating habits, and more; after accusing Antonio di Guido of being a glutton and a sodomite, Bonciani adds that "you use your mouth in the same way as your ass."[66] While the verve that Bonciani brings to his accusations is impressive, these are traditional elements of the *tenzone* genre. As such they reveal little about the character of Antonio di Guido but do reveal Bonciani's mastery of a literary genre widely cultivated in this period, especially among poets known for improvisation. Within Lorenzo de' Medici's circle, Luigi Pulci was the most renowned master of this type of poetic invective, as exemplified in his infamous *tenzone* with Matteo Franco.[67]

The protagonists of the *Uccellagione di starne* are Lorenzo's friends, the members of his youthful *brigata*. In all likelihood, the original inspiration for the composition was a real hunting trip undertaken by the *brigata*, the events of which were then celebrated (and creatively distorted) in verse by Lorenzo and his friends. The poem offers a rich representation not only of the hunt itself but also of the way in which the *brigata* transforms the events into stories and rhymes. In the narration, three of Lorenzo's friends participate actively in the hunt. Among these is Giovan Francesco Ventura (1448–78), a close friend of Lorenzo's youth who is also immortalized in comic fashion in several of Poliziano's *Detti piacevoli*.[68] Ventura is also the dedicatee of a much more sombre poetic composition by Lorenzo: his *capitolo* "L'amoroso mio stil, quel dolce canto," written to console Ventura on the death of one of his daughters. Guglielmo de' Pazzi (b. 1436) is also among the hunters in Lorenzo's poem: he was Lorenzo's brother-in-law, having married Bianca de' Medici in 1460.[69]

The third member of Lorenzo's *brigata* who actively participates in the hunt is Foglia Amieri, but Lorenzo's poem also features many other members of his *brigata*, including Sigismondo della Stufa, Giovansimone Tornabuoni, Piero Alamanni, and Braccio Martelli. Some of these appear as bystanders (as does Lorenzo himself, who serves as narrator but does not participate in the hunt) or are discussed because of their conspicuous absence from the hunting party. The member of the *brigata* whose absence is discussed at greatest length is Luigi Pulci, explained by the character Braccio Martelli as follows:

> Luigi Pulci, too, has stayed behind:
> today he has gone off into a wooded grove
> because his head was filled with fantasy,
> and probably he's going to fashion some sonnets.
> Watch out, Corona: believe me,
> this morning he was muttering a lot in bed.
> He kept repeating the name "Corona";
> I'll bet he's going to put you into a *frottola* or a *canzona*.[70]

The "Corona" referred to here was a falconer employed by the Medici, mentioned repeatedly in Lorenzo's letters. Corona must have had either a particularly good sense of humour or particularly poor skills as a falconer (or both), because in the *Uccellagione* the members of Lorenzo's *brigata* (in particular Braccio Martelli) amuse themselves making fun of his inability to catch partridges:

> Corona never caught a partridge,
> except by accident or by chance,
> and he has killed more hapless sparrowhawks
> than Orlando ever killed Saracens.[71]

Braccio believes that Pulci, instead of hunting with the rest of the *brigata*, has gone off to use his powers of poetic imagination to invent poems about Corona, presumably in this same vein of good-natured mockery. Thus Pulci is represented as even more dedicated than the rest of the *brigata* to poetic invention. But all of the men who are mentioned within the poem are implicated in the *brigata*'s abiding interest in the transformation of reality into poetry – Lorenzo himself, as the primary author of the poem (perhaps with the participation of others), as well as the other members of the *brigata* who constitute the poem's ideal first audience. The final verse of the poem points to this process of the transformation of lived experience into poetry: the members of the *brigata*, the hunt behind them, turn their attention to the improvisation of poetry ("mille rime") – the process, we may understand, from which the *Uccellagione di starne* itself emerges. The preceding verses, too, trace the process through which real events undergo a process of magnification and manipulation in the retelling, in a process driven by competitive boasting among male friends:

> Next they all gather in a circle around a cask of wine
> with cups floating inside.
> Then another hunt begins.
> In the retelling every butterfly becomes a crane ...
> Each man tells a different story,
> and each crowns his own hawk the champion,
> finding some ready excuse for any failings.
> And he who didn't do much with his hawk
> now lets off steam talking and drinking.[72]

Scholars have appreciated the *Uccellagione di starne* as a rich document of historical hunting practices in fifteenth-century Tuscany, revealing facets of this patrician pastime that are not detailed in other surviving sources. Yet for all of the technical elements of falconry that flesh out the narration, the poem clearly does not aspire primarily to provide a realistic representation of this pursuit. Indeed, for a poem ostensibly about a partridge hunt, very little proper hunting takes place. Rather, the focus of the poem is on the representation of Lorenzo's male friends and the social dynamics within the *brigata*. Tension arises in the narration when the hunting rivalry between Guglielmo de' Pazzi and Foglia Amieri escalates into an argument and nearly a fight after Foglia's hawk kills Guglielmo's. Guglielmo seethes with anger for some time, but finally Dionigi Pucci diffuses the tension with a well-timed joke at his own expense, and the party ends the day united in friendly banter.

The dynamics of male friendship are thus the central theme of the work, and the composition and circulation of the poem would have served to reinforce these friendships within Lorenzo's circle. Lorenzo makes a point of working into the poem a number of humorous references to friends of his who have no real role in the narrative (perhaps because they were not present at the real hunt that inspired the poem). The circulation of the poem, and likely its oral performances, among this first audience of insiders would have served to reinforce the social cohesion of the *brigata* itself. Solidifying these bonds of friendship between Lorenzo and the sons of other wealthy and influential Florentine families had significant political value for Lorenzo and the Medici regime. Many of the young men represented within the *Uccellagione di starne* would go on to hold major governmental posts, their loyalty to Lorenzo helping to ensure the Medici regime's continued grip on power in the Republic of Florence.

Part of the strategy that Lorenzo's *Uccellagione di starne* uses to reinforce in-group identity among the privileged audience of *brigata* members is the use of terms that carry a hidden meaning readily decipherable only to group members. Often the hidden meaning of such terms is a sexual double entendre. The deployment of such wordplay was a prominent element in Florentine comic poetry beyond Lorenzo's circle and was particularly associated with the barber-poet Burchiello. Within Lorenzo's circle it was Pulci who was especially known for developing a sophisticated lexicon of code words, which he shared in particular with his young patron Lorenzo. Some of Pulci's compositions that rely on this so-called "lingua zerga" (jargon) would be incomprehensible to modern readers were it not for the survival of a handwritten list, by Pulci himself, of some of these terms with their hidden meanings.[73] With the aid of this word list it is possible, for instance, to decipher the meaning of an encoded letter that Pulci sent to Lorenzo, inviting Lorenzo to return to Florence because "there will be some beautiful fish here these evening" ("Qui saranno stasera di be' pesci").[74] Since Pulci's word list confirms that in his jargon fish ("pesce") means young woman ("fanciulla"), he is evidently encouraging his young patron to join him at a gathering where he knows young women will be present. The shared use of code words and double entendres to discuss sexual adventures (whether real or imagined) was a major facet of the poetic style of the young Lorenzo during the years he was most influenced by Pulci, and the *Uccellagione di starne* shows clear examples of this (and, no doubt, contains other examples that are no longer clear to a modern reader). Such double meanings within the text generally appear intended to amuse in-group readers by alluding to supposed sexual exploits, failings, or proclivities of the men who belong to Lorenzo's *brigata*. For example, the poem quite clearly makes fun of Dionigi Pucci for his laziness, but his inability to get his hawk to stand up (9.2) can also be understood as a humorous reference to impotence. When Foglia tells Guglielmo "tu pigli assai villani e stran' trastulli; / ma io pazzo a 'mpacciarmi con fanciulli!" ("you're into very rude and strange amusements; / but I'm crazy to get involved with boys!"), the remarks are evidently a reference to pederasty.[75] Competition and playful insult were prominent components of the culture of the *improvvisatori*, and in the case of Lorenzo's *brigata* it is clear how these cultural features served to create and strengthen social bonds within a network that increasingly included oral poets.

One of the most brilliant (and widely discussed) chapters in Lorenzo de' Medici's long career of cultural politics was his initiative of compiling, between 1476 and 1477, the *Raccolta Aragonese* as a gift to Federico d'Aragona, the son of Ferdinando I, then king of Naples. The manuscript anthology, containing 499 poems, was meant to demonstrate the nobility of vernacular poetry (and its potential parity or even superiority to classical poetry) and to showcase Tuscan and especially Florentine hegemony over the rest of Italy in the sphere of vernacular literature. While Lorenzo's personal involvement in the initiative is undoubted, most scholars believe that Angelo Poliziano had a significant role in the execution of the *Raccolta Aragonese*, including perhaps in the composition of its dedicatory letter (although it is signed by Lorenzo). The opening of this letter is organized around the figures of Homer and Peisistratus. If virtue is to flourish, the letter claims, we need great poetry – just as, in ancient Greece, it was thanks to Homer's poetic excellence that the heroism of Achilles was remembered and served as an inspiration for valorous Greeks of later centuries, like Alexander: "Had the divine poet Homer never lived, Achilles's fame would have been buried along with his body" ("se 'l divino poeta Omero non fusse stato, una medesima sepultura il corpo e la fama di Achille averebbe ricoperto").[76]

But, the letter argues, poetry in turn can only flourish when political leaders are committed to it:

> After the death of Homer, when the sacred work of this most celebrated poet had been scattered and as it were dismembered across many different regions of Greece, Peisistratus, prince of Athens, a man of many virtues, exceptional both in spirit and in body, having offered vast rewards to whoever brought him any Homeric verses, with the greatest diligence and care reassembled the whole body of the most sacred poet.[77]

The letter goes on to assert that Lorenzo (supposedly at Federico's request) has now done something analogous for the body of Tuscan vernacular poetry, assembling scattered fragments into a single corpus. Implicitly, then, the letter casts Lorenzo as a modern-day Peisistratus, ensuring an enduring future for a poetic corpus that had its roots in oral traditions and was still only tenuously preserved in writing.

Comparing the cultural achievements of Quattrocento Florence to those of ancient Athens had been a mainstay of Florentine political rhetoric since Leonardo Bruni's *Panegyric to the City of Florence* in the first years of the century. Lorenzo's *Epistola* develops this traditional comparison between Florence and Athens in a surprising direction that readers opposed to Medici power might well have found troubling, in that it compares Lorenzo, who wielded illegitimate power over what was nominally a free republic, to the tyrant who had seized illegitimate control over Athens. Emphasizing the literary, indeed philological, contributions of both Peisistratus and Lorenzo while remaining silent about more strictly political matters, the letter may appear to suggest that a leader's capacity to elevate his city's cultural standing is more important than questions of political legitimacy.

Given the reputation of *canterino* poetry as a plebeian art form, one might imagine that the *Raccolta Aragonese* would have passed over this type of poetry as unsuited for the collection's goal of advertising Florence's preeminence in literary matters. Not so: the collection in fact highlights contemporary Tuscan poets who were known above all as oral poets and improvisors, although the considerable body of scholarship that has been devoted to the *Raccolta Aragonese* has rarely considered the significance of the inclusion of *canterino* poetry. The most salient example is Niccolò Cieco, who was, at the height of his career, the most celebrated of the performers to entertain audiences in Piazza San Martino.[78] Sixteen poems attributed to Cieco were included in the collection. Michele del Giogante – the impresario who organized *canterino* performances in Piazza San Martino and who attempted to employ a team of scribes to surreptitiously transcribe Cieco's improvised verses – was also represented. By including a number of poems by Tuscan *canterini* who performed in Piazza San Martino, the *Raccolta Aragonese* positions *canterino* poetry as an integral part of the prestigious vernacular poetic tradition. Lorenzo's anthology aims to demonstrate that Tuscan and especially Florentine cultural hegemony in the Italian peninsula rests not only on the achievements of the *Tre Corone* of the fourteenth century but also on the excellence of recent and contemporary Tuscans and Florentines. Lorenzo and Poliziano, keenly aware of Florence's status as the leading Italian centre of *canterino* poetry, are eager to marshal this flourishing contemporary tradition as part of the case for Florence's present-day cultural preeminence.

As we have seen, a survey of the Medici family's many entanglements with *canterini* and their art in the fifteenth century reveals a complicated and robust network. The overlap between the categories of *canterini* as performers for public audiences in Piazza San Martino and official *araldi* in the context of the Signoria predated the Medici rise to power, but the role of these performers developed in new directions during Medici rule. There were complex links between the Medici palazzo in Via Larga and the stage of San Martino, especially since *canterini* patronized by the Medici, like Antonio di Guido, moved back and forth between these two performance contexts. And the possibilities for instrumentalizing *canterino* performance were many; as we have seen in examining the specific case of Florentine poetic engagement with Francesco Sforza, *canterini* could be engaged to perform panegyrics in private for essentially diplomatic functions or to articulate political ideals in public performances. The inclusion of *canterino* poetry in what amounts to a foreign policy dossier prepared for Piero de' Medici suggests the degree to which this art form was integrated into politics. At the same time, we can observe the Medici family's engagement with oral poetic performance evolve from appreciative spectatorship and politically motivated patronage to increasingly active involvement in poetic production. From the rather plodding sonnet attributed to Cosimo il Vecchio, to Lucrezia Tornabuoni's active artistic engagement with *canterino* forms and techniques, to the young Lorenzo's extensive poetic productions, the entanglements between members of the Medici family and oral and improvisational poetic forms were becoming more robust and complex, like their personal connections with individual *canterini*.

The fact that *canterino* poetry was included in the *Raccolta Aragonese* demonstrates that its status was not merely that of popular entertainment but also a cultural form that the Medici family took seriously and sought to promote in pursuit of their own political goals. Still, the promotion of this art form for political purposes did not automatically transform the dismissive attitude of humanist intellectuals like Poggio Bracciolini regarding the sort of improvisational performances that enchanted crowds in the piazza. The real change in humanist attitudes towards improvisational and oral poetry in the fifteenth century would come about with a radical rethinking of its historical, intellectual, and spiritual identity, shaped decisively by the contributions of Marsilio Ficino.

Chapter Two

"Inspired and Possessed":
Marsilio Ficino and Oral Poetry

When Marsilio Ficino collected his own correspondence for publication, he chose to open the collection with a letter from Cosimo de' Medici, written shortly before the Florentine magnate's death. In it, the ailing Cosimo asks Ficino to visit him as soon as possible at his estate in Careggi and to bring Ficino's recently completed translation of Plato's *Philebus*. No less insistently, at the close of the letter, he requests that Ficino bring along another item of paramount importance: "Farewell," he writes. "Come, and bring your Orphic lyre with you."[1]

These two objects, the Platonic book and the Orphic lyre, can serve as the twin emblems of Ficino's contribution to Florentine cultural life. It is a pairing – the book and the lyre – that Ficino's admirers evoked, at times playfully, during his life and subsequently. Andrea Ferrucci's 1521 bust of Ficino in Florence's Duomo, for instance, depicts Ficino holding a book – certainly representing his textual legacy, and perhaps to be interpreted specifically as his translations of Plato's dialogues. More intriguingly, Ferrucci seems to represent Ficino gripping or even playing this book as though it were his famed Orphic lyre, his rapt expression suggesting that he is in the grip of the divine frenzy that Ficino himself had popularized (see figure 5).[2]

These two projects of Ficino – Platonic translation and Orphic musical-poetic performance – are clearly central to his reputation among his contemporaries, and not by accident: as we will see, he carefully crafted his own image as the authority in both of these fields. The nature of the connection between these two pursuits, though, has yet to be fully explored. In fact, these two interests would appear to be somewhat incompatible: Plato is well known for articulating the "ancient quarrel" between philosophers and poets. Yet Ficino's laborious work to learn Greek was motivated in large part by an interest in oral poetic performance. Nor was this interest merely abstract or scholarly: Ficino was intrigued by

Figure 5. Andrea Ferrucci, *Bust of Marsilio Ficino* (1521). Florence, Cathedral of Santa Maria del Fiore. Photo by author.

the compositional and performative practices of Florentine oral poets and saw their activities as integrally linked with descriptions of altered states of poetic inspiration that he found in ancient discussions of oral poetic performance. He sought to interpret these works by bringing to bear both theories derived from his study of Plato and practice on his "Orphic lyre."

Both of these interests for which Ficino was famed are clearly part of the intellectual fascination with classical culture in fifteenth-century Florence. Ficino's translations of Plato not only made it possible for his contemporaries to engage with these works but also set the intellectual preoccupations of his world on a particular Platonic trajectory. Ficino's Orphic lyre, too, is also clearly of a piece with the humanist desire to interrogate and reanimate ancient traditions. Yet at the same moment when Ficino and his contemporaries were cementing the reputation of Florence as a centre of classical learning, the city was also, as we have seen, famed for its excellence in oral and improvised poetry and music as performed by the *improvvisatori*. This tradition has rarely been considered in connection with Ficino's activities, but it is central to understanding both of Ficino's projects and their far-reaching impact on poetry in the fifteenth century and well beyond.

The lyre itself, much discussed by Ficino and his contemporaries, was for Ficino an emblem of his engagement with ancient oral poetic traditions, and particularly with Orphic texts, but it also reflected Ficino's close and long-standing relationships with Florentine *improvvisatori*. Ficino's performance practices and philosophical interpretations were influenced by these relationships, and Ficino in turn exerted an influence on the practices of the *improvvisatori*. Scholarship on fifteenth-century Italian culture often relies on oppositional frameworks (Latin versus vernacular; elite versus popular; ancient versus contemporary; textual versus oral) which separate Ficino's intellectual interests from the tradition of improvised musical-poetic performance for which Florence was famous. For this reason the extent and implications of these fruitful relationships have not been fully recognized, but they can serve as a key to understanding Ficino's thought and its influence within fifteenth-century musical, intellectual, and political circles.

Though his commitment to his Orphic lyre was unique, Ficino was by no means the only fifteenth-century Florentine gripped by a fascination with Orphism, a vogue resulting from an intellectual paradigm shift concerning the figure of Orpheus. The mythological figure was hardly a new discovery: the Orpheus myth was, throughout the Middle Ages, one of the most widely known stories from antiquity. The importance of Orpheus for most of this period, though, consisted in his status as the protagonist of various mythical exploits, most notably his journey to the underworld and attempted rescue of Eurydice; Orpheus was invoked for centuries to characterize powerful musical performance. But the arrival in fifteenth-century Italy of Greek poetry attributed to Orpheus made possible an entirely new way of thinking about Orpheus: Orpheus could be examined not simply as a mythical character but as the purported author of a surviving poetic corpus – a possibility that particularly excited humanist textual scholars. Direct analysis of these Orphic verses seemed to offer a path towards gaining a far deeper understanding of Orpheus than had been possible for earlier generations: the poems, humanist thinkers suspected, could reveal the secrets of Orpheus's mystical theology and even his crypto-monotheism. The claims about the power of Orpheus's verses which figure so heavily in classical myth – the stories of his power to charm the natural world with his song – could now be tested against actual surviving examples of his poetry (or so it was thought).

Today it is well established that the various poems which were once attributed to "Orpheus" could not have been the work of a single poet and that most of them date from the first centuries CE, far later than the remote antiquity in which Orpheus was supposed to have lived. Much of this Orphic poetry was far removed from what Italian humanists were accustomed to regarding as the standards of aesthetic excellence for classical poetry, exemplified by the refined verses of Virgil and Horace. The *Orphic Hymns* and Orphic fragments were often obscure, repetitious, and unbalanced. These puzzling qualities did not extinguish humanists' interest in the Orphic poems, though; rather, they forced humanists to seek new approaches that might allow the poems to speak with their original force.[3] Marsilio Ficino was the most important of the early protagonists of this humanist rethinking of Orpheus, and in his view recapturing the power of Orphic verse required performing the material as sung poetry, restoring the original union of word and music that Ficino considered the key to the power of Orpheus's song.

Ficino's Orphic singing was the subject of several influential studies by D.P. Walker, whose focus – and that of most scholars who have subsequently examined the topic – was the relationship between Ficino's musical practices and his magical and astrological theories.[4] Following his readings of the Greek Neoplatonists (especially Iamblichus and Proclus), Ficino came to believe in the power of music to channel beneficent influences from the stars. Ficino expounds a theory of this type of astrological singing in his 1489 *De vita* and, although he does not discuss Orphic singing specifically in that text, there is good reason to think Ficino came to believe that his own Orphic singing could achieve the same kinds of magical efficacy that he theorizes in the *De vita*. But there is evidence that Ficino's Orphic singing was not inspired only by his magical interests and that it had a broader impact on his thought and on his literary and intellectual milieu than has been acknowledged. Rather than examining the connections between Ficino's Orphic singing and the astrological and magical theories he developed over the course of the 1480s through his study of the Greek Neoplatonists, this chapter will focus on the connections between two of the major facets of Ficino's work that occupied him from the very beginning of his career: his fascination with Orpheus and his promotion of the theory of divine poetic frenzy described in the Platonic dialogues. Orpheus served as a model – one that Ficino pursued himself and recommended to fellow poets and performers – for the way that musical-poetic performance could elevate the soul through the cultivation of divine frenzy.

These Orphic texts that captivated Ficino had first arrived in Italy in 1424, thanks to the efforts of the humanist and book hunter Francesco Filelfo, who in a letter to Ambrogio Traversari, dated June 1428, mentions a manuscript containing the *Orphic Hymns* and the *Orphic Argonautica* which he brought to Italy from Constantinople.[5] He translated at least part of the latter text into Latin; isolated sections of the *Orphic Argonautica* in Filelfo's translation survive in several manuscripts.[6] Sometime between 1458 and 1465, the Byzantine refugee Constantine Lascaris, then living in Milan, wrote an introduction to the *Orphic Argonautica*, the bulk of which consists of a biography of the poem's supposed author, Orpheus. The text illustrates the range of fifteenth-century perspectives on Orpheus, since Lascaris acknowledges that some of his contemporaries nurtured doubts about Orpheus's status as a real historical personage. Lascaris, though, vigorously rejects these concerns: to question Orpheus's historicity would be absurd, according to Lascaris, since his life has been written about by so many poets, historians, and geographers.[7]

Lascaris's contemporaries – especially Ficino – were clearly interested in the material. Around 1462, Ficino produced a translation of the *Orphic Argonautica*, and around the same time Leodrisio Crivelli (Filelfo's friend and former student) also completed a translation of the text, dedicated to Pope Pius II.[8] Ficino was thus one of the first Europeans to complete a translation of the *Orphic Argonautica*, and his translation of the *Orphic Hymns* was very likely the first of that text. Though he was clearly enthusiastic about working with the material, Ficino was less convinced of the wisdom of publishing his translations, and for this reason Ficino's translations of the Orphic texts have survived today only in fragments. In a letter that Ficino wrote several decades later (around 1492) to his friend Martin Prenninger, he explains why he decided not to publish the translations:

> It never seemed a good idea to publish the *Argonautica*, the hymns of Orpheus, of Homer or Proclus, or the *Theology* [i.e., *Theogony*] of Hesiod, which, as you saw when you were recently a guest in my house, I had translated, word for word, just for myself in my youth (I know not how). I was afraid I might seem to be calling readers back to an ancient worship of gods and daemons that was justly condemned long ago.[9]

Ficino's anxieties about accusations of heresy that could have resulted from publishing his translations of the Orphic poems (and what he regarded as related works by Homer, Hesiod, and Proclus) did not, however, prevent him from including translated excerpts from these texts in his own works. Dozens of translations of Orphic verses appear throughout Ficino's major works the *Theologia platonica* and the *De amore*. Ficino seems to have believed that presenting these texts together with his own interpretations and commentary could prevent dangerous misinterpretations and avoid provoking suspicions that he harboured heretical beliefs. In one of his works, Ficino alludes to his intention to explain the rites of Orpheus and Pythagoras elsewhere – a remark that Paul Oskar Kristeller interpreted as showing that Ficino at one point intended to produce a commentary on the Orphic writings along the lines of his commentaries on Plato.[10]

While Ficino declined to publish his personal translations of the Orphic works, he was eager to share them with his friends and associates – especially through the medium of oral performance. Ficino's fascination with the musical performance of poetry like the *Orphic Hymns* endured throughout his life. In a letter to Paul of Middelburg on 13 September 1492, looking back on the major achievements of his time, Ficino writes:

> For, as if golden, this age has brought back into the light the liberal arts, which were almost extinct: grammar, poetry, rhetoric, painting, sculpture, architecture, music, and the ancient art of singing to the Orphic lyre. And all this in Florence.[11]

Given the magnitude of the contributions of Quattrocento Florentines to the other fields mentioned – the paintings of Botticelli, the sculptures of Donatello, the architecture of Brunelleschi – a reader today could be forgiven for finding the final crescendo to Orphic singing a puzzling anticlimax. This sense of incongruity is perhaps only heightened as the letter continues and Ficino lists more of the achievements of his time, including the invention of printing and the revival of Platonic philosophy. How, the reader might wonder, could Ficino consider the revival of Orphic singing a development comparable in magnitude to the invention of printing, or even to the revival of Platonic philosophy that Ficino himself led, the contribution on which Ficino's fame would primarily rest?

This revival of Orphic singing, like the revival of Platonic philosophy, was spearheaded by Ficino himself, not least through his own activities as a performer of poetry and music based on what he took to be Orphic models. Ficino clearly attached great significance to this practice, and writings from throughout his life reveal him crafting his own image as a performer of Orphic verse. In a letter to Cosimo de' Medici dated 4 September 1462, Ficino frames a significant early-career milestone in the context of his Orphic singing. As he tells Cosimo, "For the last few days

I have, for mental relaxation, been taking my lyre in hand and playing over to music the hymn the divine Orpheus sang to the Cosmos, that is, to the world."[12] This hymn, which concludes with the line "Hear thou, o Cosmos, our prayers, and grant to the pious youth a tranquil life," was apparently a good choice, as Ficino recounts that his singing was interrupted by the arrival of a letter informing him that Cosimo intended to generously patronize the young scholar's Greek studies by, among other things, gifting him a manuscript of Plato's complete works.[13] Since Ficino had no direct access to most of the Platonic dialogues before Cosimo procured this manuscript (likely from the Byzantine Gemistus Pletho), this development was of great importance, marking the genesis of Ficino's career as a translator of Plato.[14] Ficino's translations and interpretations made the full range of Plato's thought available, for the first time, to Latin-educated readers across western Europe, and this translation project is rightly regarded as Ficino's signature contribution. As Ficino's letter emphasizes, though, he had begun his translation career not with Plato's prose but with Orphic poetry; in the letter to Cosimo, Ficino includes his Latin translation of the Orphic hymn that he describes singing to the lyre, entitled "Ad Cosmum."[15]

Ficino had some success in convincing his contemporaries that his revival of Orphic singing was a major achievement. In a letter to Ficino, the poet Johannes Pannonius praised him for having revived the ancient Orphic style of song: "You restored to light the ancient sound of the lyre and the style of singing and the Orphic songs which had previously been consigned to oblivion."[16] Ficino and his lyre made many a cameo in the literary works of his contemporaries, who amplified the older trope of describing a musician as a new Orpheus with vivid descriptions of Ficino impersonating Orpheus through song. In Ugolino Verino's *Carlias*, for instance, Ficino makes an impressively Orphic cameo at a banquet scene:

> But once hunger has been driven away, the Etruscan poet Marsilius stands up and strikes his lyre. Then with a sonorous voice he harmonizes verses of the sort which Rhodopeian Orpheus sang mournfully on the lyre when he had lost Eurydice, weeping in vain in wicked Tartarus while the shades looked on: what is the boundary of the sea, the earth, and the sky; what are the causes of things, what is the spirit, whence and wherefore were men created, and whither fly the swift souls that have departed the body, whether they seek the sky and the Stygian swamp; the Lydian poet was singing these things with his learned plectrum.[17]

Within Ficino's immediate circle, his Orphic exploits were also celebrated in a memorable poem by Naldo Naldi, which describes how the soul of Orpheus transmigrated through various classical bodies – those of Homer, Pythagoras, and Ennius – before being reincarnated as Ficino, after waiting 1,600 years,

> until divine fate should give rise to Marsilio, whose pure limbs Orpheus might willingly put on. Hence with his lyre and song he charms hard oaks and softens again the hearts of beasts.[18]

From Naldi we also learn that the instrument Ficino played, his Orphic lyre, bore a painted image of Orpheus. In Naldi's poem "To Marsilio Ficino, Regarding the Orpheus Painted on His Lyre" ("Ad Marsilium Ficinum de Orpheo in eius cythara picto"), the painted Orpheus speaks: "I am that Orpheus who moved forests with his song."[19] In addition to these rather grandiloquent celebrations of Ficino's Orphic alter ego, there are more playful allusions to Ficino's Orphic identity, like the shirt Filippo Buonaccorsi sent to Ficino from Poland, accompanied by these verses: "This barbarian costume will make you a true Orpheus, since you already have his singing and his lyre."[20]

However, Ficino's Orphic singing was not merely an early example of historically informed performance, as a colourful description of Ficino's Orphic performance style in a poem by Giannantonio Campano makes clear:

> If curly-haired Apollo should play upon Marsilio's cithara, Apollo would fall defeated in both dexterity of hand and singing. There is frenzy; when he sings, as a lover to the singing of his beloved, he plucks his lyre in harmony with the melody and rhythm of the song. Then his eyes burn, he leaps to his feet, and he discovers music which he never learnt by rote.[21]

This description of Ficino entering an altered state as he performs on his lyre very likely reflects another facet of what Ficino thought Orphic performance entailed. As Campano's verses suggest, it is probable that Ficino affected a state of poetic frenzy during the course of his Orphic performances.[22] That Ficino would have sought to access this state comes as no surprise in the larger context of his work: exploration of the idea of poetic frenzy was one of Ficino's most singular contributions to fifteenth-century Italian thought.

The most important ancient source for the concept of divine frenzy is a famous speech by Socrates in Plato's *Phaedrus*, which Ficino translated between 1466 and 1468. Socrates begins his speech by assuring his young interlocutor that madness should not be considered merely an evil, since some of humankind's greatest blessings result from madness, when it is sent as a gift from the gods. He then outlines the principal types of divine frenzy, beginning with the frenzies which seize prophets and priests. Socrates continues:

> And a third kind of possession and madness comes from the Muses. This takes hold upon a gentle and pure soul, arouses it and inspires it to songs and other poetry, and thus by adorning countless deeds of the ancients educates later generations. But he who without the divine madness comes to the doors of the Muses, confident that he will be a good poet by art, meets with no success, and the poetry of the sane man vanishes into nothingness before that of the inspired madmen.[23]

As we will see, Plato's *Ion* also deals significantly with the concept of the divine inspiration of poets. However, prior to September 1462, when he received as a gift from Cosimo de' Medici the famous codex (today held at Florence's Biblioteca Laurenziana) containing the dialogues of Plato, Ficino did not have access to the *Ion*. Hence, when he wrote his letter *De divino furore* in 1457, Ficino's most important Platonic source on the subject was the *Phaedrus*, which he would then have been able to read only in the partial Latin translation of Leonardo Bruni.[24]

Bruni was Ficino's most important immediate predecessor as translator of the *Phaedrus*, and he also preceded Ficino to some extent in seeking to re-elaborate the Platonic doctrine of divine frenzy, devoting particular attention to the poetic frenzy. In 1429, having evidently reflected at length on the theory of divine frenzy contained in the *Phaedrus*, Bruni wrote a letter to the poet Giovanni Marrasio, explaining his understanding of the Platonic concept of divine frenzy, particularly as it applies to poets:

> Not every work is a poem – not even indeed if it consists in verses – but that most excellent work, that work most worthy of that honoured name, which is sent out from a certain divine inspiration. And so just as much as prophecy is superior in dignity to conjecture, to the same degree the poem that is from frenzy is to be placed before the craftsmanship of sane men ... Poets also prove to be good only when they are seized by that frenzy. For which reason we call them *vates*, seized by a certain fury, as it were. But he who approaches the poetic gates without the frenzy of the Muses, as Plato says, hoping that he will emerge as a good poet by a certain craft, as it were, is himself hollow, and his poetry, which comes from prudence, is demolished before that which comes from frenzy.[25]

Here Bruni not only approves Plato's notion that frenzied poets are superior to those who retain their habitual state of mind, but he also asserts that the phenomenon of poetic frenzy can be accessed by contemporary poets. Ficino adopts both of these conclusions, and it is reasonable to think that Ficino was influenced by this reflection on the subject of poetic frenzy as well as by Bruni's translation work.

Outside of this text, Bruni's writing on poetic frenzy is limited, but he does offer some brief remarks on the subject in a crucial passage of his 1436 *Vita di Dante*. Reiterating the sharp distinction between those who create poetry while inspired by the poetic frenzy and those who create poetry through patient work and study, Bruni unequivocally assigns Dante to the latter category, asserting that "Dante was of this second type: he acquired learning through the study of philosophy, theology, astrology, arithmetic, and geometry, by reading histories, poring over numerous and varied books, working into the night and sweating in his studies, and it was this learning which he rendered beautiful and clear with his verses."[26] In contrast, Bruni cites Orpheus and Hesiod as examples of poets of frenzy.

There can be little doubt about the real reasons for Bruni's characterization of the *Divine Comedy* as a product of erudition: Bruni's primary goal in writing his *Vita di Dante* is to portray the poet as praiseworthy above all for his dedication to civic affairs, an ideal central to Bruni's brand of humanism. Bruni's fundamental privileging of civic over contemplative ideals is ultimately the reason not only for his conclusion that poetic frenzy could not have produced the deeply political poetry of Dante, but also for the relatively measured interest that he shows in the entire Platonic framework linking poetic inspiration to contemplative rapture – the framework that he himself, through his pioneering (albeit incomplete) work translating the *Phaedrus*, had played a crucial role in recovering.

Ficino, by contrast, embraced and elaborated the theory of divine frenzy with far greater zeal than his predecessor. While following in Bruni's footsteps as an interpreter of Plato, he turned the concept of poetic frenzy into the cornerstone of a larger theoretical framework about poetry that he articulated in numerous writings. His fascination with Plato's four categories of divine frenzy, and in particular with the implications of the poetic frenzy, is evident beginning with the composition of his 1457 letter *De divino furore* to Pellegrino Agli. This extremely important text – Ficino's first widely influential work – offers a theoretical framework that is essential to understanding Ficino's lifelong efforts to revive ancient theories and practices of poetry along what he took to be Orphic and Platonic lines. It also contains Ficino's earliest known quotation of Orphic poetry: Ficino quotes several verses that he had found attributed to Orpheus in the pseudo-Aristotelian *Liber de mundo*. He read (and quoted) the text not in the original Greek but in the thirteenth-century Latin translation by Nicholas of Sicily.[27]

Ficino, ostensibly replying to two letters (one in verse and one in prose) Agli had composed, praises Agli's poetry as the product not merely of refined technique but of divine frenzy. In the treatise, Ficino explains that every human soul has the potential to channel poetic frenzy, because all souls were exposed to the divine harmonies of heaven before they descended to Earth. The longing to experience again that celestial harmony can inflame the soul and cause it to burst into a divine poetic frenzy:

> In Plato's view, this poetic frenzy springs from the Muses; but he considers both the man and his poetry worthless who approaches the doors of poetry without the call of the Muses, in the hope that he will become a good poet by technique. He thinks that those poets who are possessed by divine inspiration and power often utter such supreme words when inspired by the Muses, that afterwards, when the rapture has left them, they themselves scarcely understand what they have uttered.[28]

In this letter Ficino makes a bold pronouncement about what constitutes true poetry, as opposed to vulgar song: true poetry must not only imitate the harmony of the spheres through euphony of sounds and rhythm but must also contain profound and prophetic meanings, and by these means kindle the soul of a listener with "the desire to fly back to its rightful home." Such poetry cannot be produced through technique alone; it must be inspired directly by the Muses. Following Plato's *Phaedrus*, Ficino wrote that poetic inspiration of this kind was one of four categories of ecstatic state that could lift the human soul into contact with divinity. In the *De amore*, Ficino explains how the poetic frenzy relates to these other types of ecstatic states:

> There are four species of divine madness. The first certainly is poetic madness, the second, mysterial, the third, prophecy, the fourth, amatory feeling ... Therefore first there is need for the poetic madness, which, through musical sounds, arouses those parts of the soul which are asleep, through harmonious sweetness calms those which are perturbed, and finally, through the consonance of diverse things, drives away dissonant discord and tempers the various parts of the soul ... That Orpheus was seized by all of these madnesses, his books can testify.[29]

While this section of the *De amore* explains how Ficino conceptualized the internal experience of the inspired poet, and the role of the poetic frenzy in the ascent of the ladder of contemplation, it does not explain how this inner experience gives rise to outward expression – that is, to the composition of poetry. In his commentary on Plato's *Phaedrus*, Ficino attempts to answer this question:

> Whoever experiences any kind of spiritual possession is indeed over-flowing on account of the vehemence of the divine impulse and the fullness of its power: he raves, exults, and exceeds the bounds of human behavior. Not unjustly, therefore, this possession or rapture is called frenzy and aliena-tion. But no man possessed is content with simple speech: he bursts forth into clamoring and songs and poems. Any frenzy, therefore – whether the prophetic, hieratic, or amatory – when it proceeds to songs and poems, seems to be released, and properly so, as poetic frenzy.[30]

Here Ficino clarifies that, in terms of inner experience, the poetic frenzy is the first of the four stages of contemplative ascent, while in terms of outward expression, the poetic frenzy is the faculty that gives a suitable form (i.e., verse) to the insights achieved through all four of the frenzies. It is the poetic frenzy that enables the individual who has glimpsed divine truths to communicate these truths to an audience.

Further evidence for the idea that Ficino's interest in poetic frenzy was not merely theoretical is provided by the letters which Ficino wrote to the many poets whom he counted among his friends and acquaintances. In these letters, Ficino offers his theory of poetic frenzy not as a philo-sophical or literary curiosity but as a practical road map for reforming contemporary poetic practice around Platonic and Orphic principles. For one thing, Ficino is eager to affirm that the poets with whom he corresponds are vessels of the divine poetic frenzy. At the opening of *De divino furore* Ficino declares that he recognizes in the poetry of his corre-spondent, Pellegrino Agli, the true inspiration of divine frenzy:

> This I ascribe not just to study and technique, but much more to divine frenzy. Without this, say Democritus and Plato, no man has ever been great. The powerful emotion and burning desire which your writings express prove, as I have said, that you are inspired and inwardly possessed by that frenzy; and this power, which is manifested in external movements, the ancient philosophers maintained was the most potent proof that the divine force dwelt in our souls.[31]

At the closing of the letter, Ficino reiterates that Agli has received di-vine inspiration and exhorts him to regard his inspired poetry with the proper humility, since its merits come not from the poet but from God:

> I have chosen to describe at greater length the frenzy belonging to divine love and poetry for two reasons: first, because I know you are strongly

moved by both of these; and second, so that you will remember that what is written by you comes not from you but from Jove and the Muses, with whose spirit and divinity you are filled. For this reason, my Pellegrino, you will act justly and rightly if you acknowledge, as I believe you do already, that the author and cause of what is best and greatest is not you, nor indeed any other man, but immortal God.[32]

As we can see in this last passage, Ficino's intention in ascribing divine inspiration to his poet friends is not merely to flatter them but more importantly to direct their attitudes and poetic practices towards his own ideals. This strategy is also evident in a letter that he wrote to the poet Alessandro Braccesi, entitled "True poetry is from God and for God" (*Vera poesis a Deo et ad Deum*). Ficino starts the exposition of his thesis immediately by addressing Braccesi as "a priest of the Muses" and goes on to discuss some of Braccesi's "songs" that Ficino had received the previous day. Having, in essence, subjected them to testing by performing them on his lyre, Ficino concludes that, since they roused "both singer and audience to frenzy," Braccesi's works meet the criteria for divine inspiration according to Plato. And having apparently sought a second opinion for good measure, Ficino reports additionally that "a little later this was confirmed by our friend, Giovanni Battista Buoninsegni, the Greek and Latin scholar." Following this confirmation of the divine inspiration behind Braccesi's poetry, Ficino exhorts Braccesi,

> From now on, my friend, I beg you to forget mortal men and, since your song is God-inspired, to sing of God. For not only Moses and David but the other Hebrew prophets clearly warned us to do this by their religious songs, as also did Zoroaster, Linus, Orpheus, Museus, Moses, Empedocles, Parmenides, Heraclitus and Xenophanes. So besides did Pythagoras and Plato, who banished Homer and Hesiod from the company of men to the Underworld, partly because they improperly ascribed divine qualities to men and partly because they impiously ascribed human qualities to the gods. Similarly, if you sing of men alone, as if you were perhaps ungrateful to God, which heaven forbid, you will sing mostly of men who are ungrateful and dumb. But as often as you sing of God (which I hope you will do), so often shall Echo sweetly and happily accompany your song.[33]

From Ficino's comments about the poetry of Agli and Braccesi we can identify a number of qualities that Ficino actively encouraged the poets of his circle to cultivate. Poetry that displays "powerful emotion and burning desire" gives evidence of divine inspiration, he writes; presumably the desire he refers to is the soul's longing for its maker, a recurring theme in Ficino's philosophy. Ficino stresses that both Agli and Braccesi should openly declare that their verses are created not by them but by God (or the Muses, which for Ficino amounts to an alternate way of describing the same kind of divine inspiration). Ficino discourages Braccesi from composing poetry about humans: his poems, inspired by God, should also have God as their subject. However, poets must avoid impiously ascribing human qualities to God (one of the mistakes which caused Homer to earn Plato's disapproval). The proper subject matter for poetry, then, is true theological insights – which in Ficino's perspective means theology consistent with Christian doctrine but also with Platonic philosophy and the other teachings of the *prisca theologia* (Orphism, Hermeticism, etc.). This last point is confirmed by Ficino's apparently rather miscellaneous list of authorities, which includes biblical prophets alongside *prisci theologi*. Some of the figures (like Plato) wrote authoritatively about poetry, while others (David, Orpheus, Parmenides) wrote poetry themselves and therefore offer a model of the sort of poetry that Braccesi should aspire to write.

It is not always clear what Ficino's correspondents made of his pronouncements regarding their inspired verse, but there is evidence that Agli, to whom Ficino dedicated his letter *De divino furore*, was genuinely interested in the phenomenon of oral poetry and accepted, to some extent, Ficino's framework of poetic frenzy. Not only was Agli a poet himself; he also demonstrated a special interest in Homer's life and the oral performance of Homeric poetry and produced the earliest translation of the pseudo-Herodotean *Life of Homer* from Greek into Latin. The translation was never printed; it is preserved in an elegant manuscript at Florence's Biblioteca Medicea Laurenziana (MS Plut. 65.52), partly in the hand of the humanist Bartolomeo Fonzio.[34] Agli's preface to the translation, dedicating it to Lorenzo de' Medici, reveals that his familiarity with the theory of poetic frenzy shaped the way in which he interpreted the biography of Homer. Deploying the familiar dichotomy of inspiration versus craft, Agli remarks that Homer's works "appear to have been poured forth by instinct and by divine inspiration, rather than worked out by human application."[35] He goes on to paraphrase the Platonic theory that, as Agli puts it, poets "are not able to write anything outstanding without that heat and that power of the mind which is called divine frenzy."[36]

In his letter to Braccesi, Ficino acknowledges Plato as the authority who allows him to identify Braccesi's poetry as divinely inspired, but he is not citing the *Phaedrus*; rather, Ficino refers specifically to the *Ion*, to which he attributes the criterion that divinely inspired poetry puts both performer and audience into a state of frenzy. Ficino's reliance on the

Ion is worth exploring in greater depth, since the text itself offers a more complicated picture of poetic frenzy than Ficino implies.

Ficino's *De divino furore*, with its exposition of the Platonic theory of poetic frenzy, had a significant effect on Florentine intellectual preoccupations, awakening interest among his contemporaries in studying Plato's articulations of frenzy.[37] When Ficino completed his translation of Plato's *Ion*, it served to bolster this interest – perhaps surprisingly, given that the *Ion* does not portray poetic frenzy as an entirely admirable phenomenon. Kristeller has argued that Ficino must have completed his translation of the *Ion* by April 1466.[38] When Ficino undertook his translation of the *Ion*, he dedicated it not to Piero de' Medici, the head of Florence's ruling family at the time, but to his son Lorenzo, then seventeen years old. Lorenzo's poetic gifts were already evident at this early age, and the text of Ficino's dedication suggests that his choice of Lorenzo as dedicatee was determined by Lorenzo's poetic vocation. At the conclusion of his introduction to the *Ion*, Ficino claims – in Platonic terms – that Lorenzo has been inspired by Phoebus, the same god who inspired the ancient poet-singer Linus:

> The same god who seized Linus, and who even now inspires you, O Lorenzo, best of men, is Phoebus – it is Phoebus who gave prophecy to your grandfather Cosimo, but the bow and healing cures to your father Piero, and who at last bestows on you his lyre and his songs.[39]

The passage suggests that Ficino recognized that Lorenzo's own gifts for performing oral poetry to the accompaniment of the lyre could serve as a point of connection with Ficino's evolving Neoplatonic theories of poetic inspiration. Ficino dedicated his translation of the *Ion* to Lorenzo in part because, as a budding oral poet himself, Lorenzo could be expected to take particular interest in Plato's most extended discussion of the frenzy of the oral poet.

So it is clear why the subject matter of the *Ion* was of particular interest to Ficino, given his dedication to musical-poetic performance, and why he saw it as potentially of special interest to the young poet Lorenzo. The *Ion* is the only Platonic dialogue focused throughout on the topic of oral poetic performance, and the representation, within the dialogue, of Socrates's interlocutor – the bard Ion, prize-winning performer of Homer's poetry – is one of the most detailed portrayals preserved in classical Athenian literature of a practitioner of this type of oral poetic performance.

It is not a flattering portrayal. In the dialogue the naive bard's initial claims to being a skilful and knowledgeable performer and interpreter of Homer's poetry are dismantled by the relentless ironic questioning of

Socrates. Socrates forces Ion to confess that he does not in fact possess the skill and knowledge that he had claimed. After all, the Homeric poems deal with a range of subjects – warfare, seafaring, medicine, etc. – and since Ion has no training in these fields, his success as an interpreter cannot be based on this sort of skill and knowledge. Moreover, other poets (like Hesiod) treat similar topics, but Ion, by his own admission, excels only at performing and interpreting Homer. Ultimately Socrates proposes an alternative explanation: that Ion's success as a rhapsode, and Homer's as a poet, is made possible not by knowledge but by a divine force that takes possession of the bard. Socrates compares the grip of this power to the force of a magnet:

> For, as I was saying just now, this is not an art in you, whereby you speak well on Homer, but a divine power, which moves you like that in the stone which Euripides named a magnet ... For this stone not only attracts iron rings, but also imparts to them a power whereby they in turn are able to do the very same thing as the stone, and attract other rings; so that sometimes there is formed quite a long chain of bits of iron and rings, suspended one from another; and they all depend for this power on that one stone. In the same manner also the Muse inspires men herself, and then by means of these inspired persons the inspiration spreads to others, and holds them in a connected chain. For all the good epic poets utter all those fine poems not from art, but as inspired and possessed.[40]

Ion eagerly confirms to Socrates that he experiences a kind of ecstatic state while performing Homer's poetry and seems pleased to accept the notion that he is a subject of divine possession. Yet whatever divine possession might have passed through Ion has clearly not left him with any stable understanding of the true or the good; the dialectical method exemplified by Socrates is presented, implicitly, as the superior path to achieving such understanding. Socrates's arguments, then, seem designed to undercut the authority that had traditionally been ascribed to the oral poets. As Reginald E. Allen has commented, "To describe rhapsody or poetry as a matter of divine apportionment without intelligence is not to praise it but to dismiss it."[41]

Ficino does not seem to have seen it this way.[42] In his introduction to Plato's *Ion*, Ficino offers a definition of the term *rhapsode* and asserts that rhapsodes can possess divine frenzy:

> But "rhapsode" in this book signifies a reciter, interpreter and singer of poems. Ion interpreted the poetry of Homer, and in the presence of an audience he sang to the lyre and was so moved that he could expound no other poet except Homer ... [A]s an interpreter of a poet, Ion and many

other rhapsodes who have been similarly affected interpret poetry that is not theirs by divine instinct [only]. But if [ordinary] human intelligence is not enough to perceive poetry that has already been handed down to us, then much less will it suffice to discover or invent poetry.[43]

Ficino's inability or unwillingness to recognize irony or ambivalence in Plato's treatments of the poetic frenzy had major consequences on those who followed him – beginning with his friend Cristoforo Landino. Since Landino did not have advanced knowledge of Greek, his interpretations of Platonic thought depended crucially on Ficino's translations and interpretations. Landino assumed, following Ficino, that the conceit of the poet as vessel of divine inspiration found in the *Ion* and *Phaedrus* corresponded to Plato's own earnest belief; he also went on to elaborate, on this basis, his own exalted conception of the poet as a semi-divine creator. In his 1482 Horace commentary, Landino writes:

Man makes out of matter whatever he makes. God creates out of nothing. But the poet, although he does not quite produce something out of nothing, yet, inspired by Divine madness, he does form something in an elegant song, so that he seems, by his fictions, to have produced highly admirable things nearly out of nothing.[44]

We have already seen, in the discussions of Ficino's correspondence with Pellegrino Agli and Alessandro Braccesi, how Ficino's collected letters reveal a programmatic outreach on Ficino's part towards the poets with whom he had personal relationships, aimed at promoting a wider dissemination and implementation of concepts and practices of poetry founded on what Ficino believed to be a Platonic theory of divine poetic frenzy. Ficino's approach to the performance of poetry (including the poetry of Agli and Braccesi) involved soloistic singing of verse to instrumental accompaniment. Ficino's musical instrument itself, his Orphic lyre, survived as an artefact for some time – at least into the second half of the sixteenth century, when it was in the possession of the jurist Bartolomeo Romuleo.[45] Enough is known about Ficino's lyre, then, to draw some general conclusions about the nature of the instrument; D.P. Walker wrote, "It seems to me likely then that Ficino accompanied his planetary songs on the *lira da braccio*." Walker goes on to propose, albeit tentatively, a further possible conclusion: "If this conjecture is correct, one might suppose that Ficino's music was like that of the 'improvvisatori sulla lira,' of which, unfortunately, we know very little."[46] The notion that Ficino's Orphic performance might have been directly modelled on the practices of Italian *improvvisatori* is a significant observation, but Walker does not explore possible connections between Ficino and the *improvvisatori* in greater depth. Given that, as far as can be determined, Ficino's music was never set down and preserved in musical notation (nor would this be surprising for improvised performance), it is indeed impossible to directly verify Walker's supposition that Ficino's performance style was modelled on that of the *improvvisatori*. But we do not need access to transcriptions of Ficino's performances to know that his engagement with the work of the *improvvisatori* was deep and fruitful: surviving sources reveal that Ficino was fascinated with improvisation as a popular practice in the world around him. And while scholars have recognized that Ficino's activities as a theorist and practitioner of oral poetry were influenced by his engagement with ancient texts, it has not been acknowledged that these activities took shape in the context of a dialogue between Ficino and important oral poets of his time. Many of the poets who belonged to Ficino's circle and corresponded with him on literary and other matters had a documented interest in musical-poetic performance, including some who were famed as *improvvisatori*.

We have already seen, briefly, the letter in which the humanist Giannantonio Campano describes the frenzy that supposedly possessed Ficino while singing and playing his Orphic lyre. While these verses by Campano have been discussed in relation to Ficino's Orphic singing by scholars including John Warden, the larger context of Campano's verses has rarely been considered.[47] The poem is part of a letter that Campano wrote while residing in Germany to the Florentine Gentile Becchi, best known as teacher of the young Lorenzo de' Medici. Together with the poem about Ficino, the letter contains a series of verse tributes to Campano's Italian friends, expressing his nostalgia for the rich intellectual, social, and poetic world he had come to know in Florence and Rome, which he keenly misses during his sojourn in Germany. Improvisatory performance of sung poetry emerges as a central facet of the cultural life of this circle, not just in Campano's verses about Ficino but also in those which follow them, dedicated to Baccio Ugolini and Cherubino Quarquagli, who were mutual friends of Campano's and Ficino's and both famed improvisors.

Ugolini was among the best known of the Florentine *improvvisatori* of the fifteenth century. According to the testimony of Paolo Cortesi, in fact, Ugolini was, along with Jacopo Corsi, considered the greatest improvisor of his day in Italy.[48] Discussing Ugolini, Campano's letter evokes the improvisor's penchant for wandering the city after dark performing verses to the accompaniment of a string instrument:

> Does Baccio, as he once did, still carry his cythara all over town, singing to the windows that are closed for a night of sleep? Does his song still praise Amasina? Does he still remember Campano? Or, now that I have been

compelled to leave both Rome and Latium, am I nothing to him? Has he drunk from the river of oblivion?[49]

The fact that Campano juxtaposes descriptions of Ficino's Orphic singing and Ugolini's musical wandering in the context of a panegyric to Italy's improvisatory music scene is important evidence. It demonstrates that Ficino's Orphic music was seen by contemporaries as closely connected with the kind of improvised music that was then popular in Florence. Furthermore, Campano's letter uses the same classicizing term – *cythara* – for Ugolini's instrument as for Ficino's, though we know from other contemporary accounts of Ugolini's music that Campano is referring here to the instrument usually called the *lira da braccio*.

The situation described in Campano's letter – that of the sleepless love poet singing the praises of his beloved through the streets – likely refers to Ugolini's performances in the musical-poetic genre known as the *strambotto*: vernacular lyric love poetry in the *ottava rima* metre, a form widely cultivated by Quattrocento *improvvisatori*, including Ugolini. Because of the genre's oral and improvisational nature, far fewer *strambotti* survive in written form than one might otherwise expect for a widely popular literary genre. Only a few *strambotti* attributable to Baccio Ugolini have been preserved. One example, discussed by Nino Pirrotta, is contained in MS 55 of the Biblioteca Trivulziana of Milan, which preserves both text and music of a *strambotto*.[50] If the music contained in this manuscript was indeed composed by Ugolini, it may offer some clues to the type of melodic elements that would have been used (improvised or otherwise) to accompany *strambotti* in the elite musical and poetic circles of Medicean Florence and in the initial performance of Poliziano's *Orfeo*, with Ugolini playing the role of Orpheus, as will be discussed in greater depth in the next chapter. *Strambotti* attributed to Ugolini (with no music preserved) are also found in the Vatican Library MS Urb. 729, a collection of *strambotti* by various poets of the late Quattrocento and early Cinquecento, many of them connected with the Roman circle of Paolo Cortesi.[51]

Thanks to his skill as an instrumentalist and singer, Ugolini was often praised, like Ficino, as a kind of modern-day Orpheus. Ugolini played the part of Orpheus in a more literal sense, too, acting the role of Orpheus in at least two dramatic performances that we know of: the debut performance of Angelo Poliziano's *Fabula di Orfeo* and an earlier Orphic spectacle staged in Rome in 1473 in honour of the impending marriage of Eleonora d'Aragona and Ercole d'Este.[52] Porcellio Pandone recounts that, as part of this Roman spectacle, the "Thracian priest" Orpheus appeared on stage dressed in a long robe, playing "the *cythara* which moves the weapons of Jove, and soothes tigers."[53] The identity of the actor playing Orpheus is revealed in a poetic account of the event by Paolo Emilio Boccabella, a member of Pomponio Leto's Roman Academy, who gave a positive review, writing that Baccio/Orpheus "outdoes all other extemporaneous poets." Playing on the similarities between Baccio Ugolini's name and that of the god Bacchus, Boccadella's text claims that Baccio/Orpheus "runs riot" (*exultat*) during this extemporaneous performance, seemingly given over to a Bacchic frenzy.[54]

Ficino and Ugolini shared a lifelong friendship, as witnessed by a pair of letters that Ficino published in his collected correspondence. In one of these, a famous 1492 letter addressed to Martin Prenninger, Ficino includes a list of his friends and students. He lists Baccio Ugolini as one of his old friends, a group that he characterizes as "friends through close association, conversation-partners so to speak, those who share in to-and-fro discussions and liberal studies."[55] On 15 June 1493 Ficino sent a letter to Ugolini with a copy of his *Liber de sole* – a sophisticated philosophical text expounding Ficino's Neoplatonic solar theology. Ficino's correspondence with Ugolini thus embodies the sort of shared intellectual discussion that, in the letter to Prenninger, he describes sharing with Ugolini and his other old friends. This deep friendship between Ficino and Ugolini is important as further evidence that the worlds of humanist learning and poetic improvisation were not separate but often intimately connected – and that this connection applies not just to experiments in improvisation and poetic performance in Latin but to the sort of vernacular improvisation widely practised in both urban and courtly contexts in this period.

There is evidence, too, that Ficino sought to bring *improvvisatori* like Ugolini on board with his theories of poetic frenzy, connecting his interpretations of Plato's writings on frenzy with the activities of contemporary *improvvisatori*. We see this in a letter written by Ficino on 4 March 1474 to Antonio Pelotti and Baccio Ugolini, offering a concise exposition of his theory of Platonic frenzy. In the letter, Ficino names several poets whom he says Plato regarded as "true" poets inspired by frenzy – the first is Orpheus, followed by Homer, Hesiod, and Pindar. The central focus of the letter is the skill/frenzy dichotomy dealt with at length in Plato's *Phaedrus* and *Ion*. As Ficino puts it, "No one, however diligent and learned in all the arts, has ever excelled in poetry unless to these other qualities has been added a fiery quickening of the soul. We experience this when we are inflamed by God's presence working in us. Such force carries the seed of the divine mind."[56] He thus presents divine frenzy as an experience with which both he and his correspondents are personally familiar, evidence that Ficino viewed the theory of frenzy as particularly relevant to the performative poets of his circle.

Campano's letter, alongside its praise of the musical-poetic performances of Ficino and Baccio Ugolini, also praises those of Cherubino
Quarquagli, another of Ficino's friends and correspondents who achieved
fame as an oral poet and improvisor.[57] Campano recalls Quarquagli improvising while the two of them wandered the streets of Rome:

> Apollo loves Quarquagli, dark in face but serene in mind, and Quarquagli
> has the spirit of Apollo in his breast. He sings happy things, and calls
> out with his sweet voice to nymphs, for whom he even lost two teeth. For
> when he preferred Cyrrha to Nisa, Hyacus became upset and smashed a
> glass against his face with his enraged hand. But he was not able to make
> Quarquagli drop his cithara.[58]

Quarquagli was an early member of Ficino's circle – according to Ficino,
he was among those who attended the first lectures Ficino gave in 1468.[59]
Ficino insists on his closeness with Quarquagli in a letter to Giovanni
Niccolini, in which he writes, "Be so good as to tell me: did you think that
our Quarquagli had now slipped from our memory? Anyone who thinks
I have forgotten my Quarquagli would also think I have forgotten myself."[60] In fact, Ficino wrote a philosophical treatise, De officiis, as a letter to
Quarquagli, which discusses, among other things, the duties of the poet
and of the musician. Echoing a theme found in the letter to Alessandro
Braccesi cited above, Ficino writes, "David and Hermes Trismegistus command that, as we are moved by God to sing, of God alone we should sing."[61]
Surviving sources reveal that Quarquagli produced poetry both in Latin
and in Tuscan. As a vernacular poet he, like Ugolini, was known for his
cultivation of the *strambotto* form. His *strambotti* were reportedly admired
and imitated by none other than Serafino Aquilano – perhaps the most
renowned performative poet of early Cinquecento Italy. Angelo Colocci –
humanist papal secretary and editor of Serafino's works – claims that some
of Serafino's *strambotti* were based on those of Quarquagli.[62] His fame as
an *improvvisatore* is also reflected in the inclusion of *strambotti* attributed
to Quarquagli in some of the most important collections of *strambotti* as-
sembled around the turn of the sixteenth century. The MS Vat. Urb. 729
is one such manuscript: it contains two *strambotti* by Quarquagli alongside
strambotti by numerous poets known for their skills as improvisors, including Baccio Ugolini, Girolamo Benivieni, Chariteo, and Tebaldeo.[63]
Another poet who had close ties to Ficino based on their mutual interest in musical-poetic performance was Sebastiano Foresi, the author
of a dream-vision poem in Dantean *terza rima* entitled *Trionfo delle virtù*;
Ficino wrote a letter presenting Foresi and his poem to Lorenzo de' Medici.[64] In a letter that Ficino wrote to Foresi dated 11 August 1476, Ficino

alludes to their shared interest in instrumental performance on the lyre and to an agreement the two men had apparently made that neither was to play the lyre except in the presence of the other:

> What are you doing today, my Foresi? Are you playing the lyre? Take heed that you do not play it without Marsilio! Otherwise, if you break faith with me, the strings of your lyre will sound completely out of tune to you. As often as I sing with my lyre, I sing in harmony with you. To me no melody is sweet without the sweetest friend.
>
> Commend me to my Landino, a true friend.[65]

In another letter to Foresi, Ficino expresses concern about his friend spending time on the construction of a lyre – time which might, he implies, be better spent playing music with Ficino:

> There is no one amongst all my friends with whom I converse more profoundly and more enjoyably than with you, my sweet Foresi. For I address others with only the tongue or the pen, but you I often address with lute and lyre. In fact, without you my lutes are silent, my lyres mute. Come, I beseech you, my Foresi, whenever you sing to the lyre, sing in harmony with me. But I see that while you are so intent upon constructing one lyre, you are forgetting the music of the other. Amongst the heavenly beings, Sebastiano, even Phoebus does not both play the lyre and make it, while Mercury makes the lyre but does not play it. Therefore, let no-one on earth presume to exercise equally the skills of making and of playing the lyre.[66]

Ficino's letters to Foresi dealt with the intellectual as well as the practical aspects of musical performance, however. On 8 September 1479, Ficino wrote a letter to Foresi in which he asserts that musical talent often goes hand in hand with intellectual gifts, and especially with aptitude for humanistic and literary studies. After closing the body of the letter, Ficino adds a postscript describing how he was seized with the urge to take up his lyre and sing the hymns of Orpheus:

> Now, my Foresi, just after I had written farewell, I rose to my feet, and hastened to take up the lyre. I began to sing at length from the hymns of Orpheus. Get up yourself, get up as soon as you have read this second farewell and, if you are wise, willingly take up the lyre, that sweet solace of labour.[67]

Ficino was also in frequent correspondence with a poet named Antonio from San Miniato – identified by Arnaldo Della Torre as the *canterino* Antonio d'Agostino da S. Miniato, who is documented as having held public performances in Florence's Piazza San Martino.[68] One of the poems that Antonio performed has survived, thanks to a manuscript, today in Florence's Biblioteca Nazionale Centrale, that originally belonged to Michele del Giogante, the impresario who organized and promoted many of the performances held in Piazza San Martino.[69] The work in question is a *terza rima* narrative poem about the 1448 siege of Piombino; a note appended to the text claims that the poet was an eyewitness of the events described. In the opening stanzas the poet invokes the inspiration of Apollo, the Muses, and other pagan divinities. The text points emphatically to an oral performative context: the poet addresses his audience as "circostanti" (bystanders) and refers to them listening to, hearing, and seeing the performance.

The correspondence between the two men implies that Antonio regarded Ficino as a theorist of oral poetry who could provide feedback on his verses. Antonio apparently sent Ficino some verses he had written in the form of a prophecy, to which Ficino replied rather hesitantly:

> I hesitate to call you mad, but nevertheless I will not call you a prophet until I see those things come about which you predict for the future. I am about to go to Rome, and shortly thereafter to return; on my return I will come to you right away with my lyre: thus you will teach me these things.[70]

In this response we get a glimpse of two important and overlooked facets of Ficino's relationship with performers like Antonio. First, it is evident that Ficino's performances on his Orphic lyre were not merely the product of deep study of ancient texts but emerged from close connections and collaborations with contemporary varieties of oral poetic performance. And second, it is clear that over the course of Ficino's decades of engagement with both improvisational practices and Plato's poetics of frenzy, he became an authority within a circle of oral poets intrigued by the possibility of linking their own performative activities with Ficino's theories of inspired poetry. The theory of frenzy promoted by Ficino was used by *improvvisatori* within and beyond Ficino's network as a conceptual framework for describing the altered state of consciousness associated with improvisation.

Ficino's efforts to disseminate his version of the Platonic theory of poetic frenzy were highly successful, and the impact of these theories on *improvvisatori* can be clearly documented in surviving written sources. Given the ephemeral nature of improvised performance, there is little doubt that the landscape of oral poetic performances displaying the influence of Ficino's theories in his own time was far more extensive than what has survived. Among the rare examples of Quattrocento *improvvisatori* whose orally composed works were entrusted to writing and survive, perhaps the most prominent is Cristoforo Fiorentino, known as l'Altissimo. The influence of Ficino on l'Altissimo, as we will see, is not hard to detect.

The skill of l'Altissimo as a singer and musician earned him – like many of his colleagues – fame as a kind of modern-day Orpheus. Niccolò degli Agostini, who claimed to be a proficient improvisor of poetry himself, authored a *strambotto* in which he asserts that l'Altissimo's song has showed itself to be more powerful than that of Amphion, Arion, and Orpheus:

> If Amphion, with his song and his sweet lyre
> built the walls around ancient Thebes;
> If Arion, scorning the ire of Neptune,
> plied the sea upon a dolphin;
> If Orpheus dragged his Eurydice from the very centre
> where every soul sighs, up through the dark strata;
> You, Altissimo, have accomplished more
> with song alone than all of them ever did.[71]

The apex of l'Altissimo's career as *improvvisatore* was a cycle of ninety-four performances he gave in Piazza San Martino beginning on 4 June 1514 and concluding on 15 July 1515, in which he retold, in verse, the major episodes of Andrea da Barberino's prose romance *I Reali di Francia*. The following year, 1516, saw l'Altissimo's first known publication, the full printed title of which was *La Rotta di Ravenna, cantata in san Martino di Fiorenza all'improviso dal Altissimo poeta fiorentino, poeta laureato: Copiata dalla viva voce da varie persone mentre cantava* (*The Rout of Ravenna, sung extemporaneously in San Martino in Florence by the Florentine poet Altissimo, poet laureate: Transcribed from the live performance by various persons while he was singing*). The title makes it clear that the printer was eager to advertise the improvisational gifts of the poet and the status of the printed book as a faithful transcription of an actual oral performance. Similar claims appear in the paratexts accompanying l'Altissimo's *Primo libro de' Reali*, which was printed posthumously.

Until recent years, the few scholars who have written about l'Altissimo have tended to assume that these claims could not be accurate – that the massive poetic text, while it might well have been recited orally, must have been composed in written form and that the printed text must derive from this written text composed by the author. Luca Degl'Innocenti's recent work has challenged such assumptions. Degl'Innocenti has convincingly argued that the printed text of the *Primo libro de' Reali* is in fact the product of the transcription of an oral performance, probably carried out using the technique known in Latin, from antiquity to the Renaissance, as *reportatio*, which typically involved a team of scribes who, working together, could successfully keep up with the pace of a poem's oral delivery. In support of this argument Degl'Innocenti has marshalled an array of textual details – references to objects visible to the audience, internal inconsistencies, and so on – that are readily understandable in a work composed and delivered orally but would be difficult to account for in a text composed in writing.[72]

Texts attributed to l'Altissimo reveal that Ficino's poetic theories were an important influence on this *improvvisatore*. For one thing, his invocations often mention divine frenzy, a theory which Ficino was responsible for popularizing among his contemporaries. In the first of the invocations of the *Primo libro de' Reali*, the divine frenzy that the poet hopes to harness in his performance is explicitly identified with the inspiration of the Holy Spirit:

> O virtue that the Egyptians called Mind,
> Divine Mind, and then somewhere the Greeks
> called burning divine frenzy,
> because this frenzy so enflames everything
> that it lifts the soul up to God; and in the present day
> we call the Holy Spirit,
> that inspires poets with the secrets of God;
> let this pour into my breast.[73]

As Degl'Innocenti notes, the reference to "Egyptians" in this invocation is probably to be understood as referring to the Hermetic writings, which had been translated by Marsilio Ficino. L'Altissimo also refers to the source of his own inspiration as divine frenzy at numerous other points in the poem – often in the invocations with which he customarily began performances. For instance, the opening *ottava* of the seventy-first *cantare* of the poem ends with these verses: "Infondi in me del tuo divin furore, / tanto ch'io piaccia a ciascun auditore" ("Pour into me your divine frenzy / so much that I might prove pleasing to every listener"). The same pair of verses (with small variations) is also found at two other points in the poem.[74] L'Altissimo's habit of discussing his own improvisations as products of divine frenzy is clearly a reflection of the success of Ficino's efforts to popularize the Platonic theory of frenzy.

There can be no doubt that l'Altissimo was intensely interested in other aspects of Ficino's philosophy, too. As Degl'Innocenti has shown, *cantari* 74 and 75 of l'Altissimo's *Primo Libro de' Reali* are essentially a long verse adaptation of Ficino's 1457 philosophical treatise *Di Dio et anima*.[75] The case is fascinating for what it reveals about the pathways by which the work of a leading philosopher like Ficino could reach individuals of different class and educational backgrounds. This example not only highlights the impact of Ficino's efforts to personally prepare *volgarizzamenti* of his own Latin writings – which in this case found an eager reader in l'Altissimo. It also shows that the popular oral performances by l'Altissimo served as another channel for the diffusion of Ficinian thought to wide and diverse audiences that included illiterate Florentines. The situation inevitably calls to mind the metaphor of the magnet from Plato's *Ion* that Ficino restored to cultural currency. Ficino's thought not only exerted a magnetic sort of attraction over *improvvisatori* like Cristoforo l'Altissimo but was also transmitted, by these modern-day rhapsodes claiming to be influenced by poetic frenzy, to the large and diverse audiences that they, in turn, mesmerized.

A final example of the influence Ficino's theories of poetic frenzy exerted on the improvisational practices which had informed his interpretations in the first place is provided by the Brandolini brothers. Raffaele Brandolini (c. 1465–1517) and his elder brother Aurelio Brandolini (1454–97) were both celebrated improvisors. Both brothers also suffered progressive loss of vision culminating in near blindness and therefore, confusingly, shared the same nickname, Lippo – a term referring to inflammation of the eyes. The brothers came from a Florentine family but grew up in Naples, where Aurelio's precocious skill as an improvisor of poetry attracted the attention of Gioviano Pontano and his humanist circle. Raffaele describes Aurelio's rise to fame: "At about the age of seventeen, then, he began first with vernacular verses, soon also with Latin ones. And ... he celebrated heroic praises in extemporaneous song at the court of Ferdinand I King of Naples."[76]

Later in life Aurelio performed for and was supported by a number of powerful and wealthy patrons, including popes Sixtus IV and Innocent VIII, King Matthias Corvinus of Hungary, and Lorenzo de' Medici. Raffaele writes that his brother remained in Florence for a year, "enjoying the liberality of Lorenzo de' Medici, then ruler of the Florentine republic, although targeted by the sharp attacks of Poliziano."[77]

A remarkable testimony to the improvisational skills of the elder Brandolini brother, Aurelio, is found in an account of a performance that he gave in Rome, probably in 1485, for an audience of Venetian patricians that included Bernardo Bembo and his son Pietro (then a boy of fifteen). This account, too, reveals some of the technical challenges associated with improvised poetry. Bernardo Bembo proposed a theme for Brandolini's song – the superiority of antiquity to present times – and Brandolini, without hesitation, began singing and accompanying himself on the *lyra*, extemporaneously producing forty-nine Latin distichs on the subject. The exceptional fact that these verses – unlike the vast majority of those produced extemporaneously on such occasions – are preserved in written form (whether accurately or not) is due to the diligence of the young Pietro Bembo, who transcribed the verses as they were being sung. The extemporaneous poem itself contains an internal reference to the unusual fact of its transcription; the poet, boasting of the rapidity of his composition, challenges his transcriber to a race of sorts:

> Ready your pen, friend scribe.
> You will not be able to keep up with my words; I will go faster;
> you will not be able to write down my verses.[78]

The text also includes a disclaimer regarding the difficulty of accurately transcribing such a performance:

> If you find any verses that are not so good, ascribe that to an error on the part of those who were writing while Lippo the blind Florentine was singing.[79]

After improvising in Latin, Brandolini concludes by improvising two stanzas in vernacular Italian.

Given that both brothers' activities as performers of improvised poetry are well documented, it is illuminating to read Raffaele Brandolini's theoretical perspective on the art of musical-poetic improvisation in his Latin treatise on this subject, *De musica et poetica* (*On Music and Poetry*), which he dedicated to Pope Leo X in 1513. Raffaele's defence of improvisation reveals the extent to which improvisors practising their art within circles permeated by humanist culture drew on the Platonic theory of divine poetic frenzy, as promoted by Ficino, to elevate the value of their own art form. First Raffaele claims that "an extempore song unquestionably merits greater credit and admiration than one carefully composed."[80]

To bolster this argument Raffaele turns to familiar ideas, first invoking the distinction between "ars" and "natura" to argue that true poetry cannot be achieved merely through study, requiring divine inspiration:

> Or will you dare condemn that to which we are not educated by art but initiated by nature, and which we did not learn, accept and read with the aid of any human teacher, but seized, took in, and poured forth by divine will and inspiration, and which proceeded not from some dishonor and worthlessness, but from divine worship, from piety, from questions about nature, from the regular motions of the stars, from the institutions of human life?[81]

Raffaele also turns to ancient precedents to prove the superiority of improvisational performance, arguing that the performative dimension of poetry – as well as oratory – was considered of foremost importance in the ancient world, and reiterating that extemporaneous poets should be especially admired for their performative talents: "I maintain that the extemporaneous style in oratory or poetry deserves a higher recommendation than – or certainly an equally great one as – a long and much-polished style."[82]

Drawing ever more directly from Platonic theories of poetry recently popularized by Ficino, Brandolini uses the metaphor of the magnetic chain from Plato's *Ion* to describe the frenzy of poets, which he believes can be transmitted to others:

> Or have you not heard that poets are divinely inspired by the furor by which they are touched ... Plato said that the class of poets was divine and that poets themselves, stirred by divine instinct, imparted that same furor to their interpreters, whom he called "rhapsodes." They imitated the nature of magnetic stones that not only attract iron rings, but pass on invisibly that same attracting force to the rings themselves.[83]

While scholars have long recognized the impact of the revival of the Platonic theory of divine poetic frenzy on the theory and practice of poetry in the Renaissance, they have largely overlooked the extent to which Ficino's integration into a social world that highly valued improvisatory musical-poetic performance shaped his interpretation of the relevant Platonic texts, with deep implications for the way in which Plato's theories would be understood for centuries. Had the return of these Platonic texts to western Europe been shepherded by an interpreter without Ficino's musical and poetic interests and commitments, a quite different view of what constituted a Platonic approach to poetry might have become dominant. The very dialogues that articulate the theory present at best a mixed view of the value of poetic frenzy: the rhapsode Ion is an object of ridicule, and the theory of divine frenzy is deployed by Socrates to undermine Ion's pretentions to knowledge of his subject matter. In the *Phaedrus*, even as Socrates proposes poets as potential vessels of divine frenzy, he also ranks poets a low sixth among nine categories of human occupations – below household managers and financiers and just ahead of tyrants. The banishment of Homer from Socrates's ideal polis in the *Republic*, while not turning on the issue of frenzy, raises serious questions about the ultimate value of oral poetry from a Platonic perspective.

Yet Ficino, even as he translates the Platonic texts that speak to the "ancient quarrel" between philosophers and poets, tirelessly promotes a vision of a contemporary Platonic cultural revival that assigns a central and exalted role to oral poetic performance. One of the cornerstones of Ficino's efforts to popularize Platonism, beginning with his *De divino furore*, is his promotion of the idea that his own contemporaries can elevate their souls through the frenzied rush of inspiration experienced by poets and improvisatory performers. Ficino, whose interest in the theory of poetic frenzy was likely inspired by his early engagement with musical and poetic improvisation, quite successfully tailored his interpretation of a Platonic theory of poetry in order to speak to the values and tastes of the social and intellectual milieu in which he lived and worked. As we have seen, Ficino's two accessories, his Platonic translations and his Orphic lyre, both contributed to, and were shaped by, his lifelong interest in oral poetic performance.

And if Ficino's particular approach to Plato and poetics was influenced by his interest in improvised oral performance, the theories he developed also exerted an important influence on poetic practices of his circle. Scholars have generally not recognized a programmatic effort by Ficino to influence poetic practices in his milieu: perhaps this is because Ficino never wrote anything like an *Ars poetica*, in a period that produced countless *artes poeticae*. But this is hardly an inconsistency: the approach to poetry that Ficino called for was fundamentally based on a distinction between *ars* (skill) and *furor* (frenzy), in which he rejected the relevance of *ars* for true poetry in order to valorize *furor*. Ficino's theory addresses itself to an audience primed by the humanist thought currents of Quattrocento Italy (and Florence especially) to value poetry highly. The vision of poetry that Ficino promotes is not, however, primarily written, intellectualizing, and highly controlled but oral, spiritually and emotionally potent, and spontaneous. These are values whose resonance for Ficino, and for his milieu, depended on their immersion in the culture of oral poetic performance that, as we have seen, played such a prominent role in the life of Quattrocento Florence.

Chapter Three

"Secret Frenzies": Angelo Poliziano and Invention

In 1482, when the young scholar Angelo Poliziano began teaching a new lecture course on Virgil at Florence's university, he did so in style, delivering one of the most stunning opening lectures in the history of higher education. Instead of giving the customary prose lecture, Poliziano delivered a poetic performance, launching into an elegant Latin poem of nearly 400 verses that he had composed for the occasion: the *Manto*. We can imagine the shocked looks that Poliziano's students must have exchanged as they heard their professor begin his lecture as follows:

> It stood there still on the shore of Pagasae, the craft that first crossed the waves, its oars yet untried. But while the furled sails remain fastened to the yard-arms ... the Minyans gather at the cave of biformed Chiron ... When the meal is ended, faithful Orpheus stirs his lyre and his skillful fingers accompany the tuneful song ... And now he had charmed all things with his maternal song when suddenly he broke off and set down his plaintive lyre. Boldly Achilles takes it up and rubs his fingers upon it, and the young boy sings an unpolished tune in his untrained voice.[1]

What was the twenty-eight-year-old scholar hoping to achieve with this performance? Surely he thought a virtuoso verse production would impress his students, but the answer is more nuanced than that. As unconventional as it is, the poem is intended, on one level, as an explication of Virgil. The character Orpheus in these opening verses is usually read as standing for Virgil, while the young Achilles who imitates Orpheus represents Poliziano himself, admirer of Virgil.

This description of Orpheus's performance for the Argonauts (Minyans) is based, in part, on the *Orphic Argonautica* – the only ancient text in which Orpheus sings in the presence of Chiron and Achilles along with the Argonauts – and in this textual allusion we can detect the influence of Marsilio Ficino.[2] The *Orphic Argonautica* was part of the newly recovered Orphic corpus translated by Ficino and perhaps part of his Orphic performance repertoire; Ficino also discussed the relevant passage from the *Orphic Argonautica* in his popular work *De amore*, so awareness of this intertext would have extended beyond the privileged few who witnessed Ficino's performances.

There is another sense, too, in which we can detect the influence of Ficino's performances within the Orphic scene that opens Poliziano's poetic lecture. The description of Orpheus inspiring the younger Achilles to take up the lyre recalls a passage from Poliziano's 1473 *Elegy to Bartolomeo Fonzio* in which Ficino, compared to Orpheus, inspires the younger Poliziano to play the lyre:

> [Marsilio Ficino] often drives away heavy cares with his learned lyre and adds his voice to his melodious fingers. Just as Orpheus, the singer of Apollonian song, is said to have charmed the Thracian beasts, so [Ficino] would be able to calm African lions with his singing ... From here, when he has fallen silent, inflamed by the frenzy of the Muses I am immediately carried back to my usual dwelling, and again I ponder rhythms and provoke Phoebus and, inspired, I strike the sacred lyre with a plectrum.[3]

In this passage, Poliziano echoes the many other descriptions of Ficino we saw in the previous chapter presenting Ficino as a performer of frenzy and embodiment of Orpheus. By evoking Ficino at the beginning of his poetic lecture on Virgil, Poliziano signals its emphasis on the theme of poetic frenzy.

As we saw, Marsilio Ficino's reintroduction of the Platonic theory of divine poetic frenzy quickly attracted wide interest, first in Florence and soon in other areas of Italy and Europe, thanks in part to Ficino's dedicated outreach to literati and especially to practising poets. The appeal that the theory of frenzy held for poets and improvisors is readily understandable on a number of levels. The idea that true poetry was the product of divine inspiration could be deployed by poets to present the value and dignity of their poems in the loftiest possible terms. The prominence of oral and improvisational poetry in Florence heightened the impact of Ficino's theories, as poets like Cristoforo l'Altissimo drew connections between Plato's poetic frenzy and the rush of inspiration that fuelled their own feats of spontaneous performance.

But the Ficinian framework that celebrated poetry produced through divine frenzy (*furor*) also involved a corresponding devaluation of the importance of skill or training (*ars*), which Ficino presented as at best unnecessary and at worst a hindrance to the production of great poetry.

Given that so many of the poets of Ficino's milieu (including many of those renowned as improvisors) were erudite humanists whose poetry was profoundly shaped by diligent study of the classical tradition and by imitation of Latin and vernacular literary models, many might well have objected to this aspect of the theory of poetic frenzy as Ficino interpreted it. Surprisingly, though, Ficino's devaluation of skill and erudition in poetry for the most part did not provoke direct objections from the humanist literary elite: his detractors attacked his ideas on other grounds, while members of his own Neoplatonic circle, such as Bartolomeo Fonzio, adopted Ficino's version of the theory of poetic frenzy enthusiastically and largely without modification.[4]

Angelo Poliziano, however, who studied for a time with Ficino and became one of the most renowned classical scholars of his age, engaged with Ficino's theory in a more nuanced way. Taking Ficino's writings as a starting point but refusing to regard them, or even Plato's dialogues themselves, as the final word on the subject of *furor*, Poliziano constructed his own understanding of the phenomenon of poetic frenzy throughout his career, drawing on his deep classical learning as well as his practice of improvisation to argue that *ars* and *furor* – and oral improvisation and written composition – are mutually relevant to the creation of inspired poetry.

Poliziano's rather surprising lecture course on Virgil (whose poetic introduction, the *Manto*, would be published as the first of his Latin poems called *Silvae*) was not his first engagement teaching at the Florentine Studio. In fact, he had begun teaching two years previously, in 1480, and his initial choice of lecture material was rather polemical. He chose to begin his teaching with two texts that had not been the topic of previous lectures at the Studio: the *Institutio oratoria* of Quintilian and the *Silvae* of Statius. This choice subverted institutional expectations and generated considerable controversy. Poliziano had, after all, been hired to teach oratory and poetry, two genres of Latin literature that purists regarded as all but synonymous with the writings of Cicero and Virgil, respectively, and indeed these authors had been among the mainstays of Cristoforo Landino's earlier teaching at the Studio. Certainly in part Poliziano's choice of material was meant precisely to combat the purism of his humanist colleagues who saw any deviation from the golden Latin of Cicero and Virgil as decay. But why did he choose these texts in particular? The special merit of the *Silvae*, according to Poliziano's teaching commentary on the work, was that the author had composed them spontaneously, in a state that Poliziano identifies as a frenzy. In his introduction, Statius writes that the *Silvae* "flowed from me with a sudden zeal and a certain pleasure in haste" ("mihi subito calore et quadam festinandi voluptate fluxerunt"). About the idea of "sudden zeal," Poliziano writes, "This is, as it were, a characteristic of the *silva*. For, as Quintilian said, those who compose *silvae* write extemporaneously, following heat and impetus."[5] He goes on to explain that Statius had "a rather passionate and fiery disposition, the sort which excels in impetus and rapidity," and that his "innate talent was equal to the task" of writing the *Silvae*. By contrast, Poliziano argues, Statius's *Thebaid* is "an extremely polished work," and he does not intend this entirely as a compliment. As he explains, in writing the *Thebaid* Statius was "forced to rely on the help of art. But there is no skill which can imitate that inspiration of the mind which the Greeks call *enthusiasmos*, which is the reason for the opinion of Plato, and Democritus before him, that 'no one can become a good poet without a kindling of the spirit and without, as it were, a certain infusion of frenzy.'"

Poliziano regards Statius's *Silvae* as superior to his *Thebaid* because the latter work is primarily the product of artifice, while the former is the product of frenzy. Poliziano is clearly employing here the same dichotomy (*ars* and *furor*) that had been popularized in Florence by Ficino. It is important to note, however, that Poliziano uses this dichotomy to compare two works by the same, highly learned poet. The learned Statius achieved better results, Poliziano says, when he composed rapidly in a frenzy than when he relied on his controlled erudition alone.[6]

Even while explicitly connecting the fervour of Statius with the divine poetic frenzy theorized by Plato, Poliziano makes clear that, in his interpretation, the frenzy that Statius channelled in writing the *Silvae* originated not in a transcendent divine source but in his own "rather fiery disposition" – whereas the more controlled *Thebaid* was the result of this fiery disposition itself having cooled off. And while he argues that poetry produced through frenzy is (at least in the case of Statius) superior in aesthetic terms to poetry produced through erudition, Poliziano devalues Ficino's argument that the primary value of poetic frenzy is as a conduit for divine truth.

The process that led to the renewal of interest in Statius's *Silvae* in Quattrocento Italy began in 1417, when Poggio Bracciolini discovered a manuscript of the text in St. Gall and had a copy made for him. Previously the text had been known to Italian humanists only by its reputation and was feared to have been lost forever. In the wake of Poggio's discovery, a number of humanists eagerly read the newly available text, including Francesco Barbaro and Niccolò Niccoli. In Florence itself, though, where Poggio returned with his manuscript in 1435, the initial curiosity aroused by Poggio's discovery did not lead any major humanist before Poliziano to dedicate sustained attention to the text. One factor behind the limited early impact of the rediscovery of Statius's *Silvae* was the frustratingly corrupt state of the text available for humanists to study; apparently the scribe who produced the manuscript that Poggio brought back to Italy was inept, or, as Poggio says in a letter, "the most ignorant of all living people."[7] No significant work was done with the text until the early 1470s in Rome, when the two earliest humanist commentaries on the work were produced, by Niccolò Perotti and (shortly thereafter) Domizio Calderini, both members of Pomponio Leto's Roman Academy. The interest these two Roman intellectuals directed towards Statius's *Silvae* was shaped by another text that had been one of Poggio's major discoveries: Quintilian's *Institutio oratoria*, the complete text of which, like that of the *Silvae*, Poggio had found in St. Gall.[8]

In pairing Quintilian with Statius in his 1480–1 lectures, then, Poliziano was essentially offering the latest in philological scholarship, but the pairing is also illustrative of Poliziano's attitude towards the theory of frenzy. Quintilian was among the ancient rhetoricians who addressed the issues of nature and training as relevant to the study of rhetoric. He argues that nature can accomplish much without education, but not vice versa: "For if you isolate one of the pair from the other altogether, nature will be able to do a lot without teaching, but without nature there can be no teaching."[9] Similarly, the *Rhetorica ad Herennium* (the subject of Poliziano's lectures the following academic year, in 1481–2) explores the distinction between nature and training as it applies to memory, concluding that the two are mutually reinforcing: "As in everything else the merit of natural excellence often rivals acquired learning, and art, in its turn, reinforces and develops the natural advantages."[10] In pairing Statius and Quintilian, and framing Statius's work in terms of an interplay between "innate talent" and "polish," Poliziano seems to be drawing on these rhetorical frameworks. In Quintilian Poliziano also found discussions of talent and polish applied as assessments of certain ancient writers. Quintilian sees Homer as a poet of genius, Virgil as a poet who had to work with diligence and care to achieve excellent results: "Indeed, though we must yield to Homer's divine and immortal genius, there is more care and craftsmanship in Vergil, if only because he had to work harder at it."[11] These assessments, too, were key to Poliziano's attitude towards the production of poetry.

To understand the model of poetic frenzy articulated by Poliziano, we can turn to his introductory oration for the course on Statius and Quintilian. As we have seen, Poliziano discusses the *Silvae* primarily as a model of improvised composition. Poliziano argues that Statius's claim of indecision about whether to publish the *Silvae* is actually a rhetorical move calculated to convince others "that those poems flowed from him extemporaneously and with a 'sudden zeal.'" While insisting that the work reveals "genuine" evidence of spontaneity, Poliziano is practical in his assessment of its value, identifying two advantages of the spontaneous approach. First, he argues on aesthetic grounds that artists often compromise their own output when they are unable to stop tinkering with their work: "We think that no work is complete unless we have laboured over it extremely. Yet in practice it often happens conversely that our writings become worse from excessive attention, and they are worn away rather than polished by the file of revision."[12] Poliziano's second argument in favour of extemporaneity is equally practical: improvisation is impressive to an audience, and this matters to "a man caring greatly about his reputation" inasmuch as "respect for his ability to compose rapidly would likely win him freer indulgence from his readers, readier favour, and greater admiration."[13]

It is clear that, while Poliziano finds the concept of poetic *furor* useful, his understanding of the relationship between *furor* and *ars* is quite different from Ficino's. While Ficino sees *furor* as the necessary and sufficient route to worthy poetry and divine truths, Poliziano takes a much more practical approach to the value of *furor* – and, as a rhetorician, he also stands up for the value of *ars*. While he finds the spontaneity of the *Silvae* "genuine," Poliziano also praises the work's rhetorical and literary craftsmanship: "There is nothing in these poems that was not invented very skilfully, nothing which was not arranged very prudently, no passage that was not tested and examined so that delight could be coaxed forth from it ... everything that he wrote seems to have been composed for display, carefully arranged to achieve renown." Poliziano's admiration for the rhetorical invention (*inventio*) and arrangement (*dispositio*) of the *Silvae* would hardly seem to leave room for uncontrollable *furor*, but it is the improvisatory qualities of the work that carry it – the "flashes of brilliance" from a poet "so accessible in his thoughts, so bright in his words."[14] It is clear that Poliziano saw *ars* not as an impediment to *furor* but (in keeping with the ancient rhetoricians' attitudes towards nature and art) as its mutually beneficial counterpart.

Poliziano's long engagement with Statius's poetry helped him to develop his own interpretation of poetic frenzy, overcoming the aspects of Ficino's theory of frenzy that he found less compelling: not only the notion that *ars* is at best unnecessary and at worst counterproductive to the achievement of poetic greatness through *furor* but also the idea that poetic *furor* entails becoming a mouthpiece for unmediated divine truths whose purpose is to spiritually elevate audiences. For Poliziano, Statius offered a model of an alternative *furor*: inspired, impressive, and enhanced by the deployment of rhetorical expertise. In short, this was a *furor* customized for Poliziano and his fellow humanists to emulate.

Poliziano devoted much attention to fine-tuning Ficino's theory of poetic frenzy according to his own reading of ancient texts. And in his wide-ranging literary output – Latin and vernacular, performed orally and published in writing – Poliziano strove to present much of his own work as the result of improvisational composition. Even in his first *Miscellanea*, a collection of erudite philological studies, Poliziano emphatically ascribes to his work an improvisatory character, insisting that these have been produced "extemporaneously, rather than with labour" ("ex tempore potius quam a cura").[15]

In his letter dedicating the *Manto* to Lorenzo di Pierfrancesco de' Medici (second cousin to Lorenzo il Magnifico), Poliziano represents his poem as an ephemeral creation produced for oral delivery on a particular occasion. In doing so he deploys the very same rhetorical move that he had identified in Statius: projecting indecision about publishing a work as a means of bolstering its improvisational credentials. He writes, "You compel me, Lorenzo, to publish an unpolished, uncorrected poem; even to have recited it once in public would have seemed too shameless. Surely it would have been enough that such an imperfect creature, which might be numbered among those insects called ephemera, should have lived but for a day."[16]

Along similar rhetorical lines, Poliziano also presented his twelfth elegy as a swiftly composed work. In the prose lines dedicating the poem to Lorenzo di Pierfrancesco, Poliziano writes:

> I present to you the elegy which you were demanding from me – an almost extemporaneous work; for while I began it this morning, while the priest was preparing himself for the mass, I have completed it this afternoon, while riding back in a carriage.[17]

In addition to describing it as "almost extemporaneous" and pegging its quick composition to the events of his day, Poliziano also argues for its improvised nature within the poem itself, in the exact terms he used to describe Statius: "And now we present writings poured forth with sudden heat."[18]

Scholarship on Poliziano has long been hampered by a stubborn and problematic division between studies of Poliziano's vernacular poetry and studies focusing on his philological work. The year 1480, when Poliziano began his career as professor at the Florentine Studio, often serves as a chronological boundary separating these two scholarly discourses: as Lucia Cesarini Martinelli has noted, scholarship on the vernacular poetry of Poliziano tends to focus on works written before this year (especially the *Orfeo* and the *Stanze*), regarding his later output as less vibrant, while scholarship on Poliziano's philological work often disregards his writings prior to 1480 as mere poetic *juvenilia* with little relevance for understanding the serious work of the mature philologist.[19]

When we consider Poliziano's poetic output throughout his career in light of his interest in the issues of improvisation and frenzy, it is particularly obvious that this chronological and thematic division is unhelpful. Poliziano's abiding interest in improvisation is in fact a unifying thread linking all of his intellectual output, as critic of ancient texts and creator of new texts, Latin and vernacular author, and composer of oral and written material. It makes sense, then, to consider Poliziano's poetic work over the course of his career, pre- and post-1480, with a focus on his engagement with issues of improvisation.

It is helpful to begin by surveying Poliziano's engagement with popular forms of improvised musical-poetic performance.[20] Evidence shows that Poliziano was known as an avid singer of poetry – both his own poems and those of others. For instance, a letter that Poliziano wrote to Lorenzo de' Medici on 2 May 1488 confirms that the singing of popular poetic forms was a passion and a pastime that Poliziano shared with Piero de' Medici, as with Lorenzo; in the letter, Poliziano, who was then travelling to Rome with Piero, explains that they have been passing the time by performing popular forms of sung poetry, such as the *Canzone di Calen di maggio*.[21]

In addition to Poliziano's documented enthusiasm for singing improvised forms, there are some intriguing hints that he may have been a talented instrumentalist as well. As we saw in chapter 1, a number of writings from Lorenzo de' Medici's circle refer to an individual known as "il compare della viola," admired for his ability to accompany the singing of poetry on the viola, and Paolo Orvieto has argued that it was Angelo Poliziano who went by this nickname.[22] Not all scholars have accepted Orvieto's conclusion, but it is clear that Poliziano was an active participant in the improvisational musical-poetic performances of Lorenzo's *brigata*.[23] Two texts that discuss the death of Poliziano also present the humanist as a player of the lyre. Paolo Giovio, writing about the illness that led to Poliziano's death, describes Poliziano suffering from a burning fever and claims that in his final moments he took up his lyre and "sang songs of supreme frenzy" ("supremi furoris carmina decantavit").[24] In a Latin poem entitled "Politiani tumulus" lamenting the deaths of Lorenzo and Poliziano, Pietro Bembo casts the latter as an Orpheus figure. Bembo imagines Poliziano playing the lyre and singing, attempting to recover his deceased patron from the underworld as Orpheus had attempted to recover Eurydice. Poliziano's Orphic song is cut short in the poem by the personification of Death, who, resenting the poet's efforts to break the laws of the underworld, strikes Poliziano dead.[25] Giovio's account may have only a loose connection to the facts surrounding Poliziano's death, and Bembo's is clearly a flight of poetic fancy. Still, both authors evidently expect their readers (including those who knew Poliziano personally) to recognize the humanist in these portrayals of a frenzied singer and Orphic lyre player, suggesting that Poliziano's engagement with musical-poetic performance was widely known.

The artificial division between alleged phases of Poliziano's career shows its limitations with particular clarity when one considers Poliziano's lyric *Rime*. These vernacular poems, as we shall see, show clear links to the culture of musical-poetic improvisation actively cultivated by Luigi Pulci and other members of Lorenzo de' Medici's youthful *brigata*. On that basis, many scholars have tended to group Poliziano's vernacular lyrics among the poet's *juvenilia*, supposing that, in his maturity, Poliziano the philologist abandoned his earlier interest in the composition of vernacular lyrics. However, the leading authority on Poliziano's *Rime*, Daniela Delcorno Branca, has argued that Poliziano's production of *ballate* and *strambotti* was not confined exclusively to his youth. In particular, Delcorno Branca has identified a substantial group of Poliziano's vernacular poems that she argued must have been composed between 1478 and 1487.[26] The majority of these poems are in the *strambotto* (also called *rispetto*) genre – a genre particularly associated with the *improvvisatore* tradition. Antonia Tissoni Benvenuti considers it highly likely that many of Poliziano's vernacular poems were in origin extemporaneous, or at least presented as such: "Possiamo supporre, anche se non ne abbiamo testimonianza scritta, che presentasse come estemporanei parecchi suoi testi in volgare" ("We can hypothesize, even though we lack written testimony about this, that [Poliziano] presented many of his vernacular texts as extemporaneous").[27] She considers it particularly likely that Poliziano's *strambotti* were originally presented as improvisational.[28]

The hypothesis that Poliziano's *strambotti* were initially delivered as sung poetry is supported by the pervasiveness of the theme of singing within the texts of these poems. Poliziano's *strambotti* present themselves as part of a tradition of oral poetry through frequent references to the lover/poet singing poetry: "Ascolta el canto con che ti favella / colui che sopra ogni cosa t'ama" ("Listen to the song with which the man who loves you above all else is speaking to you," 27.1.2–3); "Io ho cantato" ("I have sung," 27.12.6).[29]

These details about Poliziano's enthusiasm for musical-poetic improvisation and its contemporary forms serve as important context for understanding Poliziano's *Fabula di Orfeo*. Considered to be the first secular

drama in vernacular Italian, the work reveals Poliziano's commitment
to both the performance and the intellectual analysis of improvisational
poetry on a number of levels.[30] In the first production of the *Fabula*,
Baccio Ugolini was chosen to play Orfeo, thanks in large part, no doubt,
to Poliziano's admiration for Ugolini's skill as an *improvvisatore*. Many
contemporaries praised Ugolini for his ability to play the *lira da braccio*
while improvising poetry, including Poliziano, who wrote in a letter to
Francesco Pucci about Ugolini's various modes of composition: "What
is sweeter, purer, more polished, or more charming than [Baccio Ugolini's] songs – either the ones that he sings extemporaneously on the
cithara, or the ones that he composes at leisure?"[31] As Nino Pirrotta per-
suasively argued, the text of the *Fabula di Orfeo* would have been in large
part sung, with some of the stage performers, including Ugolini, also
providing improvised musical accompaniment.[32]

The stanzas sung by the character Orfeo in Poliziano's *Fabula di Orfeo*
(that is, in the initial performance, by Baccio Ugolini) are *strambotti*, and,
like Poliziano's other *strambotti*, they refer frequently to singing. There
is therefore considerable formal and thematic continuity between the
Fabula di Orfeo and Poliziano's *Rime*. Another, perhaps more surprising,
point of continuity is that both the *Fabula di Orfeo* and the *Rime* represent
not only the poet/lover but also the beloved lady as a singer whose song
wields marvellous power. In the *Fabula di Orfeo*, the character Tirsi says,
of Eurydice, that "parla e canta in sí dolce favella, / che i fiumi isvolger-
ebbe inverso il fonte" ("she speaks and sings with a voice so sweet / that
it could turn rivers back towards their source").[33] The power that Tirsi
attributes to Eurydice's song is one of the powers traditionally ascribed,
in myth, to Orpheus's song – as it is in Poliziano's *Nutricia*: "Following the
lyre of Orpheus from a winding valley, the waves of a river turned back
on liquid foot to their source."[34]

The beloved lady of Poliziano's *strambotti* is, like Eurydice in the *Orfeo*,
described as a singer whose song has the power to enchant. For example,
her song has power over the angels of heaven: "Gli angioli al canto suo
sanza dimoro / scendon tutti dal cielo a coro a coro" ("When she sings,
the angels, without delay, all descend from heaven, one chorus after another").[35] The enchanting song of the lady (like that of the sirens of
classical mythology) can ensnare and imperil the helpless listener:

> Is it any wonder that such beautiful singing
> has made me full of desire, and eager for more?
> This woman would make a dragon fall in love,
> Or a basilisk, or even a deaf asp.
> I fell for it, and now I pay the price,

For I find myself trapped like a thrush.
When she laughs, everyone should flee:
She traps you with her song and kills you with her laugh.[36]

These descriptions of the Eurydice of the *Fabula di Orfeo* and the beloved of the *strambotti* in rhetorical terms typically associated with Orpheus's ability to enchant beasts and men raise interesting questions about the inclusion of women in the poetic culture of improvisation. Though there is little evidence for women's direct participation in the practices championed by Ficino in Florence, the theories articulated by Ficino and his contemporaries, as we will see in chapter 5, served to open the door to more active engagement with these poetic conversations in the sixteenth-century courts of Italy.

Poliziano himself acknowledges his desire to reach a large and not exclusively erudite audience in his dedicatory letter to the *Fabula di Orfeo*, where he writes that he composed the play "in the vernacular so that it could be understood better by the audience" ("in stilo vulgare perché dagli spectatori meglio fusse intesa").[37] For these original spectators, the musical and performative dimensions of the play would have been foremost. We have seen how frequently humanist authors made recourse to the myth of Orpheus in their descriptions of performances by Renaissance *improvvisatori*. Such descriptions – like Poliziano's verses comparing Antonio di Guido to Orpheus – can, by suggesting a kind of ideal continuity between ancient and modern forms of oral poetry, serve to elevate the status of the modern *improvvisatore*'s art.

Putting his friend the *improvvisatore* Baccio Ugolini onstage in the role of Orpheus, Poliziano in effect invites from his audience an extended reflection on the relationship between ancient and modern oral poetry. Original stage directions demonstrate that Ugolini's gifts as a singer and lyre player were important to the impact of the performance. Nino Pirrotta highlighted three moments in the play in which Ugolini must have performed his lines musically: First, at his initial appearance onstage, when he descends a mountain singing Latin Sapphic verses in praise of Cardinal Gonzaga. Ugolini as Orpheus also sang Latin verses, adapted from Ovid, while ascending with Eurydice from the underworld before his infamous turn. Between these scenes, during Orpheus's descent into the underworld, stage directions state that "Orfeo cantando giugne all'inferno." These sung verses (verses 189–229, according to Pirrotta) are in vernacular Tuscan, not Latin. More specifically, we are dealing with *ottava rima* lyric stanzas – sung *strambotti*, which as we have seen were particularly favoured by Quattrocento *improvvisatori*, including Ugolini.

The choice by Poliziano, Pirrotta observes, to have his Orpheus sing *strambotti* effectively "puts the strambotto on a par with the Latin verses as the representatives of the noblest form of sung poetry."[38]

Orfeo is not, however, the only character within the play to express himself in *strambotti*. While the *strambotti* of Orfeo maintain an elevated, noble register, with other characters Poliziano explores the expressive range of this popular verse form, introducing comical forms and humble terminology usually excluded from poetry – for example, in the *strambotto* delivered by the old shepherd Mopso at verses 88–95, based entirely on the *rime sdrucciole* (with the antepenultimate syllable stressed) traditionally considered a comic effect:

> The murmuring of refreshing waters
> streaming down a rock are not so pleasant,
> Nor the sound that is made when a smooth breeze
> Blows through the treetops in a stand of pines,
> As your rhymes are pleasant,
> Your rhymes that echo all around:
> If she hears them, she will come like a puppy.
> But look: here comes Tirsi, sliding down the mountain.[39]

Pirrotta believes that Mopso would have sung this *strambotto* (alternating song with Aristeo, who has declared "canterem sotto l'ombrose foglie" – "we will sing beneath the shady leaves") and that the song has to be understood, at least thematically, as a poetic improvisation: after all, in the final verse of Mopso's *strambotto* he is responding, in song, to Tirsi's sudden and unexpected arrival.[40]

It is clear that the *Orfeo*, particularly in its original performance, was a celebration of improvisation on several levels. The performers, led by Baccio Ugolini, impressed the audience with their gifts for musical improvisation. The characters themselves are presented as improvisors of music and poetry. And Poliziano wants his audience (and his readers) to believe that he too, as author of the *Orfeo*, has performed a feat of near-extemporaneous poetic composition. In the dedicatory letter to Carlo Canale, Poliziano claims to have composed the text "in two days' time, amid continuous chaos" ("in tempo di dua giorni, intra continui tumulti").[41] As we have seen, Poliziano emphasized the near-spontaneity of his artistic process in discussions of many of his other works. And, as Francesco Bausi has noted, by prefacing his work with this letter emphasizing its rapid composition, Poliziano seems to be pointing his readers towards the classical text that increasingly captivated him as a model of spontaneous poetic excellence: Statius's *Silvae*, which open with the author's dedicatory letter to his friend Stella, in which he claims that "none of them took longer than two days to compose."[42]

As we have seen, the period after Poliziano began to teach at the Florentine Studio is often considered the beginning of his mature scholarly and literary career. The Virgil lecture discussed earlier was ultimately published as one of the four poems, composed between 1482 and 1486, that Poliziano entitled *Silvae*, in an obvious reference to the ancient genre of the *silva* and particularly to the work of Statius that he admired for its "sudden zeal" and rhetorical brilliance. Poliziano's effort to channel Statius was apparently convincing to at least to some of his readers: Nicolas Bérauld, reading Poliziano's *Silvae* in early sixteenth-century France, identified the improvisatory quality of the verses as their defining characteristic. Bérauld, who was well aware of the significance that Poliziano's studies of Statius and Quintilian had for his approach to composing his *Silvae*, defines the genre of the *silva* as follows: "Here we call 'sylva' a poem that is poured out with a kind of heating-up of one's innate talent, and with a sudden frenzy and poetic spirit."[43] Bérauld is particularly struck by the improvisatory quality of the opening verses of Poliziano's *silva*: "Whenever I read these words, I seem to hear Poliziano himself, struck by a sudden divine frenzy, pouring out these verses extemporaneously from his rounded mouth, and modulating them with his sonorous voice, more beautiful than a swan's."[44] Bérauld was something of an expert on improvisation and in 1534 published a treatise on improvisation, in which, as Terence Cave has noted, the French humanist draws on Quintilian's theories of improvisation as expressed in the tenth book of the *Institutio*.[45]

It is easy to see why readers of Poliziano's *Silvae* would have identified these poems with extemporaneity, since in the poems themselves Poliziano describes the composition process in terms of *furor*. In the *Nutricia* (the last of the *Silvae* to be published), Poliziano presents himself as composing in the grip of a frenzy:

> Where, rash piety, do you constrain me to go, dazed with wonder? What kind of passion is this in my trembling spirit? Am I in error, or do my innermost feelings bring forth of their own a work appropriate for my mistress, and gradually conceive sounds and words in harmonious rhythm and pour forth flawless songs that shall never be at the mercy of the Fates' spindles? Thus may it go. Come, wherever ardent frenzy impels me, wherever my mind, my piety, my prayers lead me, let us follow.[46]

This framing of the poem in terms of *furor* and spontaneity is quite clear, and other language in the poem also highlights compositional frenzy in Ficinian terms:

The celestial modulations fashion and enflame the luminous and puri-
fied spirits of poets. This ardor carries off the one who cries "*euoe*" and
in a surge of frenzy his mind is first overwhelmed; then the god, shut
up in the depths of his heart, seethes, arousing frenzied feelings in his
breast. Resenting association with man, he frightens him and drives him
into the deepest recesses against his will; the god himself takes possession
of the empty place, occupies and pervades his limbs, and instills his song
in the human heart.[47]

Given this attention to poetic frenzy, it is not surprising that Orpheus, a
central figure in Ficino's vision of oral poetry based on *furor* and the protagonist of Poliziano's effort to engage a broad audience in the *Fabula di
Orfeo*, is prominently featured in Poliziano's *Nutricia* as well. The poem at
one point describes Orpheus charming the denizens of the underworld
with his song, heroically calming the "threefold barking" of Cerberus.[48]
Later, an extended passage recounts Orpheus's downfall and death,
complete with a description of "the lyre floating by itself on the water,
emitting a plaintive sound and carrying the bloody head of its master
and alas! seeming to utter weary cries of lament."[49]

Poliziano's *Nutricia* deals directly with the topic of the use of the lyre in
contemporary varieties of musical-poetic performance, too, in the context of lavish praise of Poliziano's young pupil Piero de' Medici. According to Poliziano's poem, alongside exercises in translating Greek texts
into Latin, Piero's education includes learning to perform poems to the
accompaniment of the lyre, an art for which the Medici scion supposedly
shows remarkable talent: "Behold, he has not yet completed fifteen years
yet he summons the masterpieces of Greek antiquity into Latium and
moulds poems on his sweet lyre."[50]

A motivating preoccupation in Poliziano's *Silvae*, as in the *Fabula di
Orfeo*, is the relationship between ancient and contemporary cultures of
improvisation. One key component of his investigation of these issues
in the *Silvae* is his reworking of the metaphor articulated in Plato's *Ion*
where Socrates illustrates the way a god inspires a poet, a poet inspires
a rhapsode who recites the poems, and the rhapsode inspires an audience, by invoking the concept of a magnet attached to a series of rings.[51]
An insightful interpreter of ancient contexts, Poliziano recognizes that
the metaphor describes a culture in which literature is performed and
transmitted primarily through oral modes. This insight into a significant
difference between Poliziano's own literary world and that of Plato (a
difference which did not attract Ficino's attention) led Poliziano towards
a modification of the metaphor.[52] In Poliziano's *Nutricia*, poetic inspiration is transferred through writing:

The poems themselves, committed long ago to the Nile's papyrus, trans-mitted the Apollonian inspiration and breathed the music of the celestial lyre; indeed a sacred contagion excites the throng of readers with a like en-thusiasm and the same ardor passes from one poet to engender inspiration in the heart of others, like the iron ring lifted up by the hidden force of a Magnesian stone that attaches to itself a long chain in a pendant bond and fastens them together with invisible hooks.[53]

This adjustment to Plato's metaphor entails an important shift in think-ing about literary tradition and inspiration. Plato's chain in the *Ion* rep-resents a hierarchical transfer of inspiration through particular groups: god, poet, rhapsode, audience. In Poliziano's modification, the chain is no longer hierarchical: each link represents a literate poet, composing poetry with the inspiration of previous texts. The chain can thus repre-sent not just the effects of a single poetic performance but the entire tradition of literature unfolding over generations – in other words, pre-cisely the topic of the *Nutricia*. Whereas Ficino valued the metaphor as evidence that inspired poetry could serve as a direct conduit for divine truths, Poliziano characteristically turns the emphasis towards histori-cally contingent, textual processes of literary composition.

In his interpretations of Statius, Poliziano argued that Statius drew on a "fiery disposition" and "innate talent" in order to compose the *Silvae* extemporaneously. In his own *Silvae*, Poliziano appears to suggest that poetic inspiration can begin not only with a spark of innate fire but also through the reading of other poets' works. For Poliziano, then, poetic *fu-ror* is linked with *ars* – the training that enables one to engage with earlier literary traditions. This represents a deviation from Ficino's claims that unlearned poets can produce divinely inspired poetry through frenzy.

It would hardly seem possible to assess the relationship between an-cient and contemporary cultures of oral and written poetry without tak-ing Homer into account, and indeed Poliziano offers some surprising insights into oral improvisational poetic traditions when he discusses Homer in the *Silvae*. At the beginning of the *Ambra*, Poliziano pays hom-age to Homer as the source of poetic frenzy: "The great Maeonian, from whose fresh-flowing torrent the whole throng of poets imbibed their se-cret frenzies." Drawing on Plato's magnetic chain metaphor once again, he continues:

As the stone of the laboring Hercules draws the iron upwards and inter-twines at a distance the long rings of metal and breathes its power into them all, so the sacred impulse of poets depends entirely on Homer alone. He, reclining at the table of Jupiter, gives us to drink from cups offered by the

Trojan youth that drive away the sad decrepitude of the years and prolong life into eternity.[54]

We can begin to understand how Poliziano's contemporaries responded to this discussion by turning to a commentary on the *Ambra* written by a little-known humanist called Petreio, who was a member of Pomponio Leto's Academy, was implicated in the anti-papal conspiracy of 1469, and later resided for a time in Florence.[55] Petreio first notes that the concept of divine frenzy derives from Plato and that it has more recently been expounded by Ficino: "Our own Marsilio Ficino writes about the same topic in his *Letters*."[56] He continues by noting that Poliziano deviates from Plato:

> This is a simile taken from Plato and applied to a different thing. For Plato says that all poets are attracted by a divine frenzy, as iron is attracted by a magnet. Poliziano, taking poetic licence, says that all other poets are dependent on one poet – Homer – just as many iron rings hang down from a magnet. But he calls the magnet the "Herculean stone." For Plato attests that it is called this by Euripides, because in attracting it uses a kind of "Herculean" force – that is to say, a heroic force. If I am not mistaken you will not find this in any other Latin writer.[57]

Petreio is correct to note Poliziano's relatively loose treatment of Plato's metaphor, in which Homer is represented by one of the intermediate iron rings in the magnetic chain, rather than the magnet itself and ultimate source of inspiration for all poets. Poliziano's adjustment of the metaphor here probably reflects the fact that the *Ambra* is intended to serve as an encomium to Homer. However, there are reasons to believe that Poliziano is also making a more specific argument about Homer. Tellingly, Poliziano connects the magnetic draw of Homer with what he says is the improvisational, unpremeditated quality of Homer's poetry:

> Certainly that light of a heavenly and clearly immortal nature shines in this poet, because those most beautiful songs, which every age has rightly admired, flowed to him without labour and spontaneously ... while by contrast Varus has it that the Mantuan poet [Virgil] composed very few verses in a day.[58]

Here Poliziano is echoing Quintilian's critical judgments on Homer: for Quintilian, as we saw, Homer is a poet of "superhuman genius," while Virgil writes with "diligence and exactness." For Poliziano, these qualities are the function of a relationship with improvisation and *furor* specifically:

Many poems transcribed while [Homer] was singing ... were placed into him by a certain sudden and unexpected inspiration and (as they say) with a spirit bearing them, so that they are easily perceived not to have come, as it were, from the anvil of human craft, but rather to have been sent forth from his sacred breast with a certain divine impulse and inspiration, as if from an oracle's cauldron or shrine.[59]

In his analysis here, Poliziano relies on his reading of the pseudo-Herodotean *Life of Homer*, which asserts that Homer had improvised much of his poetry and that the *Iliad* and *Odyssey* had been recorded by an unscrupulous grammar teacher named Thestorides while Homer sang.[60] The terms that Poliziano uses to describe Homer's inspired improvisation recall his descriptions of Statius composing the *Silvae*. Homer composed "in a sudden and hasty inspiration" ("subito ... repentinoque instinctu") and Statius "in a sudden zeal" ("subito calore"). It is clear that Poliziano's attitude towards what he sees as Homer's improvisational composition is a development of his earlier assessments of Statius's poetic inspiration.

Having devoted seven years of his youth to the project of translating the *Iliad* into Latin, Poliziano was arguably the most prominent expert on the Homeric poems in Quattrocento Italy. Not unexpectedly, he paid a great deal of attention to Homer in his lectures at the Florentine Studio: the year the *Ambra* was composed, 1485, began a five-year period in which Poliziano lectured on the Homeric poems.[61] Poliziano's expertise in the study of Homer allowed him to recognize the depth of Homer's influence on the literary tradition; it also gave him insight into the apparent absence of earlier influences on Homer. For Poliziano, Homer represented a sort of literary horizon, beyond which one could imagine Homer in direct contact with the divine.

Modern scholarship has recognized that the reason Homer appeared as a literary horizon to Poliziano is that the Homeric poems were written down at the conclusion of the Greek Dark Ages, a period when literacy was lost in Greece. In the wake of the pivotal Homeric scholarship of the twentieth century (in particular the comparative studies conducted by Millman Parry and Alfred Lord of oral poets in the Balkans), there is now general agreement that the Homeric poems represent a uniquely successful intersection of two modes of textual transmission that rarely overlap within a given society: on the one hand a highly refined art of extemporaneous oral composition, on the other the technology of the written word.[62] Poliziano did not have access to all of the information that would have allowed him to reconstruct the precise place of the Homeric poems in the history of Greek literacy and literature (and indeed many questions remain unanswered today on these issues). However, in his treatment of Homer Poliziano seems to anticipate the contours of important discussions that have continued to unfold in Homeric scholarship in later centuries.

By citing the anecdote that the unscrupulous Thestorides had written down the orally composed epics of Homer and tried to pass them off as his own, Poliziano introduces an important argument in his theory of poetic inspiration: Homer appears as the magnet in the chain of poetic inspiration because he, uniquely, had composed without the benefit of a written model to study. For Poliziano, who values both *furor* and *ars*, the conversion of Homer's oral composition to written text represents, for subsequent poets, both a source of inspiration and a technical model.

As we have seen, at the start of his career at the Florentine Studio, Poliziano embraced Ficino's terminology of *furor poeticus* as a means of explicating the style of Statius's *Silvae*. However, in the way that Poliziano manipulated this concept, it must have been clear to his colleagues – many of whom were members of Ficino's circle – that his articulation of the concept diverged from Ficino's. As Poliziano himself noted admiringly, Statius's occasional poetry, while genuine and inspired, in Poliziano's view, was characterized by craftsmanship and careful arrangement – hardly the mystical utterances of an unlearned mouthpiece for the divine. Homer, however, represented a different interpretive task. For late antique Neoplatonists, the Homeric poems represented an opportunity to mine supposedly inspired poetry in search of philosophical wisdom, which could be extracted through the application of allegorical interpretation. Poliziano's predecessor at the Florentine Studio, Cristoforo Landino, had applied a similar hermeneutic approach in his analysis of Virgil and then of Dante, and he almost certainly would have taken a similar strategy to interpreting Homer if his Greek expertise had been robust enough to permit it. The Homeric poems, vital material for Porphyry and Proclus, represented a significant gap in Florentine intellectual processing of Greek Neoplatonic culture. With his expertise in Greek and the Homeric poems specifically, and his motivating fascination with orality and improvisation, Poliziano would have seemed well positioned to fill this gap.[63]

However, although Poliziano pronounces the Homeric poems a product of *furor*, his objectives in exploring the composition of these poems lie elsewhere. In his mature work as a Homeric scholar, Poliziano's lines of inquiry are not designed to carry on the methodology of Ficino and Landino in searching inspired ancient texts for divine insights.[64] Poliziano expresses his awe for Homer's encyclopedic erudition, even calling it "divine" in a moment of hyperbole. But his intent is not to demonstrate that Homer acquired theological enlightenment through his poetic *furor*. During the years he spent translating the *Iliad* in his youth, Poliziano had studied philosophy with Ficino, whose agenda and methods in seeking divine secrets from ancient texts informed the approach of the young Poliziano, as is evident from some of the notes he added to two manuscript copies of his translation. For instance, in a gloss to the scene in *Iliad* 5 in which Diomedes wounds Venus's hand, Poliziano interprets the passage according to Platonic methodology: "Venus is wounded in the hand because that heavenly Venus of Plato, when she is wounded in the sense of touch, becomes vulgar."[65] In this gloss Ficino's influence on Poliziano is evident: in his *De amore*, Ficino had used the Latin names *Venus Coelestis* and *Venus Vulgaris* as translations for the Greek names *Aphrodite Ourania* and *Aphrodite Pandemos* that appear in Plato's *Symposium*. No doubt Ficino would have been pleased with Poliziano's work here, and probably he hoped that the younger humanist would go on to deploy his erudition and experience with the Homeric texts to produce allegorical explanations that would carry on Ficino's approaches, as Landino did in his interpretations of Virgil and Dante. However, Poliziano's interpretive interests did not develop in that direction. Over the years he spent studying Homer while lecturing at the Studio, Poliziano's growing philological skill enabled him to uncover a wealth of information about the historical world of the Homeric texts.[66] If extracting transcendent theological truths from Homer had ever been his plan, it was not one that he pursued as a mature scholar.

When Poliziano continued to engage with the concept of poetic *furor* in his late interpretations of Homer, he was motivated less by a Ficinian search for the divine than by more proximate interests. Throughout his life, Poliziano worked to understand the nature of the flashes of poetic inspiration that he himself, as a composer and performer, apparently experienced; his scholarship on Homer can be understood not as an abandonment of his earlier interests but as part of his ongoing historical and philological inquiry into the nature of improvisatory performance. In other words, Poliziano saw poetic frenzy as inspiration that could be drawn not only from divine assistance but from close engagement with literary models from the past, all of which ultimately reached back to the poetic harmony of the first great (oral) poet, Homer.

Poliziano's youthful participation in the circle of scholars, poets, and improvisors that surrounded Ficino had a lasting influence on his career: he continued to engage in improvisation through his life, honing his skill at extemporaneous composition in Latin and even in ancient Greek – clear evidence that his philological work and his extracurricular interest in improvisation were mutually reinforcing.[67] As we have seen, Poliziano's fascination with improvisation can serve as a persistent thread linking the apparently disparate elements of his intellectual career. There is strong evidence that Poliziano's scholarly inquiries into Statius are connected to his abiding interest in improvisation, motivated at least in part by a desire to understand how ancient writers deployed and understood spontaneity in the composition of poetry. And it seems clear that Poliziano's approach to Homer – his objectives, and perhaps to some extent his conclusions about Homer's orality and composition-in-performance as well – is informed by his own experiences engaging in, and observing, the vibrant culture of oral and improvised musical-poetic performance for which Florence was famous in the fifteenth century.

In the preface that Poliziano wrote (between 1469 and 1472) dedicating his Latin translation of the second book of the *Iliad* to Lorenzo de' Medici, Poliziano refers to his patron's skill as a performer of oral poetry to the accompaniment of the lyre and suggests that Lorenzo possesses the powers traditionally attributed to Orpheus:

> Or if, at times, you prefer to join the metres of Phoebus and sung verses to the sounding lyre, you strike the sounding strings with a plectrum, and you are able to make oak trees listen and follow you, and you have the power with your singing to tame raging lions.[68]

These are standard tropes, as we have seen in a number of texts, but Poliziano is a skilled rhetorician, and his insistence here specifically on the power inherent in the skill of oral poetic performance is not by chance. In Poliziano's poem the Orphic conceit allows Poliziano to recast the very real power asymmetry that subtends his relationship with his patron and fellow poet Lorenzo: "You alone are able to bring an Orphic plectrum to my rival songs; with you as my leader, I dare to compete with the ancient poets."[69] Poliziano's verses suggest that it is the Orphic power of Lorenzo's poetry that determines his status as "leader," artfully obscuring the real dynamics of wealth and influence that undergird Lorenzo's position of dominance over Poliziano and his fellow Florentines.

As we have seen, in the two surviving manuscripts that contain Poliziano's partial *Iliad* translation (the presentation copy that the young Poliziano gave to Lorenzo de' Medici and a draft manuscript in Poliziano's own hand), Poliziano has added glosses to the text of the poem. These notes offer valuable evidence of what Poliziano considered to be the salient qualities of Homer's poetry. As Alice Levine Rubenstein has shown, Poliziano's notes reveal his sustained interest in one aspect of Homer's art in particular: Homer's use of what Poliziano calls *enargeia*, the ability to make one's audience vividly experience that which is not present. Poliziano remarks upon Homer's *enargeia* in six separate passages from books 2–5 of the *Iliad* – all of them particularly vivid descriptive passages.[70] Later, in his *Oratio in expositione Homeri*, Poliziano would again underscore Homer's extraordinary ability to evoke vivid images in the minds of his readers – an ability that is all the more remarkable in that the blind Homer has seen these things not with his own eyes but only in his imagination: "In Homer's poetry we see images and likenesses of all human things. And he has placed these things before our eyes, visible and revealed, even though he himself surely never took them in with his own eyes."[71]

Quintilian's understanding of *enargeia* depends on his appreciation of the importance, for the orator and for the poet, of a highly developed imagination:

> The person who will show the greatest power in the expression of emotions will be the person who has properly formed what the Greeks call *phantasiai* (let us call them "visions"), by which the images of absent things are presented to the mind in such a way that we seem actually to see them with our eyes and have them physically present to us.[72]

For Quintilian, cultivating the ability to form vivid images within the mind allows an orator to exercise the power of *enargeia*, making an audience vividly experience that which is not present: "The result will be enargeia, what Cicero calls illustratio and evidentia, a quality which makes us seem not so much to be talking about something as exhibiting it. Emotions will ensue just as if we were present at the event itself."[73] Furthermore, this ability to form exceptionally vivid images in one's mind is also the key to success in improvisation, both in poetry and oratory:

> Once the heat of inspiration takes over, it often happens that deliberate effort cannot rival the success of an improvisation. The older orators, as Cicero says, used to say, when this happened, that a god was present, but in fact the reason is obvious. Deeply felt emotions and fresh images of things sweep along uninterruptedly, but the delay of writing sometimes cools them down, and once put aside they never return ... We must therefore form in our minds those images of which I spoke, and which I said are called *phantasiai*, and keep before our eyes and take to our hearts everything that we shall be speaking about – persons and questions, hopes and fears. It is the heart and the power of the mind that make us eloquent.[74]

The Ciceronian text that Quintilian is referring to here is almost certainly Cicero's defence of poetry in the *Pro Archia*, which indeed expresses approval for the traditional belief in the divine inspiration behind great poets and draws on the Platonic framework of divine poetic frenzy in particular.

One of the applications of the image-making power of *enargeia* that Quintilian particularly highlights is the power of the orator to guide listeners into a sort of virtual time travel, in which real or hypothetical events from the past or future are virtually experienced. Quintilian refers to this phenomenon as "time shift [*tralatio temporum*], strictly called *metastasis*" and explains, "We can form a picture not only of the past and the present, but also of the future or of what might have happened."[75] Quintilian also conceptualizes improvisational speaking as innately connected with a certain relationship with time: the phrase "ex tempore dicendi facultas" ("the power of improvisation") highlights the (a)temporal element of spontaneous performance (*ex tempore*, "out of time").[76] Modern theorists, too, have placed an emphasis on the element of time as a distinguishing feature of improvisational creative processes. Ed Sarath has argued that the two processes of improvisation and traditional composition

> differ fundamentally in their grounding in contrasting modes of temporal conception: composition is rooted in a linear, expanding conception that enables attending to large-scale relationships between moments and what precedes and follows them in the construction of overarching formal designs; improvisation is driven by a non-linear, inner-directed temporal experience that involves heightened attention to, and engagement in, the present moment as autonomous from past events and future possibilities.[77]

The distortion of time in the improvisational process, to which the term *ex tempore* alludes, may help to explain why many fifteenth-century improvisors and thinkers engage so extensively with ideas about non-linear time.

For Poliziano, *enargeia*, especially as used to achieve this type of transference of time, is a significant component of the poetics of improvisation. Fleeting time is a recurring theme throughout Poliziano's *rispetti continuati* (the series of *ottave* numbered 27 in Delcorno Branca's edition). The seventh stanza is dedicated entirely to the theme:

> Time is fleeing, and you are letting it flee,
> – Time, than which nothing in the world is more precious.
> And if you wait until May has passed,
> In vain you will then seek to pluck the rose.
> That which is not done quickly, will never get done:

Linger no more in thought, now that you can act.
Seize fleeing time by the forelock,
Before some strange doubt is born.[78]

This stanza by Poliziano explores the fleeting nature of time by juxta-posing two conceptions of time, both rooted in ancient Greek thought. The first four verses thematize the aspect of time that the Greeks called *chronos* – referring to the regular forward march of time that humans observe and measure through the passage of months, seasons, years, and other such extended intervals. In the second half of the stanza (and most explicitly in the penultimate verse) another conception of time is presented – what the Greeks called *kairos*, meaning the oppor-tune moment, the critical point in time when one is called upon to take swift and decisive action to achieve one's goals.[79] The Latin word generally used to translate the Greek *kairos* is *occasio*, while the Greek term *chronos* is translated into Latin as *tempus*. Cicero explains the dis-tinction as follows:

> An *occasion* is a period of time offering a convenient opportunity for doing or not doing some thing. And it is on the matter of opportunity that occa-sion differs from time: for both seem to be the same in genus, but under the category of time a space is fixed and limited in some way because the action is viewed as occurring in a period of time, several years, one year, or some part of a year, but under the category of occasion it is understood that to the space of time there is added the concept of an opportunity for performing the action.[80]

Ancient Greek literature and visual arts often represented Kairos as a male divinity with winged shoes and a distinctive hairstyle: a forelock of long hair hangs from the front of his head over his face, while the back of his head is shaved bald. This strange hairstyle was meant to convey that humans must seize the opportune moment as it arrives – meta-phorically grabbing it by the forelock – because once it has passed by it will slip away on its quick feet and can never again be grasped. The term "ciuffetto" ("tuft") in Poliziano's penultimate verse refers to the forelock of Kairos.

The ultimate source of this iconographical tradition was probably a famed sculpture by the ancient Greek sculptor Lysippos of Sicyon. Figure 6 shows a relief (probably Roman) representing Kairos with the classical attributes established by Lysippos.

This relief was once part of Lorenzo de' Medici's sculpture collection; Vasari asserts that it served as a model for Renaissance artists, including

Figure 6. *Kairos* (first century CE), marble relief, ex Medici collection (present location unknown). Photo credit: Antonio Quattrone.

Mariotto Albertinelli.[81] Poliziano was probably personally familiar with this sculpture.

One of the most important representations of Kairos/Occasio in Roman literature was rediscovered by Italian humanists during Poliziano's lifetime: Ausonius's *Epigram* 33, "For a Figure of Opportunity and Regret" ("In Simulacrum Occasionis et Paenitaentiae"), written as a conversation between an unnamed observer and sculptural figures of the goddess Occasio (Opportunity) and her companion Metanoea (Regret).[82] Poliziano, who imitated and alluded to Ausonius in a number of poems (including *Rispetto* 27, above), proved himself an astute reader by pointing out a glaring inaccuracy in *Epigram* 33. At the opening of the epigram the speaking statue declares the name of the artist who sculpted her:

"Whose work art thou?"

"Pheidias's: his who made Pallas' statue, who made Jove's: his third masterpiece am I. I am a goddess seldom found and known to few, Opportunity my name."[83]

Ausonius's attribution of the sculpture to the famed Greek artist Phidias ("Pheidias") was uncritically accepted by Latin-educated readers before Poliziano. Poliziano's exceptional command of Greek literature, though, allowed him to recognize that Ausonius's Latin poem was based on a much earlier Greek model, an epigram by Posidippos that also begins with a conversation between an observer and the speaking statue of Kairos:

Who and whence was the sculptor? From Sikyon. And his name? Lysippus. And who are you? Time who subdues all things.[84]

It is unclear why Ausonius attributed the statue to Phidias, when his Greek model text attributed it to Lysippos. Ausonius, writing in the fourth century CE, knew Lysippos and Phidias only as names, often mentioned side by side in ancient texts as among the greatest ancient Greek artists. Posidippos, by contrast, was a near-contemporary of Lysippos and may well have personally known the artist's work. Recognizing that Posidippos's text was more authoritative, Poliziano wrote about the issue in his commentary to Statius's *Silvae*, and later in his *Miscellanea*, dispelling the widespread misconception that Phidias had sculpted the original famed statue of Kairos.[85] Poliziano's skill as a philologist had enabled him, effectively, to resolve a problem of attribution for a sculptural work that had disappeared centuries earlier.

The relief of Kairos that was part of the Medici collection is likewise today a lost work.[86] In this case, though, an old photograph of the work survives (reproduced above), which is sufficiently clear to reveal the signature ΑΓΟΡΑΚΡΙΤΟΣ ("Agorakritos") inscribed below the foot of Kairos. As Beatrice Paolozzi Strozzi and Erkinger Schwarzenberg have shown, this cannot be an original signature but is in all likelihood an imposture perpetrated by a Renaissance humanist.[87] Agorakritos was a pupil of Phidias and according to Pliny used to sign some of his master's works (with Phidias's blessing).[88] The humanist responsible for the fake signature, apparently familiar both with the relevant passage of Pliny and with the tradition that Phidias had created the original Kairos sculpture, probably hoped to deceive other antiquarians into thinking that the relief was the work of Phidias himself. Once in Medici hands, though, the relief presumably came to the attention of Poliziano, on whom the forged signature could not have had the desired effect, since Poliziano himself had clarified that the original Kairos statue was not the work of Phidias (or his pupil, for that matter) but of Lysippos. It may in fact have been the false signature inscribed on the Medici Kairos that provoked Poliziano into publishing his refutation of the common belief that Phidias had sculpted the original Kairos statue.[89]

Multiple art historians have argued that Lysippos's lost statue of Kairos can be understood as a sort of artist's manifesto. José Dörig writes that, in the statue, Lysippos "seems to offer us his personal credo. It ... sums up the thought and work of Lysippos as the *Canon* did that of Polykleitos. He did not concern himself with the timeless existence of gods and men, but was intent upon catching the momentary flash of the eternal in the temporal."[90] The quest to catch and somehow render artistically the momentary flash of the eternal in the temporal was one that Poliziano pursued as a poet throughout his life (and which he shared with his fellow poet and patron Lorenzo). This artistic and poetic sensibility surely helped to determine Poliziano's long-term interest in artistic and literary representations of Kairos – including Lysippos's statue and its later echoes.

Poliziano's *Rispetto* 27, with its exhortation to seize Kairos by the forelock, strives to achieve a heightened sense of temporality. In early manuscripts and editions, this sixteen-stanza poem appears with the title "Serenata."[91] As the term "serenata" implies, the poem evokes a particular temporal and performative context: a sung evening performance, in the street beneath the bedroom of a beloved lady. The poem is a series of *strambotti* or *rispetti – ottava rima* stanzas that were traditionally performed to music and closely associated with improvisational practices: the verses themselves could be improvised by skilled practitioners, and/or the musical setting of the poetry could be improvised in performance.

The text directly evokes the moment of its sung performance before the beloved lady: "Ascolta el canto con che ti favella / colui che sopra ogni altra cosa t'ama" ("Listen to the song with which one is speaking to you / who loves you above all else," 27.1.2–3); "Io ho cantato pur" ("I have sung my part," 27.12.6). Time conceptualized as *kairos* – the fleeting moment of opportunity to take transformative action – thus operates within the poem at multiple levels. The beloved lady's youth is presented explicitly as kairotic. The singer persona (who serves as the lyric I and does not correspond to the lover) urges the lady not to allow her youth to slip away without bestowing the gift of her beauty on her lover, which would amount to a failure to seize Kairos by the forelock. The moment of sung performance evoked by the poem is also, implicitly, a kairotic moment, in the sense in which this term was used in classical rhetorical theory. In other words, the singer persona is called upon to seize the rhetorical occasion by tailoring his words to the particular situation and feelings of the lady in this moment, in order to persuade her to accept the lover's advances.

An interest in orality and improvisation pervades Poliziano's work from every phase of his career, from his youthful translations of Homer to his vernacular *strambotti*, from his pioneering secular drama the *Orfeo* to his Latin *Silvae*. It is this overriding and personal interest in oral poetry and improvisation that explains the ongoing presence, throughout Poliziano's works, of the theme of poetic frenzy that Marsilio Ficino's translations and interpretations of Plato had popularized, despite the fact that Poliziano's philological sophistication impels him to take this theory in different directions than had been possible for Ficino. Poliziano recognizes that the theory of frenzy cannot apply in the same way in conditions of what Walter Ong calls primary orality – the orality of a Homer or a Hesiod, uninfluenced by written models – as it might apply to the secondary orality of a literate poet like Poliziano himself, who improvises and performs poetry orally.[92] The recently rediscovered *Silvae* of Statius became, in Poliziano's hands, a model of improvisation that could be adapted to the realities of modern humanist poetry. For success in this type of poetic spontaneity, neither skill nor frenzy (contrary to Ficino's view) will suffice on its own; in Poliziano's framework, both must be tapped. In place of the pure orality and unmediated inspiration of Homer, Poliziano emphasizes the essential role, for the modern improvisor, of textual study to furnish the raw materials that can be spontaneously recombined in flights of improvisational inspiration.

Chapter Four

"The Power to Stir Up Others": Lorenzo de' Medici and Improvisation

In a 1491 letter to Piero Dovizi, Marsilio Ficino offers a surprising account of the ruler of Florence, Lorenzo de' Medici. Ficino describes his patron stumbling through the hilly Tuscan countryside, out of his mind and out of control:

> In the hills of Ambra and the valley of the Agnano, the Phoebean Lorenzo, intoxicated with the nectar of Dionysus, revels wildly far and wide. Then, being truly inspired from on high, he pours forth upon mankind celestial songs in elegant form, whose profound thoughts no one may ever penetrate unless his spirit has been seized by a similar frenzy. At times that patron of ours carries along with him quite a few who are listening more attentively and to better purpose, pouring especially upon them from the abundance of his frenzy. How he himself, wonderfully moved by divine will, has the power to stir up others in almost the same way, is explained by our Plato in the book entitled *Ion*.[1]

Descriptions of politicians in wine-soaked revelry are not typically meant to flatter. But Ficino's account of a drunken, raving ruler is clearly not a critique, nor is it an accidental revelation. On the contrary, Ficino is deploying carefully calculated panegyric reflecting an environment in which improvisational excellence could prove an asset not only for artists but also for rulers. At the time of the letter, Lorenzo functionally exercised one-man rule over a state that ostensibly retained its republican form of government. Since Lorenzo held no position within that government, nor any hereditary title, the vast power he wielded was fundamentally illegitimate. For Medicean apologists, justifying Lorenzo's power required creative approaches, and for Ficino, the most compelling argument drew him towards the surprising political possibilities of Bacchic frenzy.

As previous chapters have shown, Florence in the later part of the fifteenth century was a centre of both improvisation and classical studies, leading to a convergence of the two phenomena in which the nature of ancient and contemporary oral and improvisatory poetry was theorized by classical scholars like Ficino and Poliziano. This chapter examines the role of Lorenzo de' Medici – at once Florence's de facto ruler and one of its greatest poets – in these phenomena, demonstrating that improvisation and its valorization in Renaissance Florence transcended poetic and musical spheres and played a role in politics as well.

If there is no question that Ficino meant his description of the raving Lorenzo as a compliment, there is also no question that Lorenzo would have received it as one. As we have seen, Lorenzo had cultivated the skill of improvisation from his youth and placed a high value on musical and poetic improvisation throughout his life. However, Lorenzo's attitude towards the political value of such improvisational activity underwent a remarkable transformation as his own political career unfolded. References to Lorenzo's musical and poetic activities over a period of many years allow us to trace this transformation.

According to Niccolò Valori's biography, Lorenzo was a talented musician; Valori claims (no doubt indulging in some hyperbole) that Lorenzo was regarded as second to no one in the art of music.[2] He sought out the most renowned improvisors of his day, and not merely so that he could be entertained as a passive spectator by these famed performers. Rather, he sought the presence of these talented improvisors so that he could exercise his own gifts for performative and improvisational poetry in their company. Antonio di Guido, the most celebrated of the fifteenth-century *canterini* who entertained popular audiences in Florence's Piazza San Martino, was frequently invited to join Lorenzo during periods when Lorenzo was actively cultivating his own musical and poetic abilities, including in the summers of 1472 and 1473.

Surviving documents offer a rather robust accounting of these improvisational retreats. In August 1472 Lorenzo invited Antonio di Guido to join him at his estate in Cafaggiolo (calling him "maestro Antonio della Viuola," in reference to Antonio's instrument).[3] Lorenzo tasked Niccolò Michelozzi with arranging for Antonio di Guido's visit; in the same correspondence he also asked Michelozzi to bring him his own viola.[4] Lorenzo was apparently eager to exercise his performance skills together with Antonio di Guido and was frustrated that he had forgotten to bring his instrument to his rural retreat. A similar situation had occurred in August 1468, when Lorenzo had travelled to Cafaggiolo without his viola and had arranged for Luigi Pulci to send him the instrument.[5]

In August 1473 Lorenzo again invited Antonio di Guido to his country house in Vallombrosa, accompanying the invitation with a sonnet and perhaps (as Mario Martelli has suggested) hoping to have Antonio provide musical accompaniment for a performance of a poem.[6] Michelozzi, who again had been tasked with arranging the *canterino*'s visit, wrote, in a letter to Lorenzo dated 3 August 1473, that Antonio di Guido had appreciated Lorenzo's philosophically ambitious sonnet and that he intended to bring the text with him to Vallombrosa to discuss it with Lorenzo.[7] When she learned of Antonio di Guido's visit, Clarice Orsini reluctantly concluded that her husband's anticipated return to Florence would be long delayed; she was apparently well aware of how much Lorenzo enjoyed discussing and performing poetry with the renowned *canterino*.[8]

Baccio Ugolini, who, as we have seen in earlier chapters, was regarded by many as one of the most talented improvisors of his generation, was another companion with whom Lorenzo liked to perform poetry and music. In a letter addressed to Lorenzo in 1476, Ugolini describes himself in the frustrating situation (familiar, as he knew, to Lorenzo) of having gone on a rural retreat to Vallombrosa and forgotten to bring his viola; he asks Lorenzo to send him an instrument.[9] In a 1490 letter to Lorenzo's son Piero, Alessandro Degli Alessandri writes that Lorenzo has been singing while taking the baths at Vignone and predicts that, following the arrival of Ugolini, Lorenzo will spend even more time on this pursuit. It is clear that Degli Alessandri is referring specifically to Lorenzo's practice of improvised oral poetic performance, since in the same passage he praises Piero's command of this art.[10]

Lorenzo and Poliziano shared a long and fruitful literary collaboration that included a mutual passion for oral poetry and improvisation. Poliziano seems to refer to Lorenzo's abilities as improvisor in his *Nutricia*, which mentions a nymph who was supposedly a source of poetic inspiration for Lorenzo. A marginal note by Poliziano clarifies that he is referring to a nymph "whom Lorenzo elegantly sings about extemporaneously."[11]

Despite Lorenzo's clear dedication to musical and poetic improvisation, it appears that in his early life he did not regard these activities as connected with divine inspiration or promote the philosophical significance of his improvisation in the way that Ficino later would. This chapter will trace how Lorenzo's approach to possibilities of oral poetry evolved between his youth and maturity, in conjunction with his evolving political and cultural agenda and in dialogue with the intellectual contributions of the leading humanists of his circle, especially Ficino and Poliziano. As we saw in chapter 1, the young Lorenzo's musical and poetic pursuits were heavily collaborative and social, offering the possibility of instrumentalizing these pastimes to reinforce social bonds and group identity within his *brigata*. Through shared language, humour, and collaborative improvisation, the *Uccellagione di starne*, much like the hunt it purports to depict, serves to articulate the common purpose of a group. But there is little evidence that Lorenzo, as a youth, took much of an interest in Ficino's agenda of promoting divine frenzy as a lens for thinking about musical and poetic production. On the contrary, in fact: Lorenzo's early satirical poem *Il Simposio* provides a colourful illustration of the irreverent attitude which Lorenzo took towards the lofty philosophical and poetic theories of Ficino – including his concept of divinely inspired frenzy – during his early years. Lorenzo probably began writing the poem at some point between August 1466 and August 1467, when he was seventeen or eighteen years old, though he may have continued to modify the work after this initial period of composition.[12] At the time of *Il Simposio*'s composition there was no significant personal connection between Lorenzo and Ficino, though Ficino's thought was already exerting a considerable influence among Florentine intellectuals, including Cristoforo Landino, who was one of Lorenzo's teachers during these years. Ficino's tract *De divino furore* (dated 1 December 1457) had captured the attention of intellectuals in Florence and elsewhere and had made its mark on Landino's thought – an influence of which his pupil Lorenzo was probably aware.

Landino was not Lorenzo's only early mentor in literary matters, however, and he certainly did not exercise an exclusive influence in determining the ways in which Lorenzo applied his budding poetic talent. Among the many figures vying for influence over the young *princeps*, Luigi Pulci, as we have seen, was the most successful in shaping Lorenzo's youthful poetic pursuits. Pulci was a brilliant poet with a gift for satire and polemic – a talent which he employed not only against Ficino's friend the priest Matteo Franco (in a famous series of sonnets) but also against Ficino himself.[13]

Pulci's satirical bent and his suspicion of Ficino's philosophical project clearly shaped Lorenzo's *Simposio*, a work which programmatically subverts every function that Ficino, in *De divino furore* and elsewhere, identifies as the legitimate goals of poetry. The poem dramatizes the over-indulgence of bodily appetites, makes Christ's passion the occasion for a blasphemous pun, and mocks the altered mental state that Ficino's theory associated with poetic inspiration. Even the title of Lorenzo's poem highlights its intent to parody the Platonic dialogue of the same name, a text that Ficino held in particular reverence. Indeed, it seems probable that Lorenzo chose this title for his nearly completed poem sometime after the 1469 publication of Ficino's commentary on Plato's *Symposium*, which rapidly became Ficino's most popular work.

In the *Simposio* Lorenzo narrates, in the first person, a journey through the city of Florence in which he encounters the most noteworthy drinkers of the city. The style is an explicit parody of Dante; the drunkards of the poem correspond to the damned of *Inferno*. The role of Dante's Virgil is played by Bertolino Tedaldi and Nastagio Vespucci, who, themselves caricatures of intoxication, guide Lorenzo through the streets of Florence naming the various drunks. Among the ranks of the inebriated are many of Lorenzo's well-known contemporaries, such as Sandro Botticelli and Angelo Poliziano. The latter appears accompanied by Ridolfo Lotti, and of the two men Lorenzo writes:

> If they are mortal enemies of wine,
> Their mortal nemesis wine always is,
> And to their heads in all its fury goes.[14]

The pun in the last verse ("furor di-vino") is an evident send-up of the Platonic notion of divine frenzy, which from 1457 on (that is, since the publication of *De divino furore*) Ficino had made the cornerstone of his theory of poetry. Lorenzo's comic treatment suggests that the exalted madness of poetic inspiration is not really so different from the effects of wine, which also brings about a state of temporary madness – a point that Ficino's description of the frenzied Lorenzo would later acknowledge, though with much more reverence.

However, just a few years later, we can perceive a remarkable shift in Lorenzo's relationship with Ficino's "furor divino" and its possibilities. On 21 January 1473, Marsilio Ficino wrote a letter to Niccolò Michelozzi in praise of Lorenzo. The qualities that Ficino singles out for praise in the young man are striking, given that Lorenzo had mocked Ficino's theory of divine frenzy in his poem *Il Simposio* just a few years earlier. Ficino declares that Lorenzo is divinely inspired – specifically, by the three Graces that Orpheus had praised in one of his *Hymns*:

> I pray that those three Graces described by Orpheus, namely splendour, joy and vigour, will support our Medici; that is, splendour of intellect, joy in the exercise of will, vigour and prosperity of body. These Graces now inspire Lorenzo from on high, and they will do so as long as he only acknowledges that he has freely received these favours from God alone.[15]

Here it is significant that Ficino not only asserts divine inspiration on Lorenzo's behalf but goes out of his way to allude to Orpheus, who was often invoked by Ficino to synthesize Florentine oral poetic culture with ancient ideas about poetic inspiration and the power of oral poetry. In the same letter Ficino also declares that Lorenzo displays the same talents that Ficino himself possesses, and outshines his contemporaries not only as a longtime poet but also in his maturity as a philosopher:

> I for my part, Niccolo, would perhaps be unable to avoid being envious of so many magnificent qualities in a young man, which are usually associated with age, were it not that Lorenzo's qualities are mine also ... Poets, you have long since awarded him the laurel; orators, you have recently done likewise; now let us philosophers do the same.[16]

Ficino also explicitly calls Lorenzo's poetic inspiration a "divine frenzy" in the opening lines of a letter he wrote to Bernardo Rucellai, the body of which contains a prayer that Ficino had written, entitled *Oratio ad Deum theologica*. Discussing his own poem, which survives in both a prose version and a Sapphic verse version, presumably to be performed accompanied by his "Orphic lyre," Ficino comments, "On occasion I have heard our Lorenzo de' Medici, moved by divine frenzy, sing similar prayers to the lyre."[17] Here Ficino is making the rather surprising claim that Lorenzo de' Medici was not only sympathetic to Ficino's unique brand of Orphic poetic performance – as Cosimo de' Medici had been – but actually cultivated a similar type of poetry himself.

The transformation that Ficino's letters imply in Lorenzo's attitude towards Orphic poetry – from ironic detractor to divinely inspired practitioner – is not one that Ficino has merely imagined. There is evidence, both documentary and literary, for a dramatic shift beginning in 1473 in Lorenzo's stance vis-à-vis Ficino's Neoplatonic movement and its theory of inspiration in particular. Facing heavy political responsibilities following his father's death in 1469, when he was twenty years old, Lorenzo seems to have undertaken no new major literary projects for a period of several years. The work that marks his return to poetic composition is the *De summo bono*, whose character shows that Lorenzo's decision to return to poetry was accompanied by a new conception of how his role as poet should relate to his public image as leader of the Florentine state. As a young man, Lorenzo had acquired a reputation as something of a libertine. His notorious weakness for sexual temptations had become a political liability for the Medici regime.[18] Moreover, Lorenzo's literary pursuits, far from mitigating this problematic reputation, had actually reinforced it, since many of his early poems – as exemplified by the *Simposio* – thematize sensual impulses that some segments of the Florentine public were bound to consider scandalous.

Lorenzo relaunched his poetic career in 1473 not merely because he was finally able to spare more time for literary pursuits but because he understood that his poetry, which had contributed to his reputation as a libertine, could also function as a tool for reshaping his public image. The new public image which Lorenzo sought to fashion was based (at least in part) on the Platonic ideal of the enlightened philosopher-king. To burnish his philosophical credentials, Lorenzo began a carefully planned and widely publicized Platonic "apprenticeship" under Ficino. This apprenticeship is documented by the letters Lorenzo and Ficino exchanged between 1473 and 1474, which suggest an intense personal relationship: the letters written by both men draw heavily on the conceptual language of Platonic love that was one of the hallmarks of Ficino's philosophical thought and epistolary style.

The poems Lorenzo wrote during this period, breaking a long literary hiatus, are even more interesting than these letters for our purposes, however, because they show that Lorenzo, like Ficino, recognized that his poetic talents and long-standing interest in improvisation could be effectively harnessed to enhance Lorenzo's new identity as an enlightened Platonist. Since Ficino's philosophy celebrated the idea that a true poet could gain direct access to philosophical insights through the inspiration of poetic frenzy, Lorenzo was able to present himself not only as a student of philosophy but also as an authoritative witness of the insights of Christian Neoplatonism, by composing poems that embodied, in various ways, Ficino's ideals of Orphic poetry.

De summo bono is clearly the opening bid in this project. At the opening of Lorenzo's *De summo bono*, the first-person narrator, who will later be unequivocally identified as Lorenzo (or, to be more precise, "Lauro"), leaves Florence to wander in the valley of Monte Giovi, where he encounters the (fictional) shepherd Alfeo. The two engage in a debate about whether the rural or urban life is superior, with Lorenzo championing the city, Alfeo the country. At the opening of the second canto their debate is interrupted when they hear a beautiful sound, which turns out to be a song that Marsilio (Ficino, of course) is playing on his Orphic lyre as he strolls towards them. The bulk of the poem (cantos 2 through 5) consists of Marsilio's speech to Lorenzo (and Alfeo), in which he explains the nature of the highest good. Hence the *De summo bono* is not only a product of Lorenzo's initiation into Ficino's philosophy but also an idealized dramatization of that initiation. The reader observes Lorenzo embracing (as author, narrator, and character) classically Ficinian philosophical ideas on the principal question of the nature of the highest good (to be sought in the *vita contemplativa* and ultimately achieved in the afterlife), as well as on other subjects – including Ficino's theory of poetry. Whereas Lorenzo's earlier poetry lampooned Ficino's exaltations of the poet's divine frenzy, in the *De summo bono* we observe Lorenzo making Ficino's

Orphic enthusiasm his own. Here is the glowing account of Ficino's musical entrance:

> My ears, all heedful of his words, were then
> attracted to another voice which seized
> and bound them with its sweeter harmonies.
>
> I thought that Orpheus was back on earth,
> or he whose noble tones had walled up Thebes,
> so sweetly did his lyre sound to me.
>
> "Perhaps that Lyre set within the sphere
> of the fixed stars fell down from heaven's realm," I said.
> "The starry sky must miss its constellation;
>
> Or maybe, as that ancient sage once taught,
> the transposed soul of one of these was put –
> such was his destiny – inside this player."
>
> And while my eye, led on by what my ear
> could hear, looked through the boughs and leafy fronds
> to find out where such sweetness had its source,
>
> behold! the eye, the noble mind, the ear,
> all in an instant heard and grasped and saw
> the one who played, his teaching, and his lyre:
>
> Marsilio of Montevecchio.[19]

Lorenzo's verses pay homage to the reputation that Ficino had been building for himself as a new Orpheus, a philosopher-singer. Hearing the sweet music of the lyre, Lorenzo formulates various hypotheses about its origin, all of which revolve around the Orpheus myth: either Orpheus has returned to the world, or Amphion (a parallel oral poet from Greek myth) has reappeared, or the constellation of the Lyre (Orpheus's instrument which had been elevated to celestial status) has fallen to Earth, or a Pythagorean transmigration of souls has caused the soul of Orpheus to enter a new body.

In the invocation that opens the *De summo bono*'s fourth canto, Lorenzo asks Apollo to give him divine frenzy:

> If you, Apollo, still do love the chaste
> locks of your much-desired Daphne, help
> then him in whom her lovely name endures,

> and grant to me from your own sacred furor
> not the amount that I myself may need
> but what the subject of my song demands.
>
> Now let your favor wax, the more my wit
> falls short, that I may show Marsilio's thoughts
> in verse as I perceive them in my mind.[20]

It may strike the reader as a strange effort at flattery that Lorenzo invokes divine frenzy, the Platonic enthusiasm that Ficino himself had restored to cultural currency, to aid him in his effort to turn Ficino's ideas into poetry. But Lorenzo's approach aligns well with Ficino's writings to his poet friends suggesting that poets sympathetic to his cause could best help to advance it by producing poetry that would not only repackage his philosophical ideas in verse but do so through the authoritative means of divinely inspired oral poetry.[21]

The conclusion of the *De summo bono* strongly reinforces the text's function in representing the integration of Lorenzo's ongoing poetic vocation with his new allegiance to the contemplative philosophy of Ficino. After Marsilio has finished explaining to Lorenzo and Alfeo the nature of the highest good, he departs; Alfeo returns to tend his flock; and Lorenzo, reflecting on the speech he has heard, breaks out into an ecstatic hymn:

> So each went on to his own dwelling place,
> but as I glowed inside with sacred fire,
> and all my thoughts were sweetly wandering,
> Love, who inflames all things, inspired me to sing.[22]

The sixth and final chapter of the *De summo bono* consists entirely of this hymn, which, despite the fact that Marsilio has just left the narrative scene, is the portion of the text that shows the philosopher's influence on the poet most directly. For Lorenzo's hymn not only exemplifies in general terms the Orphic style of poetry favoured by Ficino; it is in fact a rather direct translation of Ficino's *Oratio ad Deum theologica*. The production of these parallel texts by Ficino and Lorenzo was clearly part of a coordinated effort to publicize the notion that the two men were collaborating closely, applying a substantially unified philosophical and poetic approach. And the publicity efforts went beyond the verses themselves: this canto is the text to which Ficino is alluding in his glowing letter to Bernardo Rucellai where he mentions that Lorenzo, under the influence of divine frenzy, produces similar songs to Ficino's own.[23]

These texts provide powerful evidence that Lorenzo embraced Ficino's philosophical program in the 1470s and allowed it to guide his own literary creations as part of a larger project to present himself as a philosopher and divinely inspired improvisor. With this project in mind, if we return to Ficino's 1491 description of Lorenzo raving through the hills of Tuscany in a divine frenzy, several details stand out. In his portrayal of Lorenzo as Orphic poet, Ficino makes three main claims about Lorenzo's verses: that they contain veiled philosophical meanings, that they are sung, and that they flow from him spontaneously. Among the poems by Lorenzo datable to this period, it is his *Selve* to which these qualities can most meaningfully be ascribed. In fact, the problem of teasing out from Lorenzo's written corpus the traces of his lifelong cultivation of improvisatory and performative poetry can help to untangle another problem that has long occupied scholars of Lorenzo's works: the puzzling structural features of his *Selve*. The Orphic poetic identity that Ficino ascribes to Lorenzo (in the above passage and elsewhere) can serve to elucidate these works, which have been regarded by modern scholars as among the most enigmatic poems of the fifteenth century.

Literary critics have produced very few strong, compelling interpretations of the *Selve* – a surprising absence, given that the first of the two *Selve* is one of the longest and most ambitious poems by Lorenzo, widely regarded as one of the greatest poets of the Quattrocento. Critics have struggled with what many have seen as the chaotic form of the *Selve*, puzzled by the absence of a clear overarching structure unifying the two works and their frequent and abrupt shifts from one theme to another. The eminent critic Mario Martelli declared himself profoundly perplexed by the "kaleidoscopic" nature of the longer *Selva* and its "constant jumping around from one topic to another, tangling up the subjects and frequently failing to emphasize suitable transitions from one to the next, to the point that, having finished reading the text, the scholar is left profoundly perplexed about the precise meaning to attribute to a work like this one."[24] Martelli concluded that the poem's chaotic structure resulted from scribal confusion at some phase in the work's transmission and sought to reorder the separate *ottave* into a more sensible sequence. However, there is no firm evidence to support the reordering proposed by Martelli or his hypothesis of a bumbling scribe's error.[25] Nevertheless, the hypothesis that the *Selva* we now read represents a fusion of originally autonomous sections can still prove fruitful, especially if we give due consideration to the fact that the work was very likely originally performed to musical accompaniment. Situating Lorenzo's *Selve* as part of the musical-poetic tradition of the *improvvisatori*, and as part of Lorenzo's self-fashioning as Orphic poet, allows us to conclude that the chaos within the *Selva I* is not a failure to be explained away through textual emendation but a key to interpreting the work. Lorenzo did not try to produce a tightly ordered poem and fail; he succeeded in producing a work styled as the song of an improvisatory oral poet, in keeping with his own civic-literary identity and the Orphic atmosphere of the Quattrocento Florentine intellectual landscape.

The formal features of the *Selve*, puzzling as they may seem, are all congruent with the improvisational style that interested Lorenzo through his life, and there is evidence that we should regard the *Selve* as improvisational: either as the product of actual improvisational composition practices or as a work stylistically inspired by improvised verse and its vernacular forms. First, the title, *Selve*, suggests an affinity between Lorenzo's poems and the *Silvae* of his close associate Poliziano, as well as Poliziano's privileged intertext, the *Silvae* of Statius.[26] Lorenzo's *Selve* indeed embody many of the aesthetic ideals that were the hallmarks of the genre of *silvae* as rediscovered and promoted by Poliziano: spontaneity, rapid shifts of theme, lack of rigid structure, stylistic variety (including the flexible deployment of a lower stylistic register), and an aesthetic valorization of the unfinished.

Lorenzo's *Selve* are, of course, not Latin poetry like Poliziano's *Silvae* and those of Statius; rather, they are vernacular poems in *ottava rima*, and as such they can also be said to belong to another vernacular literary genre. As Mario Martelli observed, they are *rispetti* (also known as *strambotti*) – the genre of vernacular love poetry in *ottava rima* that flourished in both popular and courtly contexts in the late Quattrocento and early Cinquecento, especially in Florence.[27] Such poems can take the form of an individual, isolated *ottava*, in which case they are called *rispetti spicciolati*; or (as in the case of Lorenzo's *Selve*), *ottave* can be combined to form longer poems, known as *rispetti continuati*. The short form of the individual *rispetti*, and the possibility of recombining them into larger units, made the form ideally suited for improvisational performance – hence the form's widespread deployment by *improvvisatori*.

Evidence from various quarters helps us to reconstruct the improvisational context of Lorenzo's work. Among the many surviving documents chronicling Lorenzo's interest in improvisation is an anecdote passed down by Lodovico Guicciardini in his *L'ore di ricreazione*, written in the second half of the sixteenth century. Regarding Lorenzo il Magnifico's skill as an improvisor of poetry, he writes:

> The Magnificent Lorenzo de' Medici, father of Pope Leo and a great poet, found himself among pleasant company discussing human nature, with everyone expressing a different opinion. When he was asked for his opinion, he improvised with grace, describing it in this way:

By nature we do fear, grow sad and cheer
A thousand times a day or even more.
We are by evil cheered, saddened by good.
For harm we hope and our own good we fear,
So little wisdom do we show in life.
How vain are cares and thoughts the end will show.[28]

The verses that Guicciardini transmits as an autonomous improvised poem also appear, in the textual tradition of Lorenzo's poetry, as the tercets of Lorenzo's sonnet "Fortuna, come suol, pur mi dileggia." As Brian Richardson has recently observed, this raises some questions:

If the anecdote is based on fact, was Lorenzo quoting his own verse from memory or did he improvise the lines and reuse them later as part of the sonnet? In favour of the latter hypothesis is the slight "disconnect" between the argument of the quatrains, on the variability of Fortune, and that of these tercets, on the variability of human nature.[29]

Further support for the hypothesis that Lorenzo reused, within this sonnet, verses originally produced extemporaneously may be found in the many instances of *ottave* by Lorenzo that have circulated as autonomous poems, in addition to having been incorporated into longer poems.[30] While there are multiple possible explanations for this phenomenon, it is consistent with the theory that Lorenzo reused and recombined passages of verse, some of them originally extemporaneous.

The fact that Lorenzo's *Selve* are connected with the tradition of *improvvisatore* performance has gone unnoticed by most modern readers of these poems, yet early readers (and publishers) of the text understood this connection as a matter of course. Today, readers of a modern edition of Lorenzo's *Selve* encounter a text that has been stripped of a number of important paratexts that were present in many of the early manuscripts and printed editions of the text, which would have shaped early readers' perceptions of them. The woodcut pictured in figure 7, which was printed as the frontispiece in two early editions of the *Selve*, is a particularly interesting example.[31]

The woodcut depicts a figure evidently intended to represent the poet of the *Selve* (that is, the lyric I of the poems), and he is depicted unmistakably as an *improvvisatore*: the attributes that define his identity as poet are not a pen or book but musical instruments. He is shown strumming a lute; behind his left shoulder is prominently displayed the classic instrument of the *improvvisatori*, the *lira da braccio*, casually suspended from a tree. The bow with which the *lira* would be played hangs in another

Figure 7. Lorenzo de' Medici, *Selve d'amore* (Florence, c. 1516), frontispiece. Biblioteca Nazionale Centrale di Firenze, Palat. D.4.7.25; with the permission of the Ministero della Cultura/Biblioteca Nazionale Centrale di Firenze. No reproduction or duplication of this image by any means is permitted.

tree behind his right shoulder. The figure is an elegantly dressed, clean-shaven young man without clear distinguishing personal features; as such he can be understood to represent a young Lorenzo de' Medici (a connection suggested by the Medici family crest that rests near his right leg) or a more generic figure, but this is clearly an *improvvisatore* performer.

Even when they appear as words on a page, the verses of Lorenzo's *Selve* invite the reader to imagine them as the sung performance of an *improvvisatore*. Lorenzo's Florentine contemporaries would not have needed paratexts like this woodcut in order to draw such a connection; as lyrical-descriptive poetry in an extended sequence of *ottava rima* stanzas, the *Selve* can be linked with the *improvvisatore* tradition of *strambotti/rispetti continuati* through internal metrical and generic features alone. But the frontispiece is important because it clearly demonstrates that Lorenzo's poems were being deliberately advertised to contemporary readers as works in this oral poetic genre.

In a 1492 poem by Jacopo Corsi ("Astreo, non dormir più, ché il tempo è lucido") celebrating the recently deceased Lorenzo de' Medici, we find a surprising description of Lorenzo il Magnifico engaging in musical-poetic performance: "Under the sweet shade, he often used to touch with his golden plectrum the sonorous *cetra*, which would cause rocks to crumble from its sweetness, singing how in ancient times the first age loved wood, and scorned gold, which the world now desires more and more as time passes."[32]

Corsi's poem goes on for dozens of verses describing Lorenzo singing about the Golden Age, when humans were indifferent to precious metals and other riches, lived in harmony with nature, and so on. Beyond the clear connection between this subject matter and the Golden Age myth that is among the central themes of Lorenzo's *Selva I*, the poem contains numerous clear textual echoes of specific verses from the *Selva I*. So Corsi's poem must be understood not only as a general tribute to Lorenzo's career as poet but more specifically as a celebration of Lorenzo as singer of the *Selva I*.

Why was this side of Lorenzo's literary activity so salient in Corsi's mind? A famed *improvvisatore*, Corsi was renowned as a performer of *rispetti* as well as other genres favoured by *improvvisatori*, including *capitoli* in *terza rima* (such as the *capitolo* paying tribute to Lorenzo). Corsi met an untimely end – murdered, as a contemporary reported, "near Monte Giordano by three unknown men on horseback, dressed in the Spanish style" – as a result of his imprudent decision to improvise some verses that damaged the honour of Cardinal Giuliano della Rovere.[33] Corsi is singled out for praise by Paolo Cortesi in his *De cardinalatu* as one of the most admired vernacular *improvvisatori*.[34] Vincenzo Calmeta too considered Corsi one of the most talented improvisors, grouping him with Serafino Aquilano as examples of poets "lacking letters" ("di lettere spogliati") but gifted with "good natural instinct" ("buono istinto della natura").[35] By describing Lorenzo delivering an oral poetic performance of his *Selva I*, Corsi is singling out for praise one specific aspect of Lorenzo's multifaceted poetic activity: his role in elevating Corsi's own traditional vernacular genre of the *rispetti* to a new level of sophistication and cultural prestige with the *Selve*.

In many of the early manuscripts, the main subdivisions within *Selva I* are given their own subtitles, usually in Latin but sometimes in Tuscan vernacular: *Descriptio estivi temporis* (Description of Summer), *Descriptio gelosie* (Description of Jealousy), *Descriptio spei* (Description of Hope), and *Descriptio auree etatis* (Description of the Golden Age).[36] While these subtitles likely were not created by the author, their presence in the early manuscript tradition is an important indicator of what early readers regarded as the salient features of this text. Modern interpreters of the *Selva I* have been confounded by the apparent lack of central organization in the poem and its wide array of themes. Summer, Jealousy, Hope, and the Golden Age of Greco-Roman mythology are not integrally connected themes; for this reason, many interpreters have seen the sections of Lorenzo's poem as fragmented.

As the "Descriptio" subtitles of the manuscript tradition suggests, though, a certain unity subtends all of the sections of the poem – not in the themes treated but in the rhetorical mode deployed. Lorenzo's poem is structured as a collection of vivid descriptions that draw on the power of language to allow the audience to see that which is not present. The poem is thus a tour de force of *descriptio*, or, to use the related rhetorical term favoured by Quintilian, *enargeia*. As we have seen, Poliziano viewed *enargeia* – the ability to use language to create vivid images in the minds of one's audience – as an essential skill for oral and improvisatory poets. Poliziano strives to demonstrate his own mastery of this skill in his Latin *Silvae*. Lorenzo, in his *Selve*, seeks to achieve analogous results in his own experiments with the vernacular *rispetti continuati* genre.

Drawing on the rhetorical mode of *descriptio* and the vernacular form of *rispetti* allowed Lorenzo to place the *Selve* into direct communication with both classical and vernacular forms of improvisation current in his Florentine milieu. Loosely connected as they are, the themes of the *Selve* also suggest the influence of contemporary theories of improvisation. One recurring theme in the *Selve* is the cyclical rhythms of time. The *Selve* abound in descriptions of dawns: the dawn that marks the end of a night of passion in *Selva I* 61, for instance, and the dawns that represent the anticipated return of an absent beloved in *Selva I* 19 and *Selva I* 135. The *Descriptio auree etatis* (Description of the Golden Age) that occupies stanzas 84–112 also explores time and its cyclical rhythms. During the lost ancient Golden Age, Lorenzo's verses claim, the sleep cycles of humans were conveniently coordinated with the rising and setting of the sun; dawn marked the rising of humans, animals, and flowers together with the sun: "Quando e razzi del sol le nebbie purgono, / con li animal', co' fiori insieme surgono" ("When sunshine cleared the skies of morning fog, / And beasts and blossoms woke, they too arose").[37] Other sections of the *Selve* deal with the cyclical movement of the seasons, as when the return of the beloved is compared with the approach of spring in *Selva I* 20. However, the cyclical nature of time is not an entirely joyful concept in the *Selve*: the pain of the human condition, as explored in Lorenzo's poems, is fundamentally linked to being trapped in time's cyclical movement. The negativity with which Lorenzo's *Selva I* invests cyclical time is evident in a key passage in stanza 97:

> Just so, resplendent Day who after great
> Exertions chases rosy Dawn away;
> Then Dawn disperses Night who, though she flees,
> Is destined in the end to vanquish Day;
> Yet even as the hunter sounds her horn,
> She yields to Dawn in time's eternal round.[38]

The familiar succession of the phases of the day is presented here in violent, sinister terms: the daytime is likened to a hunter who makes the dawn into his prey, only to in turn be hunted down by the night. It is implied that the night will in turn be hunted down by the dawn; this cycle of violence (like the diurnal cycle itself) has no end.

In the context of this vision of cyclical time and its oppressions, we might return fruitfully to Quintilian's theories of improvisation. As we have seen, Quintilian conceptualizes improvisation as innately connected with the idea of time; in Lorenzo's milieu, the temporal element of improvisation was well integrated into theories of improvisation by commentators like Poliziano. It is thus especially significant that the major theme of the *Selve* is central to contemporary interpretations of the improvisational act itself: *ex tempore* composition can be understood to occur outside of time in the sense that it demands a shift from *chronos* to *kairos*; the performer is called upon to seize the moment and accomplish instantaneously that which ordinarily requires long preparation. Both in its form (a series of *descriptiones*) and in its themes (cyclical time and its tyranny), the *Selve* evoke contemporary theories of improvisational composition.

The myth of the Golden Age is a prominent element of the cyclical presentation of time in Lorenzo's *Selva*, and it makes several appearances.

Lorenzo's verses in the *Selva* suggest that, once his beloved lady enters the "bel cerchio" ("beautiful circle") of Florence's walls, his own homeland has achieved a kind of perfection comparable to the ancient Golden Age: "O cara patria, or non sia più invidiata / da te già mai la prima età dell' oro" ("O dear homeland, now may you have no more envy for the first Golden Age").[39]

Lorenzo's *Selva I* also includes an account of the birth of Love, along with Jealousy, from primordial Chaos at the beginning of time. During the Golden Age of Saturn's rule, however, Jealousy was unknown, having been banished by Jupiter:

> When at the dawn of time, old Chaos bore
> His charming son Amor, this evil goddess
> Of whom I speak was born as well: Amor
> And Jealousy thus shared a common birth.
> But Jove, the kindly father, gracious to
> The world, expelled her to the shadow realm
> With Pluto and the Furies: there she dwelled
> While Saturn and the Age of Gold prevailed.[40]

The recurring Golden Age discourse in Lorenzo's poem draws on the poetry of Hesiod, revealing another important facet of Lorenzo's literary agenda.[41] In engaging so extensively with Hesiod's poetry (the *Theogony* and the *Works and Days*) within his *Selva*, Lorenzo is connecting his work with the literary and intellectual agendas of both Ficino and Poliziano, who were then among the few European intellectuals to have deeply studied Hesiod.

Along with the Orphic poems, Hesiod's *Theogony* was among the first Greek texts that Ficino translated into Latin as a young man.[42] The *ottava* by Lorenzo cited above appears indebted to the account of the beginning of time offered by Hesiod in the *Theogony*, in which Love is among the first offspring to emerge from primordial Chaos.[43] According to Ficino, this doctrine was shared by a number of other ancient authorities, including Hermes Trismegistus and Orpheus:

> In the *Argonautica*, when Orpheus, in the presence of Chiron and the heroes, sang about the beginnings of things, following the theology of Hermes Trismegistus, he placed Chaos before the World, and located Love in the bosom of that Chaos, before Saturn, Jove, and the other gods; and he praised Love in these words: *Love is the oldest, perfect in himself, and best counseled.*[44]

Ficino's precocious interest in these texts undoubtedly stemmed, at least in part, from his conviction that they contained theological and philosophical insights; a long tradition of Neoplatonic thought had regarded these texts as repositories of hidden wisdom. For Ficino, the theory of divine poetic frenzy served to justify the enterprise of searching for theological and philosophical wisdom in the verses of a poet like Hesiod, who, as a pagan without philosophical training, might otherwise seem to lack credentials in these areas. In Ficino's view, though, it was precisely Hesiod's lack of training (indeed, his illiteracy) that guaranteed the authenticity of the divine inspiration behind his poetic achievements. In Ficino's 1474 letter to Antonio Pelotti and Baccio Ugolini, "Poetic Frenzy Is from God," Ficino calls Hesiod one of the "true poets" inspired by divine poetic frenzy and asserts that, like the rhapsode Ion of Plato's dialogue, Hesiod was an "unlettered" poet who, "passing beyond the limitations of skill[,] ... suddenly produced astonishing poetry" through frenzy.[45] Ficino therefore believed that Hesiod's inspired poetry, especially the *Theogony*, could be interpreted allegorically to reveal truths consonant with Platonic philosophy. This conviction clearly underlies, for example, his citation of the *Theogony* in his commentary on Plato's *Philebus*: "What Hesiod says of Venus in his *Theogony* (when he says Saturn castrated the Sky and threw the testicles into the sea, and from these and the swirling foam Venus was born) must be understood perhaps as referring to the fertility for creating all things."[46]

Ficino's view of Hesiod as a poet inspired with divine frenzy was buttressed by the account that the poet gives of his own inspiration at the beginning of the *Theogony*, where he recounts that the Muses "taught Hesiod beautiful song while he was pasturing lambs under holy Helicon."[47] The text strongly emphasizes Hesiod's low social status prior to receiving inspiration from the Muses, who address him and his fellow rustics as "field-dwelling shepherds, ignoble disgraces, mere bellies."[48] Hesiod claims that the Muses "breathed a divine voice into me, so that I might glorify what will be and what was before, and they commanded me to sing of the race of the blessed ones who always are, but always to sing of themselves first and last."[49]

As a young prodigy of Greek studies, Poliziano, too, took an early interest in Hesiod's poetry, perhaps encouraged to some degree by Ficino (who certainly encouraged the younger humanist's work on Homer, dubbing him the "Homericus adulescens").[50] The same section of the *Theogony* that Ficino referred to in the passage from his *Philebus* commentary quoted above (the account of Saturn castrating Uranus and throwing his testicles into the ocean, from which Venus was then generated) also attracted the interest of Poliziano. In Poliziano's *Stanze*, this myth is depicted on the doors of the Palace of Venus, and Poliziano's verses contain clear direct echoes of the *Theogony*.[51] (Through Poliziano, the Hesiodic myth also influenced Botticelli's *Birth of Venus*.) Poliziano also draws on and alludes to Hesiod's poetry elsewhere in the *Stanze*, including notably in his verses on the Golden Age (*Stanze* 1.20), which, following Hesiod's *Works and Days*, describe how primitive humans were once able to satisfy their needs for sustenance by simply collecting abundant acorns and honey.[52]

Poliziano's interest in Hesiod's poetry continued to grow over the course of his career, as he increasingly established himself as a leading authority on Hesiod, ultimately teaching a course on Hesiod's *Works and Days* and Virgil's *Georgics* at the Florentine Studio in 1483 and publishing, shortly thereafter, the *Rusticus*, his *silva* introducing these texts. While Poliziano had, with his *Stanze*, become the first poet to experiment with tapping the Hesiodic poems as models for vernacular poetry, Lorenzo would go on to carry out a much more ambitious effort to integrate Hesiodic models into vernacular poetry in his *Selva I*. In Lorenzo's treatment of the myths of the Golden Age, Prometheus, and Pandora that are central to the poem, Hesiod's poetry is his most important intertext.

The myth of the Golden Age had been a key element of Medici propaganda since Lorenzo's youth. From the earliest phases of this propagandistic program, Lorenzo and his literary collaborators had deployed the juxtaposition of classical and vernacular literary models in a remarkably sophisticated way to evoke a cyclical conception of time, promoting the notion that Florence, thanks to Medici leadership, was poised to enter a new Golden Age comparable to the period of perfect human felicity that had prevailed in humankind's distant past, as celebrated by ancient poets.

The first important episode in this propaganda program was the young Lorenzo's participation in the *giostra* of 1469, an event that the Medici faction engineered as a celebration of the Medici scion's entry into public life; the celebration of the event in poetry was entrusted to Luigi Pulci. The personal trappings with which Lorenzo presented himself at this event were laden with symbolism meant to convey a precise message. Lorenzo carried a standard depicting a girl weaving a wreath from the green branches of a laurel tree, around which other dry branches could be seen. The vegetative imagery was meant to convey rebirth; the obvious parallel between Lorenzo's name and the laurel (*lauro*) conveyed the message that Lorenzo would personally preside over this rebirth. A motto, in French, displayed on the banner drove home the point: "Le Tem[p]s Revient."[53]

Pulci's poetic description of Lorenzo's banner suggested further levels of symbolic meaning behind it:

> And in his beautiful standard one could see
> A sun above, and then a rainbow,

Where one could read, in golden letter:
"Le tems revient," which can be interpreted to mean
that the time is returning, and the ages are renewed.[54]

When Pulci suggests the Italian phrase "secol rinnovarsi" as an interpretation of Lorenzo's French motto, his readers are meant to recognize the allusion to the famous verses from Dante's *Purgatorio* 22.70–2:

Secol si rinova;
torna giustizia e primo tempo umano,
e progenie scende da ciel nova.

The age begins anew; justice
returns and the first human time, and a new
offspring comes down from Heaven.[55]

These Dantean verses in turn paraphrase verses from Virgil's fourth *Eclogue*, with its proclamation of an imminent return of the Reign of Saturn/ Golden Age. The weaving together of prestigious classical and vernacular intertexts in Pulci's verses about Lorenzo's entry into public life conveys a sophisticated message, suggesting that the period of flourishing that Medici rule has brought to Florence will bring together the greatest achievements of antiquity with the greatest achievements of Florence's late-medieval past (including the vernacular literary tradition represented by Dante).

The myth of Medici rule (especially in its Laurentian phase) as a Golden Age would ultimately be consolidated most fully through the propagandistic efforts of Giorgio Vasari during the reign of Cosimo I. But, as Ernst Gombrich has shown, the use of this myth in Medicean propaganda was under way already during the life of Cosimo il Vecchio.[56] Writing about Cosimo il Vecchio, Ugolino Verino claimed, "He has honoured the sacred poets, and he has bestowed upon us the return of the Golden Age of Caesar Augustus."[57] Along similar lines, Naldo Naldi addressed these verses to Cosimo: "For me, with you as guardian, Medici, the benign Golden Age of old Saturn is already returning."[58]

Lorenzo's poem frequently links the end of the Reign of Saturn with the theft perpetrated by Prometheus, who stole fire and gave it to humankind:

Before Prometheus hatched the baneful scheme
Of perpetrating his outrageous theft,
The peaceful world was justly ruled by Saturn
During the epoch of the Golden Age.[59]

In the Hesiodic account, Prometheus's action does bring to an end a period of perfect human felicity, but one that is distinct from the Reign of Saturn, which is recounted in a separate section slightly earlier in the text. By conflating the two myths, Lorenzo sets up a dichotomy between Saturn and Prometheus that, while not present in Hesiod's *Works and Days* and other literary accounts, is posited by Ficino. In Ficino's commentary on Plato's *Philebus*, Ficino asserts that the names Saturn and Prometheus are mythical designations for the ascending and descending movements that link each successive level of the Neoplatonic emanationist hierarchy of being. The triadic scheme is completed by the figure of Jupiter, who, according to Ficino, stands for the self-reflective principle:

> So the ray of the good itself, although one in itself, becomes triple as well in the triple intelligence. When it strives towards the good, which some call the Sky, it is Saturn. When it turns back into itself, it is Jupiter. When it turns towards lower things, it is Prometheus, that is, providence.[60]

Ficino's philosophical interpretations of ancient myths of the Golden Age could also be instrumentalized for political purposes. In a letter to Giovanni Francesco Ippoliti, Ficino equated the mythical Golden Age with the rule of a philosopher-king of the sort theorized by Plato: "It is said that the Golden Age once existed because of such a ruler, and Plato prophesied it will return only when power and wisdom come together in the same mind."[61]

So close examination of both Lorenzo's poems and their paratexts strongly suggests that they are positioning themselves within the improvisational tradition – perhaps originating directly from Lorenzo's oral improvisational practice, or perhaps filtered through the aesthetic of that tradition. This insight allows us to understand the works as a thematic exploration of the improvisational state, in keeping with Ficino's own promotion of that practice. However, it also raises an important question: Why was Lorenzo, later in his life, so attached to the idea of oral poetry and poetic improvisation?

Returning once again to Ficino's description of Lorenzo in 1491, we can begin to perceive the contours of an answer. Ficino asserts,

> At times that patron of ours carries along with him quite a few who are listening more attentively and to better purpose, pouring especially upon them from the abundance of his frenzy. How he himself, wonderfully moved by divine will, has the power to stir up others in almost the same way, is explained by our Plato in the book entitled *Ion*.[62]

Ficino's reference to Plato's *Ion* is not simply a recherché allusion: it is articulating a model of leadership. By applying Plato's metaphor of the magnetic chain to Lorenzo, Ficino suggests that the power which Lorenzo exerted over those around him was not a matter of money, partisan manoeuvring, or force but rather a kind of charismatic authority.

Ficino's letter claims that only three individuals in history have attained all four of the divine frenzies: "Such were Orpheus in the ancient tradition and David in our own; and we ourselves have come to know in our time a most fortunate man who has attained these four gifts of the frenzies in equal measure."[63] This third recipient of frenzy is, clearly, Lorenzo. It is significant that Ficino places Lorenzo in the illustrious company of two ancient figures whom he considered exemplary both as inspired poets and as leaders. The biblical David was, of course, considered to have been the king of Israel and a divinely inspired musician and singer, the poet of the Psalms. The leadership role ascribed to Orpheus alongside his role as poet took different forms. He was regarded as the founder and leader of a religious movement, and the stories of the marvellous effects of his songs were interpreted allegorically as illustrating the civilizing powers of eloquence. Within Ficino's intellectual circle, this interpretation was expressed perhaps most powerfully by Cristoforo Landino, in his commentary on Dante's *Divine Comedy*:

> They say that Orpheus, with the sound of his cythara, drew wild animals to himself, and moved mountains, and stopped rivers. The meaning of this is that, with his eloquence, he drew wild men to himself, and moved stupid and unrefined men to virtue, and calmed the violence of the mad.[64]

For Landino and his Florentine contemporaries, Orpheus represented, among other things, an exemplary civic leader – one whose influence was based not on force, nor on any formal title, but on eloquence and charisma. This Orpheus served as a blueprint for a whole series of related, broadly propagandistic initiatives through which Medicean intellectuals (including Ficino and Lorenzo himself) presented an idealized, Orphic vision of Lorenzo, as a divinely inspired charismatic leader rather than a shrewd and ruthless tyrant illegitimately exerting one-man rule over what had been a proudly independent republic. This propagandistic program, exemplified by Ficino's 1491 letter, spanned decades; its fundamental contours can already be discerned in the texts that Ficino and Lorenzo authored collaboratively (including the *De summo bono*) between 1473 and 1474.

Lorenzo's continued cultivation of improvisational poetry during the period in which he ruled Florence no doubt reflects his recognition that it was politically expedient to reinforce the public image of himself as an inspired and charismatic Orphic poet that Ficino and other Medicean intellectuals took pains to construct. Lorenzo's improvisational poetic experiments also had political implications extending beyond his personal mythology. Parallels can be drawn with another, much better-known manifestation of Lorenzo's savvy command of cultural politics: the case of the *Raccolta Aragonese*, discussed in chapter 1. As we saw, the inclusion of *improvvisatore* poetry in the collection implicitly advanced the claim that this tradition and its forms were evidence of continuing Tuscan cultural and artistic preeminence. But the claim was even more precise: the inclusion of Lorenzo's own poems within the collection ensured that the rulers of Naples would not miss the underlying message – that the supremacy of Florence over other Italian states in the literary sphere had reached a new pinnacle thanks to Lorenzo's personal contributions as ruler, patron, and poet.

The *rispetto* genre to which Lorenzo's *Selve* belong was traditionally considered a less prestigious form than some of the poetic genres, such as the sonnet and the *canzone*, represented in the *Raccolta Aragonese*. Still, this genre of popular improvisatory poetry was another cultural sphere in which Florence could boast of preeminence over other Italian states. Lorenzo's *Selve* aimed to elevate this traditional Florentine genre to a new level of prestige by fusing it with the Latin *Silvae* genre recently relaunched by Poliziano in the wake of the rediscovery of Statius's *Silvae*. Lorenzo's personal involvement as leading poet of the late-Quattrocento flourishing of the *rispetto* genre held political value for Lorenzo and his regime, buttressing the claim that a new era of Florentine cultural preeminence had been ushered in by the political and poetic leadership of Lorenzo.

Chapter Five

The Improvisor and the World of the Courts

In 1441, theoretical discussions of the relative status of Latin poetry and vernacular oral poetry were put to a highly publicized test in Florence. An initiative led by Leon Battista Alberti and funded by the Medici family, the so-called *Certame coronario* was a competition designed to demonstrate that vernacular oral poetry could treat the most elevated themes of humanistic literature and achieve a level of sophistication comparable to that of Latin poetry. To this end, poets were asked to produce and perform vernacular poems on a favourite ancient theme: true friendship.

This high-profile event attracted a list of participants well known to Florentines who took an interest in oral poetic performance. Some of the entrants performed their own verses, while others handed off their works to professional singer-poets. The *canterino* Antonio di Meglio, then serving as *araldo* to the Florentine Signoria, was the most prominent voice of the competition, reciting the first three poems (those written by Francesco di Altobianco degli Alberti, Antonio degli Agli, and Mariotto Davanzati). Antonio di Meglio's son Gregorio – who would later go on to become *araldo* himself – delivered the *terza rima capitolo* composed by Benedetto Accolti. The *canterino* Anselmo Calderoni (then serving as *araldo* to the Duke of Urbino) performed his own verses. Michele del Giogante, the organizer and promoter of *canterino* performances in Piazza San Martino in this period, also performed.[1]

The event captured the attention of the Florentine public, and it has continued to captivate modern scholars as an illustration of the struggle for the legitimacy and status of vernacular literature in Quattrocento Florence. However, it has often been overlooked that the competition showcased not just the composition of vernacular poetry but the oral performance of that poetry. The prominence of the *araldi* and others linked with *canterino* performance reveals the close connections between Alberti's initiative and the vibrant Florentine culture of oral poetry.[2]

As it turned out, the panel of papal secretaries chosen to adjudicate the competition and crown the winning poet delivered a stinging rebuke to Alberti, the vernacular poets, and everyone else who believed in the worth of vernacular literature by refusing to award the crown at all. This rather harsh rejection of the premise that vernacular poetry was comparable in dignity to Latin literature is perhaps not shocking when we consider that one of the judges was Poggio Bracciolini, whose scorn for vernacular (and especially oral) literature as an art form is well documented. We have seen how Poggio's *Facetiae* took aim at the vernacular oral poetry of the *canterini*, mocking in particular the audiences who allowed the songs of the *canterini* to achieve such sway over their imaginations and emotions that they lost the ability to properly discern between the ancient past and the present, between fantasy and reality.

One of the uncrowned entrants in this competition was Benedetto Accolti (now called "the Elder," to distinguish him from his grandson, Benedetto Accolti the Younger). Benedetto was not only a practitioner and defender of Tuscan vernacular poetic traditions but one of the most respected Latin humanists of his generation as well. The Accolti family was an important Aretine family (hence the sobriquet "Aretino" applied to both Benedetto and his son Bernardo throughout their lives), though Benedetto spent most of his adult life in Florence and taught at the Florentine Studio from 1435 until his death in 1464. Benedetto Accolti was one of the established humanists who took a special interest in the promising work of Marsilio Ficino in the early years of Ficino's career. Ficino described Accolti as an early benefactor; he was involved particularly in encouraging Ficino to undertake his translation of the *Minos*, which was among the first ten Platonic translations that Ficino completed, prior to the death of Cosimo de' Medici in 1464.[3] On 17 April 1458, Benedetto reached the pinnacle of professional success for a humanist intellectual in Florence when he was named chancellor of the Florentine Republic, a position he held until his death. It appears that Poggio Bracciolini, who retired from his position as chancellor in 1458, personally designated Benedetto Accolti as his successor.

While Bracciolini and the elder Accolti were linked by a long acquaintance and mutual esteem, the two did not always see eye to eye; they held different views about the relationship and relative status of vernacular oral poetry and humanistic classical studies. For a Latin humanist of Accolti the Elder's generation, the choice to pursue the composition of vernacular poetry in earnest, and to participate in an oral poetic competition like the *Certame coronario*, drew criticism from purist classicists like Poggio, who regarded vernacular poetry (especially the oral poetry of the *canterini*) as not only incomparably inferior to classical literature but specifically unworthy of the attention of a serious humanist. The refusal of Poggio, Flavio Biondo, and their fellow humanist judges to award any prize in the competition must have been felt as a particularly harsh rebuke by Accolti, a professional peer of the judges who snubbed his poetic contribution and those of his fellow competitors (most of whom were not humanist scholars of the same calibre). And even Benedetto Accolti, however exceptional his openness to composing in the vernacular and traditionally oral medium of the *capitolo* genre (he composed six that survive today), did not apparently cultivate the performance skills that would have permitted him to present his own work, or in any case did not wish to display such skills at a public event like the *Certame*, preferring to entrust the performance to a budding professional *canterino*.

As the preceding chapters have shown, between the middle and end of the fifteenth century there was a remarkably rapid transformation in the role that practices of oral and improvisational performance of vernacular poetry played in Italian humanist culture. In the early Quattrocento, the vernacular performances of the *canterini* were a form of popular entertainment that most Latin humanists either disregarded or held in low esteem. By the end of the century, oral poetic performance had become a major interest of Italy's humanist elite, who engaged with it as spectators and as performers. Thanks in particular to the efforts of Marsilio Ficino to bring philosophical scaffolding to improvisational performance and frenzied insights to philosophy, humanists and *improvvisatori* alike embraced the notion that contemporary performance styles could embody anew the art of sung poetry practised in antiquity by Orpheus.

Therefore, while for Benedetto Accolti robust participation in the art of vernacular and oral poetry proved to be somewhat incompatible with his professional career, the art form would play quite a different role in the life of his son. Picking up his father's taste for the vernacular poetic genres traditional to Florence – especially the *capitolo* and *strambotto* – Bernardo Accolti, known by the rather grand stage name "l'Unico Aretino" ("the Unique Aretine"), also developed the performative aspects of this art that his father seems not to have cultivated: namely, exceptional skills as a singer, instrumentalist (specializing in the viola), and improvisor of both music and poetry.[4] An acclaimed entertainer, Accolti served for a time as *araldo* to the Florentine Signoria.[5]

Bernardo Accolti's career also illustrates another important aspect of the gradual humanist embrace of improvisational theories and practices: its increasingly widespread influence. Accolti's renown as a performer is attested by many contemporaries, including Pietro Aretino, who documented a sort of Accolti-mania that gripped audiences in Rome: "People used to close their shops, just as if it were a feast day, and everyone would run to the Castello as soon as news got out that Bernardo Accolti would be improvising before infinite numbers of great masters and prelates."[6] Bernardo's ability to draw both shopkeepers and prelates to his performances is indicative of his own skill and of the changing cultural role of improvisational performance in his lifetime.

As this anecdote suggests, Accolti performed not only for appreciative Florentines but in many other nodes of power in the Italian peninsula, including the papal court in Rome and the duchies of Urbino and Mantua. Blake Wilson has shown that the phenomenon of humanist improvisation, originally centred in Florence, spread outward after the late fifteenth century.[7] Bernardo Accolti's career offers an illustration of this phenomenon in progress: his improvisational skill provided him with access, influence, and prestige in the halls of power in far-flung Italian cultural centres. This geographical diffusion of improvisational poetics and its theoretical scaffolding inevitably also resulted in new approaches to that theoretical discourse. Sources allow us to observe this process, too, unfolding around the figure of Bernardo Accolti, who inspired (and contributed to) influential aesthetic conversations about the role of *ingenium* and *ars* in artistic creation.

Bernardo Accolti's courtly career therefore demonstrates the concrete influence of Marsilio Ficino's efforts to apply philosophical and theoretical scaffolding to practices of improvisation. As we have seen, the theoretical valorization of improvisational approaches to poetic composition brought humanist intellectual pursuits closer with the traditions of the *improvvisatori*. But the theories of improvisation articulated by Ficino and embraced in various forms within and beyond his circle also held a key to transforming poetic culture and practices in other ways. Ficino's theory of poetic *furor* offered a powerful argument that poetic excellence was not integrally linked with either the identity or the training of the poet. In theory, a poet of frenzy was not required to be elite, male, or learned. In fact, for some commentators, the ability of less highly educated poets to produce compelling verses spontaneously was regarded as evidence of the authenticity of poetic *furor*. This theory, therefore, held within it a radical potential to destabilize dominant cultural norms about the poetic vocation.

As illustrated in chapter 2, one of the main conclusions Ficino drew from his readings of Plato, and often reiterated in his own writings, was that study and poetic craftsmanship were not necessary to achieve poetic greatness, which only required the infusion of divine frenzy. In Renaissance Italian literary circles, literary craftsmanship and study were terms applied primarily to the activities of erudite poets writing in Latin.

Because of the substantial social barriers that stood in the way of women gaining access to the type of education needed to compose erudite Latin poetry, these were qualities typically ascribed only to male poets. In Ficino's interpretation, though, the theory of poetic frenzy provided a pathway by which even the unlearned could be elevated to the ranks of the greatest poets. As such, the theory held the potential to effect a revaluation of the status not only of *improvvisatori* of modest learning but also of Italy's female poets, most of whom, as authors of vernacular poetry without advanced Latin training, would have been habitually regarded by male intellectuals as belonging to the category of "unlearned" poets.

States of frenzy were often ascribed to women in the ancient texts that formed the core of Ficino's intellectual groundwork for the idea of poetic frenzy. The prophetesses of Delphi, the priestesses of Dodona, the sibyls, the Bacchantes, the prophetess Diotima – all of these ancient women are cited by Ficino as examples of humans who entered states of divine frenzy or related ecstatic states (*vacatio, alienatio*, etc.). The fact that so many of the classic examples of states of frenzy involve female subjects often leads Ficino to invoke examples of women channelling frenzy even in passages in which he is directly discussing a man possessed by frenzy. A salient example is Plato, whom Ficino regarded (notwithstanding his choice to write in prose) as a poet seized by inspiration, like the frenzied priestesses of Delphi: "If you hear the celestial Plato you immediately recognize that his style, as Aristotle says, flows midway between prose and poetry. You recognize that Plato's language, as Quintilian says, rises far above the pedestrian and prosaic, so that our Plato seems inspired not by human genius but by a Delphic oracle."[8]

Moreover, regardless of the gender of the individual possessed by frenzy, in Ficino's Latin this state of possession was customarily described as a grammatically masculine force (*furor divinus*, divine frenzy) taking possession of a grammatically feminine subject (*anima*, the human soul). To cite just one example, in his translation of Plato's *Phaedrus*, Ficino writes, in Latin, "furor, suscipiens teneram intactamque animam, suscitat illam atque concitat" ("frenzy ... takes a soft and virgin soul and awakens and inspires it").[9] This example is illuminating not only because of the grammatical gender of the main terms but also because of the adjective "soft" ("teneram") applied to "anima" – a quality which Ficino would have regarded as implicitly feminine. Ficino's particular terminology in his discussion of the divine possession (*occupatio*) that seizes the "teneram intactamque animam" evokes sexual possession.

Despite this range of factors that positioned Ficino's theory of divine frenzy as a conceptual tool with the potential to unsettle dominant norms concerning gender and poetry, Ficino himself, while he frequently discussed contemporary male poets as bearers of frenzy, never applied this framework to any contemporary female poets. No doubt part of the explanation for this lies in the fact that the female poets of Ficino's milieu were greatly outnumbered by male poets and also typically practised varieties of poetry different from the kind of musical, performative poetry that Ficino particularly associated with divine frenzy (and which he himself cultivated in his idiosyncratic way). The social norms of bourgeois Quattrocento Florentine society sanctioned female participation in literary pursuits only within very narrowly defined limits. Composition of vernacular devotional literature was regarded as an appropriate pursuit for a respectable Florentine woman like Lucrezia Tornabuoni; performing before an audience as an improvisor was not – certainly not on the public stage of San Martino that was the centre of Florentine *improvvisatore* performance.[10] To be sure, improvising took place in Quattrocento Florence in contexts less public than the stage of Piazza San Martino. Surviving evidence about the prominent role that improvisation played in Lorenzo's social circle – especially in the so-called *brigata* that surrounded him as a youth – suggests the significance of improvisation practised in private contexts. But here, too, female participation was largely excluded. Surviving accounts strongly suggest that musical and poetic improvisation within the Laurentian milieu was practiced mostly by men, and indeed that it served a central function in the male homosociality of the Laurentian circle, contributing to the close bonds that formed between Lorenzo and Poliziano and (for a time at least) between Lorenzo and Luigi Pulci.

But while the ascendancy of poetic improvisation as a literary form taken seriously by learned humanists was closely connected with Florentine intellectual contexts initially, the vitality of Florentine improvisatory practices soon exerted an influence on the musical and performative poetry of other Italian cultural centres – perhaps most notably, the courts of Northern and Central Italy. In these courts, far more than in bourgeois Florence, elite women played leading roles in courtly life. Noblewomen and other female elites in these courts, to be sure, still contended with gender-based strictures of many kinds, but they could also wield significant power over the social and cultural worlds that they moved within. Hence the ascendancy of improvisatory practices within these Italian courts, following Florentine models, also involved a different and richer level of engagement of women with this type of performative poetry.

To understand the ways in which Ficino's theories calling into question the roles of study, talent, labour, and inspiration in the production of poetry resulted in new paradigms, then, it is important to trace the phenomenon of improvised poetic performance beyond its fifteenth-century

Florentine context and into the Italian courts of the sixteenth century. The most influential articulation of the aesthetics of courtly culture and its many facets in the sixteenth century was Baldesar Castiglione's *Il Cortegiano*, which quickly became the sourcebook of choice on these subjects. In *Il Cortegiano*, theories about the relationship between *ars* and *ingenium* in the production of improvised music and poetry open into the more expansive and highly influential concept of *sprezzatura*, the appearance of effortless grace that the ideal courtier should cultivate, and female interlocutors play an important role in refining these discourses. Furthermore, in Castiglione's text, it is a performance of Bernardo Accolti himself that inspires and tests these theories about *ars* and *ingenium*. Before immersing ourselves in the world of Castiglione's *Il Cortegiano*, however, it will be helpful to consider the performer who animated the conversations about *ars* and *furor* in that text. What was it about the art of Bernardo Accolti, whom Ludovico Ariosto described in the *Orlando furioso* as "the great light of Arezzo, the unique Accolti" ("Il gran lume Aretin, l'Unico Accolti"), that captivated such diverse audiences?[11] Although it is impossible to establish the precise relationship between Accolti's surviving verses and his oral performances, contemporary accounts allow us to identify several significant qualities of his art. Above all, it was the improvisational excellence of Accolti's performances that struck audiences. In Paolo Cortesi's *De cardinalatu* – a conduct book in many respects parallel to *Il Cortegiano* but directed to aspiring princes of the church – Cortesi explains that, while improvisational performance is always so impressive that one can overlook occasional flaws, Accolti had no need of such concessions:

> Marvellously, we can get honest enjoyment from these men who are said to be in the habit of singing extemporaneously to the lyre in the vernacular. Up until recently Baccio Ugolini and Jacopo Corsi have generally been praised as the greatest of this sort in Italy, but now Bernardo Accolti should be most celebrated, who, though he pronounces verses extemporaneously, nevertheless fits elegant words to his thoughts so aptly that, while one is always ready to make allowances for things composed with such speed, the verses which Accolti pours forth simply demand to be praised, rather than pardoned on the basis of having been produced extemporaneously and with a rapid birth.[12]

Clearly Accolti's ability to compose verse extemporaneously was fundamental, but several other aspects of his style also stand out as significant. Cortesi, who knew Accolti and his performance style well, explains that the specific genres of sung poetry in which Accolti specialized were uniquely compelling to audiences:

It can be rightly said that the motions of the souls are usually appeased and excited with more vehemence by the *carmina* produced in this genre [*ottava rima* or *terza rima*]; for, when the rhythms of the words and sentences are combined with the sweetness of the [melodic] modes, nothing can prevent [the audience] from being exceedingly moved because of the power of the ear and of [its] similarity to the soul. And this usually happens quite often when either vehement motions are represented in the singing by the verses, or the spirits are exhorted to the learning of morals and knowledge, on which human happiness is dependent.[13]

In fact, the representation of intense emotional states in sung poetry in the *terza rima* and *ottava rima* metres was Accolti's specialty, and other accounts of the responses of his audiences confirm that the sort of emotional arousal that Cortesi describes was a hallmark of his performances. What sort of material did Accolti draw on in forming these intense emotional states, and what techniques did he employ? Other commentators offer some clues. Among the poets that he includes in his dialogue *Notable Men and Women of Our Time*, Paolo Giovio discusses Accolti:

Many of his songs, which were written down by various means, are in circulation, but he was always at his most unique and outstanding when he used to sing to the lyre, in the presence of great princes, Polyxena dying on the altar and Virgil's fourth book on the passions of Dido, which he translated with success beyond comparison.[14]

Several details here are significant. Giovio implies that the same verses, circulated outside of performance, did not have the same impact. The problem is compounded for modern observers: the question of how and to what degree Accolti's improvised poems were preserved at all is problematic. Giovio's dialogue asserts that Accolti's songs were "written down by various means" ("variis modis descripta"). The verb *describere* was commonly used to refer to transcriptions of oral dictations or performances, via the technique of *reportatio* that, as has been discussed, was used to preserve some of the verses sung by Niccolò Cieco, Aurelio Brandolini, and Cristoforo l'Altissimo. It is therefore plausible that in the case of Accolti, too, this was one of the "various means" through which his improvised verses were preserved.

In any case, Giovio's references to the two pieces that he considered the best of Accolti's work as an oral poetic performer – the poems he sang about the death of Polyxena and about the desperation of Dido abandoned by Aeneas – match the content of two poems that have been preserved in manuscript form, in the Vatican Library's MS Ross. 680.

The poems on Polyxena and Dido are two of the twenty-four *capitoli* in *terza rima* attributed to Accolti that compose the first part of this manuscript collection.[15]

Giovio's description of Accolti's verses about the passions of Dido as a "translation" from Virgil certainly hints at how Accolti's learned approach to improvisation might have appealed to an audience of erudite humanists; on the other hand, the notion of extemporaneous translation of classical texts might seem incompatible with the idea that Accolti was improvising at all. But while it is impossible to determine precisely what role Accolti's famed gifts for improvisation played in producing this text, the element of translation itself does not exclude the possibility of improvisation. In fact, the ability to rapidly or spontaneously translate works from one language or form into another was one of the core abilities that many Renaissance *improvvisatori* cultivated. As we have seen, the preeminent *improvvisatore* Cristoforo l'Altissimo relied (at least in part) on improvisational skills in adapting a prose romance (*I Reali di Francia*) into an extended oral poetic performance. And as the agenda of Quattrocento humanists expanded to include improvisational practices, it was perhaps inevitable that translations and adaptations of classical texts would come to occupy a more prominent role in improvisational performance practices. A fascinating example of classical translation-through-improvisation that has recently gained wider recognition thanks to the scholarship of Brian Richardson and Luca Degl'Innocenti is that of Niccolò Machiavelli. The most vivid testimonials of Machiavelli's cultivation of the art of the *improvvisatori* date from the decades following his death. Gerolamo Ruscelli, who had befriended Machiavelli's brother-in-law Francesco del Nero, recounts that Machiavelli could "compose [*ottave*] even while improvising ... and perfect ones at that."[16] Ruscelli provides a detailed description of Machiavelli's extemporaneous translation, including acknowledgment of observers' incredulity that he was actually composing extemporaneously, a common thread in conversations about improvisation:

> Thus many people recall Niccolò Machiavelli, who would open any Latin poet, put it in front of him on a table and, while playing the lira, would sing and turn into the vernacular or translate the verses of that poet, making from them stanzas of ottava rima. He kept to a true translation with such elegance of style and such ease that my friend Francesco del Nero, who was very close to him, told me in Naples that he and many others in Florence tried everything to assure themselves that Machiavelli was doing this extempore, since everyone thought it impossible that he could improvise what many people who were learned and of lofty talent admitted they would have struggled to do in an adequate space of time.[17]

Similarly, accounts of Bernardo Accolti's poetic performances and the surviving textual records of his body of work suggest a strong emphasis on improvised and performative translation or adaptation of classical material. The Vatican Library's MS Ross. 680 contains, in addition to Accolti's translation of part of *Aeneid* 4, numerous other poems in *ottava* and *terza rima* whose rubrics present them as Accolti's translations of works by classic authors: Ovid, Livy, Theocritus, Lucretius, and others. We know from Giovio's testimonial that Accolti's *terza rima capitoli* based on the story of Polyxena and on *Aeneid* 4 were part of the repertoire that he performed orally to the lyre, and this in turn suggests that Accolti's other *capitoli* that accompany them in this manuscript would also have been performed in a similar style.

Furthermore, while the nature of Accolti's performance style cannot be fully reconstructed from the texts that survive, we are able to detect certain rhetorical strategies deployed by Accolti in these poems that contributed to the transmission of intense affective states to his audiences. The themes that Accolti apparently favoured for his poems suggest a desire to maximize the affective impact of his verses on listeners. In the vast majority of the *capitoli* and *strambotti* included in the Vatican Library's MS Ross. 680, Accolti assumes the voice of a character from ancient history or mythology who has been placed in a difficult or impossible situation provoking intense emotions – dread, despair, grief, and so forth. Accolti's verses employ the techniques of vivid representation to which Quintilian assigned the term *enargeia* in order to describe these impossible situations and seek to convey the intensity of emotions of these characters.

Because Accolti's *terza rima* poem in three *capitoli* on the passions of Dido explicitly declares its main source text – the fourth book of Virgil's *Aeneid* – we can use it to assess how Accolti draws on and departs from his sources. At times Accolti's Italian *terzine* follow Virgil's Latin rather closely; at other points a brief phrase in Virgil's text provides Accolti with a point of departure for an extended invention. For example, Virgil's Dido, in verse 314 of *Aeneid* 4, confronts Aeneas with the blunt question "Mene fugis?" ("Is it from me you are fleeing?").[18] In Accolti's version, in place of this brief line, Dido launches a series of questions that occupy twelve verses – a rhetorical crescendo in which she invites Aeneas to imagine his son Ascanius and his beloved comrade Palinurus drowning before his eyes in the stormy sea and asks whether he would not prefer to remain in her arms, sharing her kingdom, rather than risk such a calamity by setting sail in winter. In this departure from Virgil's text, we see Accolti arming Dido with the tool of *enargeia* to move the sympathies of Aeneas, asking him to visualize the calamity of a possible shipwreck, just as Accolti's own performances rely on this technique.

In Virgil's text, Dido, aware of the risk that one of her enemies may attack her kingdom after Aeneas's departure, asks aloud, "Why do I linger? Is it till Pygmalion, my brother, overthrow this city, or the Gaetulian Iarbas lead me captive?"[19] Accolti's adaptation of this passage again displays his tendency to emphasize the visual imagination. For Accolti's Dido, anxiety about these threats manifests as vivid visualizations of invasions that intrude into her imagination, as she tells Aeneas: "I seem continually to see my cruel brother inside my kingdom with hostile flame. I seem to constantly see the naked sword of King Iarbas; with a confident bearing I shut him out, for you, but now he appears to shut me out from life itself."[20]

At the point of the speech in which Dido breaks off in Virgil's text (after musing that she would be less forlorn had she conceived a child by Aeneas), Accolti launches into a fifteen-verse rhetorical crescendo in Dido's voice entirely of his own invention. Mocking Aeneas's claims of piety (and with a nod to his Virgilian epithet "pius Aeneas"), Dido begs Aeneas to take pity on her and end her life to spare her the anguish of being abandoned: "With your fierce right hand, take out on me your vengeance against the Greeks."[21] It is probable that, during Accolti's sung performances of this *capitolo*, his singing style would have included vocal effects calibrated to enhance its emotional impact. Accolti's text gives some indication of what vocal effects might have been included: while in Virgil's text Dido's speech seems to simply trail off, Accolti's version explains that Dido's voice has failed her as other, non-verbal vocal expressions of grief take over: "Qui da sospir, sudor, fremito atroce, / Singulti inrequieti lachrymare / Fu interrocta l'affannata voce" ("At this point her exhausted voice was interrupted by sighs, sweat, awful shuddering, restless sobbing and crying").[22]

Accolti's *capitolo* on Polyxena – the second work, along with that on Dido, highlighted by Giovio as the finest among Accolti's oral performance repertoire – reveals Accolti deploying the same characteristic approach to bringing the world of ancient history and myth alive for his audiences. In adopting the voices of his classical characters, Accolti was bringing to bear on oral poetic performance a technique of classical rhetoric that had been part of rhetorical instruction since antiquity. Among the twelve elements of classical rhetorical teaching that continued to be practised into the Renaissance (the *progymnasmata*), Quintilian identified the most difficult – and most useful for "future poets" – as the technique of *prosopopoeia* or *ethopoeia*, which involved composing a speech in the voice of a particular character in a particular situation, often one involving emotional distress.[23]

In this case Accolti has chosen a story told by multiple ancient Latin sources and moves freely between them. The major Latin sources for the story are Ovid's *Metamorphoses* 13.441–80, Seneca's *Troades* 1117–61, and Servius's *Aeneid* commentary 3.321. According to most versions of the myth, Achilles fell in love with the Trojan princess Polyxena, one of Priam's daughters, who then (knowingly or unknowingly) helped facilitate the ambush that allowed Paris to fatally wound Achilles in the heel. Following the conquest of Troy, the Greeks, at the prompting of Achilles's ghost, sacrificed Polyxena on Achilles's grave. As in the poem on Dido, Accolti begins his version of the Polyxena story directly with a scene of surging tension and emotion: Polyxena, who has just been led to Achilles's tomb, addresses the crowd that has gathered to witness her impending violent death. The backstory is simply omitted; here as in the other *capitoli*, Accolti generally avoids extended narration, preferring to focus on vivid descriptions of the scenes he evokes and especially on delivering, in song, the rhetorically sophisticated and emotionally charged speeches of his characters. Among Accolti's classical sources, it is Ovid's version of the Polyxena story that he draws on most directly. But a comparison of the relative presence of direct discourse in the two versions is revealing: in Ovid's version Polyxena delivers a speech of 17 verses, while in Accolti's version fully 111 verses are spoken (or rather sung) in the voice of Polyxena.

As with many other Renaissance *improvvisatori*, Accolti's contemporaries praised him as a new Orpheus.[24] And much as the *improvvisatore* Baccio Ugolini had taken on the persona of Orpheus in the initial performance of Poliziano's *Orfeo*, Accolti also took on the voice of Orpheus in one of his own *capitoli* that appears in the Vatican Library's MS Ross. 680. Like Accolti's *terzine* on Dido, this *capitolo* can be considered an adaptation of Latin model texts into vernacular *terzine* for vocal performance with instrumental accompaniment on the *lira*. In this case there are two major Latin source texts: book 4 of Virgil's *Georgics* and portions of books 10 and 11 of Ovid's *Metamorphoses*. The rubric that accompanies the *capitolo* in the manuscript points towards both sources: "Unici Orpheus ex Virgilio et Ovidio" ("The *Orpheus* of l'Unico Aretino, from Virgil and Ovid").[25] The way in which Accolti's text oscillates between fairly close imitation of Ovid's text, imitation of Virgil's text, and original invention is illustrative of Accolti's goals as poet and performer – especially his interest in performing rhetorically powerful speeches by characters in emotional distress, thereby eliciting the most powerful emotional responses possible from his audience.

Accolti's *capitolo* has no introduction or opening narrative but begins in the voice of Orpheus as he addresses Hades, seeking to convince him to allow Eurydice to return to the world of the living. Orpheus addresses the denizens of the underworld in song, as his words make explicit

("Udite 'l mio canto" – "Hear my song").[26] This section of Accolti's poem follows the Ovidian rather than the Virgilian version of the Orpheus story. Virgil's version describes Orpheus's song and the powerful effects it produces on his listeners but does not report Orpheus's words. So it is Ovid's text, and the words it attributes to Orpheus in this situation, supplying the raw material for Accolti's creative elaboration in this initial part of the *capitolo*. Tellingly, the point in which Accolti shifts his approach, imitating Virgil more closely than Ovid, occurs at the moment in which Orpheus fatefully turns backward to gaze on Eurydice, thereby violating his oath and ensuring her return to the underworld. The moment in Ovid's text is characterized by the near absence of speech:

> And now, dying a second time, she made no complaint against her husband; for of what could she complain save that she was beloved? She spake one last "farewell" which scarcely reached her husband's ears, and fell back again to the place whence she had come.[27]

Where Ovid's Eurydice utters only a scarcely audible "Farewell," Virgil's Eurydice delivers a five-verse lament. Accolti, too, includes a lament in the voice of Eurydice, expanding the Virgilian model into eleven verses of *terza rima*. In describing how Orpheus lives out the remainder of his life, Accolti also follows Virgil more closely than Ovid, describing Orpheus as wandering among the frozen Hyperborean and Riphaean lands ("Iperborici ghiacci e valli acerbe / Riphee da neve non mai derilicte") and omitting the reference to the invention of pederasty that Ovid attributes to Orpheus. After Orpheus is torn apart by the raving Thracian women, his head, floating on the river Hebrus, repeatedly speaks the name "Eurydice," in Accolti's version as in Virgil's. (Ovid, by contrast, seems to highlight the failing power of Orpheus's song at and after his death; first his song fails to move the murderous Thracians, and then his severed head and lyre, floating on the Hebrus, produce sounds that are mournful but unintelligible.)

Accolti's *capitolo* then follows the shade of Orpheus to the underworld, where he is reunited with Eurydice, as occurs in Ovid's version. But whereas in Ovid's version the scene of their reunion is briefly described and no speech is reported, Accolti, in keeping with the general pattern he deploys elsewhere, seizes the opportunity to introduce another rhetorical flight in the voice of Orpheus – this one with no direct analogue in any of Accolti's classical models. Orpheus calls out to Charon to ferry him back across the river, declaring that no one has ever been happier than he is about being dead rather than alive. Then with "longing arms" ("cupide braccia"), he tries to embrace the beautiful Eurydice – "in vain" ("in vano"), since they are both now incorporeal shades. Nevertheless, in the final verses of the *capitolo*, Orpheus gives thanks that his body has been torn apart so that he can at least gaze upon Eurydice.

All of these preserved verses provide some clues about the qualities that Accolti's diverse audiences appreciated in his art. Earlier traditions of *improvvisatore* performance did not lean as heavily on classical source texts and models, so Accolti probably offered a new and more direct point of access to classical literature for some of the members of his audience that had not received an education in Latin. For humanists familiar with those source texts, Accolti offered a new mode of experiencing that literature – a new embodiment of familiar classical personas, made virtually present through the power of oral poetry to link the *fantasia* of the poet with that of the listener.

The two episodes that Giovio identified as Accolti's greatest hits both take the voices of female protagonists, and this is not merely a coincidence: the articulation of female emotion appears to be fundamental to Accolti's repertoire. In addition to Dido and Polyxena, Accolti also composed poetry in the voices of numerous other women, mostly from classical antiquity or mythology, including Cleopatra, Sophonisba, Venus, Queen Zenobia, the Amazon queen Thalestris, Clytemnestra, Medea, Niobe, Pasiphae, Lucretia, Helen of Troy, Semiramis, Myrrha, Byblis, Camilla, Iphigenia, Deidamia, Hippolyta, Orithyia, Julia Augusta, Argia of Argos, Phaedra, and Porcia. The fact that Accolti's repertoire was so clearly oriented towards representing the emotions of female characters specifically adds a layer of complexity to consideration of the relationship between improvised poetry and gender in Renaissance Italy. At a practical level, musical and poetic improvisation was a sphere, like so many others, in which the highest levels of achievement were often considered – by male commentators – to be the exclusive purview of men. At the same time, something significant is at work in Accolti's emphasis on representing female protagonists, a very different approach than, for example, the strikingly male and homosocial revelry of Lorenzo's early poetry. As we have seen, Ficino's theories about poetic frenzy seemed to associate it with a female-gendered state of emotional possession, even as the contemporary poets and performers he implicated in his theories were male. By specializing in the representation of female voices in his performances, Bernardo Accolti was in some ways merely closing the circle Ficino had begun to sketch. Moreover, the fact that Accolti's career unfolded not only in the social circles of Florence but also in the more expansive worlds of the Italian courts, which saw greater participation by women in the cultural and literary debates of the elites, is likely relevant to his choice of subject matter.

Isabella d'Este is, of course, among the most noteworthy examples of the powerful and talented women who exerted a decisive influence over the cultural world of the Northern Italian courts of the late fifteenth and early sixteenth centuries. It is therefore significant that Isabella engaged actively with the ascendant art of improvisation. Isabella's interactions with *improvvisatori* like Bernardo Accolti and Niccolò da Correggio offer some hints about the nature of her engagement with the art of musical-poetic improvisation. One significant document in this regard is da Correggio's *Psiche*, dedicated to Isabella in 1491.[28] His dedicatory letter describes the work as the product of improvisation:

> On one occasion, as a diversion, I was taking turns with others singing verses extemporaneously, each of us being assigned by the others a different topic to improvise on. I happened to be given the task of singing about a love story which, if not actually true, was not completely false.[29]

Having been assigned this topic at random to sing about in unpremeditated verses, da Correggio says, he began to improvise stanzas about the love of Cupid and Psyche; he claims that these stanzas were written down without his knowledge by some bystanders: "A few stanzas, without my knowledge, were recorded by certain bystanders in that place; and certainly I regretted this."[30] In true *improvvisatore* form, da Correggio expresses displeasure at having had his improvised stanzas transcribed because the impact that these stanzas would have had in the original performance – heightened by the improvisatory and musical dimensions of the experience – is much reduced when they are read "deprived of the ornamentation of the lyre."[31]

Da Correggio's claims about the improvisational nature of this text may of course be exaggerated to some extent. But the description must bear enough of a relationship to reality to appear plausible to an informed insider like Isabella, who was highly familiar with the art of the *improvvisatori* as practised by da Correggio and those around him. Whatever the origins of these particular *ottave*, the dedication may be taken as evidence that improvisation of poetry in a competitive fashion was a significant facet of courtly culture in Isabella's world.

Another work which da Correggio sent to Isabella shortly thereafter hints at the influence that Florentine theories of improvisatory forms had on literary culture in Mantua. In March 1493, da Correggio sent Isabella his poem entitled *Silva*, which, as he says in his letter to Isabella, had been "sung in the recent carnevale."[32] As critics including Antonia Tissoni Benvenuti have recognized, both the *Psiche* and the *Silva* provide evidence that da Correggio's literary production in this period was strongly influenced by recent developments in Florentine literature. In particular, da Correggio's *Silva* appears to respond to the efforts led by Lorenzo de' Medici in his own *Selve* to elevate the status of the *strambotto* to the level of a classicizing, humanist poetic form. Likewise, we can detect the influence of Poliziano and the ideals of elegant spontaneity that he found embodied in Statius's *Silvae*.[33] Da Correggio's choice of "Silva" as a title was certainly influenced by the revival of interest in Statius's *Silvae* that Poliziano spearheaded, whether or not it was also influenced by the title of Lorenzo's poems. Thus, in Mantua we see all of the familiar ingredients of the Florentine humanist theories of improvisational excellence at work: the application of humanist ideals to popular improvised forms of musical poetry, the cultivation of an instrument associated with improvisatory performance on the part of a political figure, and the emphasis on *ingegno* (*ingenium*) as the central requirement for excellence. That in this case the political figure is a woman speaks to a different kind of widening in scope of the improvisational theory of poetics developed in Florence. While Florentine figures in the fifteenth century developed Ficino's theory of *furor* in a variety of directions and for a variety of purposes, its potential as a blueprint for women's engagement with improvisation proved influential largely in other places and times.

We have evidence of Isabella's own musical pursuits from 1493, when she wrote to da Correggio requesting the loan of a particular *lira da braccio* so that she might practice. This was, of course, the favoured instrument of the *improvvisatori*, and performances of sung verse to the accompaniment of the *lira* were customarily based on musical improvisation and often the improvisation of poetry as well. There is good reason to think that Isabella, who certainly admired these abilities in others, also cultivated them herself. Da Correggio, who seems to have played the role of primary mentor for Isabella's engagement with improvisational poetry, responded helpfully, offering not only the instrument but also "uno capitulo da cantarli drento" ("a *capitolo* to sing with it"). The *capitolo*, a pastoral eclogue in *terza rima*, belonged to the category of poetic forms closely associated with performances of the *improvvisatori* in this period.[34] Da Correggio also offered encouragement, expressing confidence that Isabella would quickly succeed in mastering the *lira* because of her innate *ingegno* – considered to be a key quality for the improvisor.[35]

There are references to Isabella's continued engagement with the *lira* as time passed: in a letter from 1499, for instance, Isabella stated that she had been practising the viola with the intention of playing it while her brother sang verses.[36] Bernardo Accolti, in his correspondence with Isabella d'Este, compliments Isabella on her command of his own art form: in a letter dated 15 March 1502, Accolti praises Isabella for her expertise in, among other things, Tuscan (vernacular) compositions ("tusche compositioni"), which,

Accolti says, Isabella is capable "not only of judging, but perfectly composing, and perfectly reciting with the accompaniment of the viola or lute."[37]

These details reinforce the increasing significance of singing to the accompaniment of the *lira* and improvisational forms in the culture of Mantua during the late fifteenth and early sixteenth centuries. And as these improvisational practices spread across Italy – with performers like Bernardo Accolti – conversations about the nature and meaning of improvisation also spread. As we have already seen, Accolti's performances provoked not only appreciation in audiences but also reflection about what exactly improvisation entailed, whether it was authentically extemporaneous and inspired, and how it could inform ideas about the roles of *ars, ingenium,* and *furor* in aesthetic production. Accolti often performed for small private gatherings of elites as well as in large public contexts. The humanist Vincenzo Calmeta wrote about the home of Paolo Cortesi in Rome as the gathering place of a literary circle – Calmeta calls it an "Academia" – frequented by Bernardo Accolti and Serafino Aquilano and attests to a brotherly rivalry ("fraterna emulazione") that existed between the two singer-poets (into which the humanists Calmeta and Cortesi were drawn, too) in the composition and performance of *strambotti.*[38]

Literary circles like this were the context not only of literary creation but also of theorizing about the process of composing great poetry. Calmeta's close personal connections with these *improvvisatori* at Cortesi's house clearly shaped his thinking in an essay he wrote, entitled "Whether It Is Possible to Be a Good Vernacular Poet without Knowledge of Latin." Here Calmeta argues that a poet who has natural talent and is infused with "divino furor" (an echo of Ficino) can achieve some measure of poetic greatness even without the benefit of a classical education, though the work of such a poet can easily be marred by errors:

> For this reason, and by this authority, one could almost assert that a vernacular poet without [Latin] literacy could reach some level of perfection in the profession of poet, provided that he is naturally gifted with a poetic disposition, and moved by divine frenzy.[39]

Calmeta identifies Serafino, along with Luigi Pulci and Jacopo Corsi, as poets who relied on natural gifts:

> What greater natural instinct could you find than that possessed by Luigi Pulci, Jacopo Corsi, and Serafino, and many others? But the unevenness of their works, especially the longer compositions, allow us to clearly identify many places where they would have required the kind of learned skill [*arte*] that these poets lacked.[40]

The greatest results, though, Calmeta claims, are achieved by poets who combine this type of natural talent with the kind of literary *arte* (learned skill) that, in Calmeta's view, can only be obtained through the study of the Latin classics. Bernardo Accolti exemplifies this type of *arte*, according to Calmeta, as do Angelo Poliziano and Lorenzo de' Medici.[41]

Like Calmeta, Paolo Cortesi, too, nurtured doubts about the notion that poetic frenzy alone, in the absence of study, could lead to poetic greatness. In his *De hominibus doctis*, Cortesi writes, "No one possesses such richness of talent [*ingenium*] that they would be able to fashion things that are well arranged and splendidly invented without a measure of this art [*ars*]."[42] In the same text, reflecting on the poor results obtained by Maffeo Vegio in his attempt to emulate Virgil by writing a continuation of the *Aeneid*, Cortesi notes: "For, since a poet is inflamed with a force of nature, he does not despair of achieving the loftiest result. And in this way that charming Muse of Virgil deceives many, as a procuress might, since they are so charmed by the sweet sound of the poetry that they do not recognize its recondite artifice."[43] Cortesi suggests that learned artifice is essential for poets but that the greatest practitioners, like Virgil, deploy this artifice so subtly that readers are often deceived into thinking that the resulting verses are the fruit of natural talent or inspiration alone.

More influential than Cortesi's thought on these issues, though, was Baldesar Castiglione's *Il Cortegiano*, widely read and much admired after its publication in 1528 and now regarded as the most significant literary portrait of courtly life in Renaissance Italy. *Il Cortegiano*, in important ways, can be seen as further developing models of improvisational thought first articulated in Florence. With the court of Urbino as its setting, Castiglione's dialogue charts the evolving role of improvisation in courtly life, at a number of levels. Castiglione portrays the specific musical-poetic art of the *improvvisatori* as an integral part of courtly life, one which engages (albeit in different ways) both male and female members of the court; for Castiglione, the presence and participation of women was an integral element of ideal court life.[44] Furthermore, Castiglione's dialogue represents the sort of intellectual debates that were stimulated by the ascendancy of the *improvvisatori* in courtly society – in particular, debates about the relative importance of craft and inspiration. At a deeper level, Castiglione's dialogue thinks through how these debates about the nature and value of spontaneity can be applied to different facets of courtly life, beyond the specific pursuits of musical and poetic improvisation. Castiglione's most celebrated contribution, the concept of *sprezzatura*, is ultimately a result of this reflection. As we have seen in the preceding chapters, when Renaissance humanists turned their attention to the art of the *improvvisatori*, they drew on ancient writings from a range of areas, including ancient rhetorical theory dealing with the relationship between learned craft (*ars*) and innate talent (*ingenium*). In articulating the idea of *sprezzatura*, Castiglione expands the terms of this debate further, to embrace not just rhetoric, music, and poetry but potentially every act of the male or female participant in the life of the court.

Like many of his peers, Castiglione himself was a practitioner of music: we know that he owned and enjoyed playing the viola. As in the cases of Lorenzo de' Medici, Baccio Ugolini, and many others, in Castiglione's case, too, we have evidence that he did not like to be without access to his instrument and on multiple occasions sent letters requesting that his viola be brought to him.[45] That the singing of verses while accompanying oneself on the viola enjoyed high prestige in Castiglione's milieu, and at the court of Urbino in particular, is shown by the fact that the interlocutor Federico in Castiglione's *Cortegiano* declares this practice to be the highest form of music: "But especially it is singing recitative with the viola that seems to me most delightful, as this gives to the words a wonderful charm and effectiveness."[46] As musicologist James Haar has noted, Federico is evidently referring in this passage to "improvised song or declamatory speech-song over instrumental accompaniment" – the type of musical-poetic performance practised by courtly *improvvisatori* as well as popular *canterini* of humbler social station.[47]

Il Cortegiano highlights improvisational performance as a courtly practice and subject of theoretical discourse as well. In the dialogue, the figure who animates the most extended and direct discussions of improvisation at the court of Urbino is none other than Bernardo Accolti, called in the text by his *nome d'arte*, "l'Unico Aretino." He was a frequent presence at the court of Urbino over many years; documents from September 1504 and from January 1509 attest to his presence at the Montefeltro court at those times.[48] A letter from Pietro Bembo to Cardinal Bibbiena in 1516 mentions that Accolti had been asked by the Duchess Elisabetta Gonzaga to give an improvised poetic performance ("richiesto dalla Signora Duchessa di dire improviso").[49] Castiglione had many opportunities to observe first-hand the remarkable improvisational talents of Bernardo Accolti; the letters that Castiglione sent from the papal court of Leo X to his patrons in Mantua contain numerous references to Accolti's performances. On 6 February 1521, for instance, Castiglione wrote to Federico Gonzaga, "Yesterday evening l'Unico Aretino improvised for three hours before the pope, with a very large audience – marvellously, as is his custom."[50]

Unsurprisingly, then, Castiglione's dialogue depicts the character Accolti in the act of deploying his skills of improvisational performance. Moreover, the particular context of Accolti's performance elicits discussion of a question that we have encountered before with regard to improvisational performances: Was the performance genuinely improvised? While the improvisation of poetry was, as we have seen, an extremely widespread phenomenon in Renaissance Italy, the ubiquity of the practice did not eliminate the sense of wonder that talented improvisors provoked in their audiences, nor the incredulity that sceptics sometimes nurtured about whether such ostensibly improvisational performances were truly extemporaneous or merely dissimulated. The characters in Castiglione's *Cortegiano* are represented as displaying just this sort of mix of wonder and scepticism towards Accolti's skills.

Indicating the letter "S" appearing on the jewellery that the duchess, Elisabetta Gonzaga, is wearing on her forehead (apparently the same scorpion-shaped jewel depicted in Raffaello's portrait of the duchess; see figure 8), Accolti proposes that all the courtiers provide interpretations of the letter's meaning. The rest of the company demurs, and they instead prevail on Accolti to offer his own interpretation, which he does, then and there, in the form of a sonnet:

> Aretino remained silent for a while; then, being urged to speak, he at last recited a sonnet on the aforesaid subject, declaring what was meant by that letter s; which sonnet was thought by many to have been improvised; but because it was more ingenious and polished than the brevity of time would seem to have allowed, some thought that it had been prepared.[51]

A sonnet that seems to correspond to the one by Accolti described in the *Cortegiano* has been preserved:

> Consenti, o mar di bellezza e virtute,
> ch'io, servo tuo, sia d'un gran dubbio sciolto,
> se l'S che porti nel candido volto
> significa mio stento o mia salute,
>
> se dimostra soccorso, o servitute,
> sospetto, o securtà, secreto, o stolto,
> se speme, o strido, se salvo, o sepolto!
> Se le catene mie strette, solute;
>
> ch'io temo forte che non mostri segno
> de superbia, sospir, severitate,
> strazio, sangue, sudor, supplicio e sdegno.

> Ma se loco ha la pura veritate,
> questa S dimostra con non poco ingegno
> un sol solo in bellezza e 'n crudeltate.

[Consent, o sea of beauty and virtue, that I, your servant, be released from a great doubt: if the *S* that you wear on your snow-white face means my suffering or my salvation, if it shows succour or servitude, suspicion or security, secret or stupid, spirit of hope or screams, safe or six feet under, if my chains squeeze me tightly or set me free. Because I greatly fear that it shows a sign of self-importance, sighing, severity, scourge, shedding of blood, sweat, suffering, and scorn. But if pure truth has its place, this *S* shows, with great ingenuity, one sole sun, in its beauty and cruelty.][52]

The sceptics among Accolti's audience in *Il Cortegiano* suspect that he must have written this sonnet in advance, because it appears to them too polished and ingenious (*ingenioso*) to have been improvised. This objection is somewhat surprising, since the term *ingenioso* (as well as related words deriving from the Latin word *ingenium*, or talent) is often deployed by those seeking to account for the phenomenon of poetic improvisation. Indeed, Paolo Cortesi's admiration for Accolti, as discussed above, is founded on his conviction that Accolti relies on his innate talent (*ingenium*) in creating poetry. The widespread belief that Accolti's achievements as a spontaneous poet-performer were the fruits of his extraordinary *ingenium* is also echoed within the *Cortegiano* itself by the character Emilia, who, addressing Accolti, praises "your divine ingegno" ("lo ingegno vostro divino").[53]

As this ambiguous use of terminology suggests, Castiglione's presentation of Accolti hints at a new way of thinking about *ars*, or craft, and *furor*, or frenzy. We can also observe a blurring of *ars* and *furor* in Giovanni Matteo Toscano's description of Accolti's verse:

Reading the poems which you have poured forth in a sudden heat, or those which you have rendered polished with the frequent application of the file, one would hardly be able to discern how impulse differs from craft [*ars*]. One would think that all of the poems had been hammered out with the same labour, and one would say: "If this is craft, there is nothing more polished than this craft; if this is frenzy, then craft itself is less polished than this frenzy."[54]

According to Toscano, the most remarkable thing about Accolti is the way in which his poetry blurs the distinction between craft and frenzy. Toscano, in other words, seems to be referring to precisely the type of

Figure 8. Raffaello Sanzio, *Portrait of Elisabetta Gonzaga* (c. 1504–5). Florence, Galleria degli Uffizi, Inv. 1890 n. 1441; with the permission of the Ministero della Cultura. No reproduction or duplication of this image by any means is permitted.

doubt that confronts the characters who observe Accolti's extemporaneous versifying in Castiglione's *Cortegiano*. Accolti produces poetry so
refined that it would seem to have required careful revision, yet he appears to produce it spontaneously, in a frenzy. And, for many of these
commentators, the ultimate conclusion is the same: what matters, in the
end, is not so much how a poetic work or a courtly act came about, but
the effect it has on an audience.

It is no coincidence that Castiglione's influential ideal of *sprezzatura* –
the ability to create the appearance, or illusion, of spontaneity – emerges
from a cultural milieu in which practices of improvisation, and especially
musical-poetic improvisation, played a major role. In the preceding
chapters we have seen how, in Quattrocento Florence, the rediscovery of
key ancient texts, in conjunction with a lively culture of improvisational
musical-poetic performance, gave rise to new debates about whether poetic excellence should be considered primarily a matter of skill and study
(*ars*) or of spontaneous frenzy (either inspired by divinity or emerging
from the poet's innate qualities – *ingenium* or *natura*). The Quattrocento
Florentine humanists, seeking to understand the phenomena of poetic
improvisation that they observed all around them, and in which many
of them participated directly, turned on the one hand to ancient texts
dedicated to the subject of oral poetry (such as Plato's *Ion*). But they also
turned to texts about improvisation in the domain of the rhetorician (such
as Quintilian's *Institutio*), bringing the theories of improvised speech that
they found in these texts to bear on improvisational practices in the realm
of poetry and music. Both the Platonic texts reintroduced by Ficino and
the newly available ancient sources tapped most extensively by Poliziano
(notably Statius's *Silvae* and Quintilian's *Institutio*) pointed these Florentine thinkers to the conclusion that skill and study (*ars*) alone could not
suffice to achieve poetic greatness, that the best poets relied on a spontaneous effusion of verse, conceptualized as the product either of divine
afflatus (*furor*) or of the poet's innate talent (*ingenium*). Oral poets – both
ancient bards and modern *improvvisatori* – were regarded as the clearest
representatives of a poetics that apparently eschewed human skill (*ars*) in
favour of the superior, even divine powers of *furor* and *ingenium*.

When Emilia, in the *Cortegiano*, praises the *ingegno divino* of Bernardo
Accolti, this suggests that, in Castiglione's milieu, too, the poetry of *improvvisatori* like Accolti is being viewed through the lens of the dichotomy of *ars*
versus *ingenium*. The debate among the courtiers about whether Accolti's
sonnet was truly improvised or written in advance in effect turns on the
same issue, with the sceptics implying that Accolti is not really a poet of pure
ingenium, that he relies on hard work and craftsmanship (*ars*) more than he
would have his audience believe. Accolti's success as a courtly *improvvisatore*,

it seems, will depend on whether he is able to convince others that his poetry is a product of *ingenium*, not *ars*. What is demanded of Accolti is not that he eschew literary craftsmanship but that he disguise the role that such human skill and craftsmanship play in his performative poetry. He must appear to achieve his poetic excellence spontaneously and effortlessly.

By situating the episode of Bernardo Accolti's improvised sonnet shortly before the beginning of the dialogue's main discussion, on the ideal courtier, Castiglione signals that a central strategy in his text will be to take the *ars* versus *ingenium* dichotomy – which had shaped discussions of rhetoric since antiquity and which more recently, in Quattrocento Florence, had become commonplace in discussions of vernacular *improvvisatori* – and apply it to a much wider range of pursuits. Indeed, in any activity undertaken by the courtier, openly displaying one's reliance on training and skill is anathema, because doing so destroys any trace of grace: "So you see how art, or any intent effort, if it is disclosed, deprives everything of grace."[55] The ideal of *sprezzatura*, the most famous element of Castiglione's dialogue, is offered as a solution to this dilemma: the courtier must, Count Lodovico says, "practice in all things a certain *sprezzatura* [nonchalance], so as to conceal all art and make whatever is done or said appear to be without effort and almost without any thought about it. And I believe much grace comes of this: because everyone knows the difficulty of things that are rare and well done; wherefore facility in such things causes the greatest wonder."[56] Castiglione's attention to the marvel that can be created through the seemingly spontaneous and effortless execution of a difficult task shows parallels with Poliziano's remarks about what he believed Statius hoped to achieve by emphasizing the extemporaneous character of his *Silvae.* "Even though those poems were overflowing with numerous genuine artistic touches, nevertheless, a man caring greatly about his reputation could hardly overlook the fact that respect for his ability to compose rapidly would likely win him freer indulgence from his readers, readier favour, and greater admiration."[57]

Circulating in numerous editions and translations, *Il Cortegiano* became a courtly sourcebook of record for issues of language, gender, and politics and their intersections. As it gained in popularity, it held up the model of Urbino, where women like Elisabetta Gonzaga and Emilia Pia participated in conversations about the nature of improvised performance. Castiglione's formulation of *sprezzatura* held considerable influence, especially due to its universal applicability as an ideal of graceful conduct. However, the particular intellectual genealogy of the concept can clearly be traced to the model developed through earlier Florentine conversations about the role of *ars* and *furor* in artistic production, inspired by observation of *improvvisatori*.

Conclusion

To recognize the inspiration of Corilla, it is sufficient to have heard her sing; from the effects that we ourselves experience, it is possible to understand the nature and force of that flame, which ignites the senses, enchants the soul, makes it drunk, makes it fall in love, and infuses it with a most sweet inner pleasure. Who among you, then, would fail to recognize the clear signs of inspiration, which is an extraordinary state of the soul? Who has not seen her at first standing quiet and slack, starting out faint and uncertain, then suddenly catch fire, come to life, take flight, speed up her gestures and voice ... elevate herself to a higher sphere, and breathing a purer air, separate herself in a way from the state of mere mortals?[1]

This description of a performance powered by poetic frenzy is familiar in all of its elements. The sudden change in the poet's affect, the terminology of flame and flight, the power of the inspired poet to transport listeners: these are the common elements of the frenzied state in the descriptions of Renaissance commentators. In this case, though, the poet is not a Quattrocento *improvvisatore* but a Settecento *improvvisatrice*: Maria Maddalena Morelli, known by her performance name of Corilla Olimpica. Corilla was a member of the Roman Accademia dell'Arcadia who gained international renown as an improvisational performer and followed in the footsteps of Petrarch by receiving the title of poet laureate on the Capitoline Hill in 1776. As this description makes clear, not only did the phenomenon of poetic improvisation experience a resurgence in the eighteenth century, in which female artists participated to a much greater degree than they had in the fifteenth and sixteenth centuries, but the discourse surrounding this type of improvisational performance also drew heavily on fifteenth-century antecedents in its characterization

of the intellectual operations at work. Through Corilla and her contemporaries, these ideas about poetic excellence reached and influenced new audiences in turn.

Despite the significance of poetic improvisation as a cultural phenomenon in Italy across multiple centuries, it and its contemporary theoretical interpretations have been largely overlooked in scholarship on
Italian literature until quite recently. This omission has much to do with
the dismissive attitude of Benedetto Croce, the twentieth century's most
influential Italian literary critic, who remarked, "I confess that I am
unable to convince myself to assign aesthetic value to extemporaneous poetry" ("Confesso che non saprei risolvermi ad assegnare valore
estetico alla poesia estemporanea").[2] Croce observes that theorists of the
Romantic period who valorized the concept of genius tended to identify that quality in "producing poetry rapidly and instantaneously, or,
as it was called, 'all'improvviso.'"[3] For Croce, in other words, Romantic
critics identified Italy's *improvvisatori* as embodiments of the misguided
Romantic ideal of artistic genius. Once these foreign theorists lost
interest in Italian *improvvisatori* as manifestations of genius, he argues,
the *improvvisatori* disappeared.[4] Croce insists that poetic improvisation
was a significant phenomenon only between 1700 and 1850, arguing that
isolated examples of improvisors before the eighteenth century held no
historical importance.[5]

In the wake of Croce's dismissive writings about *improvvisatori*, no
major studies on the subject were published in Italy for decades. In a
1979 article, Bruno Gentili noted correspondences between eighteenth-
century *improvvisatori* and earlier improvised poetry: specifically, that
of ancient Greece. While highlighting the parallels between ancient
cultural practices and those of Settecento Italy, Gentili omits consideration of improvisational poetry in the intervening centuries.[6] The idea
that Renaissance practices of improvisation served a mediating function
between ancient improvisors and eighteenth-century improvisors was
later proposed in essays by Carlo Caruso and Fabio Finotti, which briefly
treat Renaissance precedents.[7]

Croce's judgment that *improvvisatore* performance was rare or insig-
nificant in Italy before the eighteenth century is wrong on multiple
counts and is particularly flawed as a characterization of the situation
in Renaissance Italy. For Florentines in the fifteenth and sixteenth
centuries, such performances were a regular source of entertainment
and a focal point of civic life, as we have seen. Luca Degl'Innocenti's
work reconstructing the calendar of Cristoforo l'Altissimo's performances reveals the frequency with which Florentines could attend
performances by the noted *improvvisatore*. Over the space of one year

(1514–15), Cristoforo gave ninety-five performances in Piazza San Martino, averaging one performance every four to five days.[8] Timothy McGee estimates that performances took place in Piazza San Martino as often as three or four days each week.[9] By this time the piazza had hosted generations of improvisors; Cristoforo was clearly regarded as a successor to performers like Antonio di Guido and Niccolò Cieco. These performers had a broad cultural appeal, performing both in public and for elite audiences in the courts. And the spread of improvised musical-poetic performance enhanced rather than dampened the sense of wonder that the extraordinary abilities of these performers provoked in their audiences, as reported by contemporary accounts like Pietro Aretino's description of urban life shutting down when Bernardo Accolti performed.[10] It was this sense of wonder in part that provoked erudite observers in the Renaissance, like Castiglione's courtiers, to consider the activities of the *improvvisatori* in connection with debates about the nature of inspiration, just as critics in the Romantic period would later do.[11] The terms of these debates naturally evolved between the Renaissance and Romanticism. Nevertheless, these two frameworks are closely linked, and the Romantic theory of genius and its application to the *improvvisatori* could not have developed as it did had it not been for these important Renaissance precedents.

To see how the discourse about poetic frenzy and improvisation evolved after the sixteenth century, it is helpful to survey some later accounts of improvisational practices. According to Giovanni Mario Crescimbeni's *Istoria della volgar poesia*, written in the early Settecento, poetic and musical improvisation was actively cultivated within the original Accademia dell'Arcadia, the literary society over which Crescimbeni presided. Crescimbeni observes that improvisation has greatly increased in prestige in his own time and is widely practised by nobles and men of letters. He credits Cardinal Pietro Ottoboni (praised in the text for his "ingegno" and "prontezza," key attributes for the improvisor) with an important role in promoting improvisation, as the host of weekly literary discussions which involved improvisation of poetry, both with and without music. Crescimbeni mentions specific poetic forms, including *ottava rima* poems and *capitoli*, in which *improvvisatori* – in keeping with established tradition – would challenge one another to feats of improvisation for four or even six hours at a stretch.[12] Crescimbeni's description of these practices, furthermore, recognizes fifteenth- and sixteenth-century *improvvisatori* as predecessors of the type of improvisation practised in his own milieu, singling out Panfilo Sasso, Silvio Antoniani, and Cristoforo l'Altissimo as noteworthy antecedents in the art of poetic improvisation.

Members of the Accademia dell'Arcadia not only engaged in poetic improvisation but also theorized about the mechanics of the process, just as their Quattrocento predecessors had done, and in strikingly similar terms. Was the ability to compose verse and song extemporaneously the result of access to a frenzied state or a more rational process? Arcadians disagreed. For Pier Francesco Versari, frenzy was not the explanation. In his "Dialogo pastorale," Versari praises members of the Accademia who have excelled in extemporaneous singing of verse ("il pronto cantare estemporaneo"). But Versari (through the mouthpiece of "Eurasio," his Arcadian title) calls the theory of poetic frenzy "ridiculous." If *improvvisatori* composed in a state of uncontrollable temporary madness, Eurasio asks, wouldn't their poetry lack logical connections and structure? The fact that their verse conforms to proper structure and metre, and advances convincing and reasonable arguments, shows that it is in fact the product of reason rather than frenzy.[13]

Others were more convinced by the idea that improvised poetry was the product of a fundamentally irrational process. In a speech to his fellow Arcadians, Giacinto Cerutti praised Corilla, "the most famous woman of our age," in terms drawn from earlier discussions of poetic frenzy. He argues that Corilla surpasses Sappho and Pindar, who boasted of possessing "estro" and "entusiasmo," but who in reality merely succeeded in concealing the efforts of their "arte" – deploying *sprezzatura* to good effect, in other words.[14] Corilla, by contrast, is "animated by an internal electric spark," allowing her to accomplish various feats of what earlier commentators would have called *enargeia*: "She shows objects as if they are alive and present, she seduces your fantasy, she inspires you with her sentiments, she enchants your heart, she makes herself master of you."[15] Here we see fully developed many of the arguments put forward about the power of poetic frenzy by Ficino and his contemporaries in the fifteenth century, now deployed in praise of a woman with the power to enchant and master her audiences.

Giovanni Cristofano Amaduzzi – one of Settecento Italy's most respected philologists and a correspondent and supporter of Corilla – agreed, attributing Corilla's performances specifically to "frenzy" ("furore"). As evidence, Amaduzzi cites the fact that Corilla claimed to be unable to understand the things she uttered while in the grips of inspiration:

> She said, however, that she understood almost nothing of what she had uttered while she was at the apex of her frenzy. And indeed she could not recognize as her own some of the resounding things she had said while inspired, which left a lasting impression on the stupefied audience and were repeated to her after the improvised performance.[16]

Furthermore, Amaduzzi speculates that Corilla's marvellous gifts may be related to her gender, perhaps due to some unknown physiological mind-to-uterus connection:

> If these merits are shared by all the women poets because they have more sensitive nerves, and more elastic and delicate fibres, and because of some kind of peculiar and wonderful connection between their minds and the uterus, I do not know. But I know for certain that she has always seemed to me superior, in her flights and fits, in her images, and in her ideas, to all of the male poets that I have seen, both those I have seen together with her and elsewhere.[17]

Anatomical considerations aside, Amaduzzi's analysis of Corilla articulates an important point about the relationship between improvisational practices and theories of inspiration. For Amaduzzi, Corilla's improvisations serve as a means of understanding ancient descriptions of frenzy:

> I would never have formed a proper conception of extemporaneous inspiration, had I not seen the beautiful fire and heard the beautiful flights of Corilla ... Corilla alone has been able to provide me with some understanding of, and convince me of the possible truth of, what is written about certain inspired women of the ancient world who were possessed by a prophetic spirit.[18]

A similar argument is articulated by the Jesuit author Saverio Bettinelli, in his work *Dell'entusiasmo delle belle arti* (1769), arguably the most important theoretical work dedicated to the concept of frenzy in poetry and the arts in eighteenth-century Italy.[19] Bettinelli's concept of the altered state of *entusiasmo* that allows for the creation of great poetry and other works of art is deeply influenced by the concept of divine frenzy as described in the Platonic dialogues. But Bettinelli argues that it is the *improvvisatori* he has observed who furnish the best evidence in favour of *entusiasmo*: "An excellent extemporaneous poet, when he is truly in the heat of his inspiration, allows one to observe all of the aforementioned effects wonderfully ... And anyone can verify this who observes one of the most excellent improvisors, as I have often had the good fortune to be able to do."[20] In other words, like Amaduzzi, Bettinelli saw the performances of improvisors as a kind of laboratory where Plato's theories of frenzy could be tested in practice.

While most of Bettinelli's writings on *improvvisatori*, including in *Dell'entusiasmo delle belle arti*, focus on contemporary practitioners, he regarded the improvisors of his own time as the successors of a performance

tradition with roots in the Renaissance. Bettinelli even identifies Marsilio
Ficino as an *improvvisatore*, ranking him among the major *improvvisatori*
of the Renaissance alongside more traditionally renowned performers
like Cristoforo l'Altissimo and Bernardo Accolti:

> Thus in Tuscany and elsewhere there were in that period many singers who
> both improvised and sung their verses, including Marsilio Ficino, Serafino
> Aquilano (as we have mentioned), Niccolò Cieco d'Arezzo, Cristoforo
> l'Altissimo, Antonio Tebaldeo, and Bernardo Accolti.[21]

It is clear that discourse surrounding improvisation and inspiration in
the eighteenth and nineteenth centuries owed much to earlier efforts to
link these concepts – in particular those of Ficino. Perhaps the clearest
example of Romantic theories of inspiration shaped by the convergence of
contemporary improvisational practices and the Platonic theory of frenzy
is the case of Percy Bysshe Shelley. Shelley's "Defence of Poetry," arguably
the most influential programmatic statement of Romantic poetics, was
composed as a response to Thomas Love Peacock's satirical critique of
poetry's value in his "Four Ages of Poetry." At the time he read Peacock's
essay and wrote his reply, Shelley's ideas about poetry were being shaped
by his encounters with another poet who made a deep impression on him:
Tommaso Sgricci, widely considered the most talented *improvvisatore* of his
time. Percy and Mary Shelley were first introduced to Sgricci in 1820 and
saw him improvise on a number of occasions.[22] After seeing Sgricci improvise a tragedy on the death of Hector in Pisa on 22 January 1821, Shelley
began writing, in Italian, a review of Sgricci's performance, perhaps
intended for publication in an Italian periodical (but never completed).
   In the review, Shelley asserts that the extemporaneous flow of Sgricci's
verses must be understood as his imagination operating independently
of his intellect. He writes that Sgricci himself seemed to be barely conscious of the words that a higher power ("superna possa") was dictating
through him, as the passions of the characters flowed through Sgricci
and into the souls of the audience members.[23] Shelley compares Sgricci
to a mirror; his soul reflects images of which Sgricci himself is not truly
conscious. In his interpretation of Sgricci's performance, Shelley seems
to be rehearsing the conception of poets as vessels channelling the "spirit
of the age" which concludes his "Defence of Poetry":

> They measure the circumference and sound the depths of human nature
> with a comprehensive and all-penetrating spirit, and they are themselves per-
> haps the most sincerely astonished at its manifestations; for it is less their spirit
> than the spirit of the age. Poets are the hierophants of an unapprehended

inspiration; the mirrors of the gigantic shadows which futurity casts upon the present; the words which express what they understand not.[24]

When Shelley wrote his review of Sgricci's performance, he had recently been rereading Plato's *Ion*, as he mentions in a letter he wrote at the time.[25] James Notopoulos has noted that Peacock's "Four Ages of Poetry" "came to Shelley's hand while he was in the process of reading Plato's *Ion*" and that Shelley "had earlier recommended to Peacock himself the discussion of poetic madness in the *Phaedrus*."[26] The Platonic theory of frenzy clearly exerted a strong influence on the way in which Shelley understood Sgricci's improvisational abilities, and it strongly informed "A Defence of Poetry." But Shelley's interpretations of Plato were in turn mediated by Marsilio Ficino. In 1818, Shelley had taken up the task of translating Plato's *Symposium*; according to Mary Shelley's journal, he completed the translation at breakneck speed, in just ten days, from 9 July to 20 July 1818. Shelley's rapid work as translator was made possible in part by the fact that he relied more on Ficino's Latin translation than Plato's original Greek.[27] Shelley also produced a partial translation of Plato's *Ion*, likely relying in a similar way on Ficino's version.

The question of the role of labour and study in the production of poetry, which Ficino's interpretations of Plato elevated to a central question in Renaissance debates about poetry and improvisation, becomes central in Shelley's reflections as well. The essence of poetry, Shelley claims, is a kind of inspiration that defies conscious control; labour and study can play at most an auxiliary role in its creation:

> When composition begins, inspiration is already on the decline, and the most glorious poetry that has ever been communicated to the world is probably a feeble shadow of the original conceptions of the poet. I appeal to the greatest poets of the present day, whether it is not an error to assert that the finest passages of poetry are produced by labour and study.[28]

Shelley is fascinated by Sgricci's ability to elicit powerful emotional responses from his audience. As Renaissance thinkers had before him, Shelley uses Plato's metaphor comparing the oral poet's emotional power over his audience to the force of a magnet transmitted through the links of an iron chain as a way of characterizing this aspect of the *improvvisatore*'s talent. Shelley deploys variations on this metaphor in "A Defence of Poetry" as well:

> The sacred links of that chain have never been entirely disjoined, which descending through the minds of many men is attached to those great minds,

whence as from a magnet the invisible effluence is sent forth, which at once connects, animates, and sustains the life of all.[29]

Shelley adapts the Platonic metaphor creatively, in an approach that shows some parallels with Poliziano's handling of it. In Shelley's text, as in Poliziano's *Silvae*, poetic frenzy is conceptualized as a kind of inspiration that can be transmitted textually, linking poets across different historical periods. Thus Shelley is able to claim that Chaucer "caught the sacred inspiration" from Dante, Petrarch, and Boccaccio.[30]

In addition to refocusing Shelley's attention on the concept of poetic frenzy, and the Platonic texts that discuss it, Shelley's encounter with Sgricci also appears to have provoked Shelley to experiment with improvisational approaches in his own poetry. One of the strongest pieces of textual evidence that survives of this experimentation on Shelley's part is the 110-line blank-verse fragment entitled "Orpheus," which manuscript evidence suggests was in some way connected with Sgricci's improvisations.[31] The text was transcribed by Mary Shelley; Percy Shelley would later use the pages surrounding the "Orpheus" fragment to write his review of Sgricci's 1821 improvised performance. Mary Shelley added a note in the manuscript describing her role in transcribing the poem from what was apparently Percy Shelley's dictation or oral performance: "Aspetto fin che il diluvio cala, ed allora cerco di posare argine alle sue parole" ("I await the descent of the flood, and then I endeavour to embank his words").[32] This apparent playful allusion by Mary Shelley to Percy's sudden inspiration, along with the presence of Percy's review of Sgricci among the same papers that contain the "Orpheus," has led a number of scholars to conclude that the "Orpheus" fragment likely represents an attempt, by Shelley, at poetic improvisation in the style of Sgricci.[33] It is possible that Shelley's *Hellas*, too, may have its origins in an attempt at improvisation in the style of Sgricci; in the preface, Shelley refers to the work as "a mere improvise."[34]

Shelley's interest in Platonic philosophy certainly made him receptive to the possibility that the Platonic theory of frenzy could be used to explain the phenomenon of poetic improvisation as practised by Sgricci. But it is important to recognize that, in drawing this connection between the *improvvisatore* and poetic frenzy, Shelley was responding to a long-standing tradition of associating the improvisation of verse with the Platonic idea of frenzy. Indeed, eighteenth- and nineteenth-century *improvvisatori*, like their Renaissance predecessors such as Raffaele Brandolini and Cristoforo l'Altissimo, often themselves actively promoted the notion that their extemporaneous verses were produced in a state of frenzy.

By the early decades of the nineteenth century, it had become unfashionable in some circles to regard *improvvisatori* like Sgricci as bearers of poetic frenzy. In 1816, the influential author Pietro Giordani published an essay entitled "Intorno allo Sgricci ed agl'Improvvisatori in Italia," meant to counter what he considered the excessive admiration that this class of entertainers commanded.[35] At the heart of Giordani's argument is an attack on the concept of frenzy:

> And here we repeat to you that an ordered succession of good thoughts, which is the property of a talent above the ordinary, and is acquired with great effort, can never (regardless of what the tricksters may say) be obtained through a sudden frenzy, or an abrupt inspiration. There is no frenzy other than talent, no inspiration other than study. Now what level of talent and study do the *improvvisatori* commonly have? Even if they had just as much as Homer and Dante, there is no talent, no study that can operate in the absence of time.[36]

Giordani's objections are framed in the same terms that structured the debates about the nature of spontaneous poetic production in the Renaissance, as we have seen – debates about whether great poetry should be regarded primarily as the product of *furor, ingenium,* or *ars.* Giordani suggests that the concept of poetic frenzy is a mere fiction, that the effects widely attributed to frenzy in fact proceed from *ingegno* or *studio*, both of which require time (the opposite of extemporaneity) in order to achieve good results. The fact that Giordani chooses to critique Sgricci and his fellow *improvvisatori* by objecting to the theory of poetic frenzy demonstrates that this theory was widely applied to the activities of the *improvvisatori* in Giordani's time, just as it had been in the Renaissance.

Studies of the historical development of ideas about poetic and artistic inspiration, and the concept of genius, have often highlighted Renaissance humanism and Romanticism as particularly significant cultural movements in these spheres. Some of the ways in which humanist reflection in these areas influenced thinking in the Romantic period have been well documented; for instance, the link postulated by Marsilio Ficino between a melancholic disposition and frenzied inspiration is widely recognized as instrumental in shaping Romantic-era notions of genius.[37] While forms of oral and improvisational poetic performance have been practised in Italy in every century, these two periods – the period from the fifteenth through early sixteenth century that saw the rise of humanism, and the period from the mid-eighteenth through mid-nineteenth century that saw the rise of Romanticism – are also those in which *improvvisatore* performance was a particularly significant facet of Italian cultural production. Italy's exceptional richness in this particular sphere during the latter period has been much more extensively documented than in the former. In part this is because visitors to Italy during the age of the Grand Tour routinely wrote about their experiences of Italian *improvvisatore/improvvisatrice* performances, which they often present as something marvellous and alien and sometimes as a characteristic manifestation of the presumed irrational quality of the Italian national character. The extent to which the Renaissance, too, was a period of particular vitality and prominence for oral and improvisational poetic practices in Italy has only recently begun to come into focus. As we have seen, the study of these phenomena (in both periods) has been held back by a degree of reluctance on the part of scholars to regard *improvvisatore* poetry as true literature and a cultural phenomenon meriting serious attention.

In the period between 1750 and 1850, observers seeking to account for the incredible performative abilities of Italian improvisors frequently invoked the example of the oral poets of the ancient world – especially Homer.[38] It became commonplace to debate whether modern *improvvisatori* should be considered the descendants of Homer and, conversely, whether Homer had been an *improvvisatore*. This, too, is a Romantic-era approach to understanding the phenomenon of poetic improvisation that follows precedents established during the fifteenth century. Greek texts like those attributed to Homer, Hesiod, and Orpheus raised tantalizing questions for Italian humanists as those texts began to circulate in western Europe for the first time since antiquity. It was clear from surviving sources (and indeed from clues within the poems) that the Homeric epics were originally performed orally. Encountering these poems as words written on a page, one could scarcely hope to understand their original presentation. And while Renaissance Italians had no direct access to the oral realities of an ancient rhapsodic performance, they did have easy access to a living and vital oral poetic tradition – that of the *canterini*.

In fifteenth-century Italy, as in classical Athens during Plato's lifetime, major developments in the cultures and technologies of verbal communication called into question the place of oral poetry in society. In the case of classical Athens between the fifth and fourth centuries BCE, the expansion of literacy and prose writing posed a challenge to the central role that oral poets and rhapsodes traditionally played as transmitters of cultural knowledge and values. According to Eric Havelock's influential argument, Plato and his fellow philosophers sought to supplant the oral poets and rhapsodes in their traditional role at the centre of ancient Greek education. The theory of divine poetic frenzy, with its conception of the oral poet as an empty vessel with no ability to understand his or her own poetic pronouncements, was deployed by Plato precisely as a means of questioning the societal value of oral poetry, "relegat[ing] the poetic experience to a category which was non-conceptual and therefore non-rational and non-reflective. Thus was invented the notion that poetry must be simply a product of ecstatic possession, for which the Greek animistic term was 'enthusiasm.'"[39]

In Quattrocento Italy, too, the culture of verbal communication was transformed by both technological and cultural developments. The technology of movable type led to the rapid proliferation of relatively inexpensive books. The mass appeal of the Italian *canterini* traditionally rested on their ability to reach a broad audience; Italians for whom private reading was an inaccessible pastime, because of either the prohibitive cost of books or illiteracy, could instead hear poetry performed in the piazza. The advent of relatively affordable printed books eventually helped to remove these limitations, posing a potential threat to the traditional role of the *canterini* (who in many cases responded to this challenge by becoming, themselves, purveyors of printed books).[40]

Like late-fifth-century Athens, Quattrocento Italy saw the ascent of a newly influential class of intellectuals that transformed society – in this case, Renaissance humanists. At the heart of Quattrocento humanism was a set of educational and intellectual ideals potentially antithetical to those of traditional vernacular oral culture: humanist education was centred on the cultivation of eloquence in neo-Latin. Based on the imitation of classical Latin style from carefully selected ancient authors, neo-Latin (even more than earlier varieties of medieval Latin) was inextricably tied to textual study. Especially since Italian *canterini* often performed narratives set in antiquity, classical humanists could perceive them as, in a sense, professional rivals offering an inferior approach to the ancient world. If humanists sought to recover the language of classical Romans and to comprehend their own historical distance from the ancient past through rational, emotionally detached textual study, the *canterini*, Poggio's anecdotes suggest, offered a debased approach to the ancient world, using the vernacular language of the common people and the blandishments of music to rouse the audience's emotions, collapsing the perception of historical distance and emotional separation between ancients and moderns.

Florence's status as a leading centre of both oral poetic performance and humanist philology created the conditions for such attitudes of rivalry and scorn but also for instances of mutual respect, curiosity, and influence between practitioners of these two pursuits – sometimes (and with increasing frequency as time progressed) cultivated by the same individuals. Humanists' attention to and involvement in oral poetic performance had decisive consequences for their approaches to issues of

improvisation, inspiration, and orality in their philological and interpretive work on ancient authors. The consequences of this intersection
of cultural practices for the reception of Plato's theory of divine poetic
frenzy were particularly long-lasting and significant. As the preceding
chapters have shown, *improvvisatore* performance and the theory of
poetic frenzy were intertwined from the time of the rediscovery of the
Phaedrus and the *Ion*. Had the return of these dialogues been handled
by a thinker less sympathetic than Marsilio Ficino towards the value of
oral poetic performance, the Platonic theory of frenzy might have been
integrated into European cultural debates not primarily as an argument
for the elevated status of poets as bearers of inspired wisdom but as a
warning about the perilously entrancing power of poetic performance
and, at the same time, its epistemological untrustworthiness.

Instead, Ficino tirelessly promoted an exalted interpretation of the
value of divine poetic frenzy, creating the conditions for the widespread
currency this interpretation would retain in European discourse for
centuries. One cannot fully understand Ficino's early focus on this
theory, and the traction it quickly gained, without recognizing that
Florentines in Ficino's milieu were accustomed to thinking of poetry
not exclusively – or even primarily – as a matter of written composition
committed to and accessed from a page but as an art form in which oral
and musical performance, and improvisation, were often integral. While
the theory of poetic frenzy may seem somewhat bizarre to twenty-first-
century readers, for both Plato's contemporaries and Ficino's, who lived
in day-to-day contact with living oral poetic performance traditions, this
theory resonated with their own observations of the states of apparent
altered consciousness that singer-poets (and sometimes their audiences)
seemed to enter during such performances. The use of the vocabulary
of Platonic frenzy by noted improvisors like Cristoforo l'Altissimo and
Raffaele Brandolini to describe the inspiration that supposedly powered
their own performances suggests the important role of the theory of
frenzy in elevating the status of the poetic improvisor in fifteenth- and
sixteenth-century Italian society.

The fact that oral poetic performance came to be seen as a serious art
form with illustrious classical precedents, commanding serious reflection
by humanist intellectuals and captivating audiences of princes, prelates,
and shopkeepers, exerted long-lasting effects, even as the prevalence of
improvisational poetic practices in Italian society ebbed and flowed over
the following centuries. While accounts of major poet-improvisors are
relatively infrequent in the later sixteenth and seventeenth centuries,
features of the culture of *improvvisatore* poetry in eighteenth-century Italy
make it clear that the revival of this art was shaped by discourse that

can be traced back to the fifteenth century. Accounts of the frenzied, supposedly uncontrollable poetic outpourings of *improvvisatori* and *improvvisatrici* thus shaped debates about the nature of poetic creativity throughout the Romantic period and beyond.

We have seen numerous cases in which observers of improvisational poetic performances expressed incredulity that performers were in fact improvising. Such reactions betray the preconceptions of a highly literate culture. For those whose personal experience of literary composition is limited to the slow and careful process of written composition, it can seem impossible that others might be able to produce poetry in an entirely different way – orally and extemporaneously. Techniques of oral poetic composition-in-performance have played a particularly vital role in societies (and among groups) without literacy. In such contexts, where oral poetry can serve as a primary means of knowledge transmission, oral poets often present their own art *not* as creating new poetry extemporaneously (i.e., improvising) but as faithfully reproducing a pre-existing poem which they have learned orally. As revealed in the studies of Parry and Lord on the poetic composition-in-performance practised by illiterate oral poets of the former Yugoslavia, when these poets were called upon to perform the same work twice, the plot of the narrative might remain fairly fixed, but the exact words would inevitably vary, as the product of composition-in-performance. Nevertheless, these singers would often claim that they were reproducing "word-for-word" the poems that they had learned orally.[41] What counted, for these illiterate performers and their audiences, was faithful transmission of a tradition; therefore, while their oral art required them to master a technique that can be considered a form of extemporaneous composition, these poets did not pride themselves on improvisational creativity.

The oral poets of Renaissance Italy all operated in a society fundamentally shaped by literacy, but the ways in which individual performers engaged with literate practices could vary widely. Some of the most famous *canterini*, including Niccolò Cieco, were blind, and thus unable to read. Popular *canterini* performing in the piazza undoubtedly drew listeners with varying degrees of literacy. Illiterate Italians who were unable to read chivalric romances and classical texts could instead listen to the same stories performed as oral poems, and this ability to appeal to illiterate audiences must have contributed to the success of some of the popular *canterini*. Still, if considered simply as transmitters of textual traditions, oral poets were bound to compare unfavourably to printed books, especially in a context where literacy and broad access to texts were expanding. But *canterino* performers were sought out by Italy's intellectual and economic elite and admired in humanist circles in particular – that is to say, by audiences that had ready access to books and were steeped in textual forms of knowledge transmission.

For such audiences, the performance of oral poetry was more than just an alternate means of textual transmission; the performance was clearly valued for what it offered that the written word could not. The affective power of sung verses, especially to the accompaniment of instrumental music, was regarded as critically important. But the literate perspective of humanist observers also pushed them to valorize the improvisational aspects of oral poetic performance above its role as a means of textual transmission; the fascination with improvisation that pervades discourse about oral poetic performance in the Quattrocento and Cinquecento suggests that this aspect of the tradition was increasingly regarded as central by humanist observers. Alongside their mastery of textual forms of knowledge preservation and transmission, Italian humanists turned to practices of extemporaneous composition with roots in the traditions of *canterino* performance. In these practices they found (as it seemed to them) a means of better understanding ancient forms of oral poetry and of experiencing for themselves, as performers or spectators, the unpredictable rush of the moment of extemporaneous inspiration.

Notes

Introduction

1 "Ciriacus Anconitanus, homo verbosus et nimium loquax ... inque ea re vehementius angi videbatur." Latin text from Poggio Bracciolini, *Facezie*, ed. Stefano Pittaluga (Milan: Garzanti, 1995), 88. Throughout the book, where not otherwise noted, translations are my own.

2 "Hic persimilis est ... viro Mediolanensi qui, die festo, cum audisset unum e grege cantorum (qui gesta heroum ad plebem decantant) recitantem mortem Rolandi, qui septingentis iam ferme annis in proelio occubuit, coepit acriter flere." Latin text from Bracciolini, *Facezie*, 88–90.

3 "Multo fletu ac dolore." Bracciolini, *Facezie*, 90. See also Blake Wilson's observations about these sections of Poggio's text, in "Dominion of the Ear: Singing the Vernacular in Piazza San Martino," *I Tatti Studies in the Italian Renaissance* 16 (2013): 284.

4 See Marco Villoresi, *La voce e le parole: Studi sulla letteratura del Medioevo e del Rinascimento* (Florence: Società editrice fiorentina, 2016); Luca Degl'Innocenti, *I Reali dell'Altissimo: Un ciclo di cantari fra oralità e scrittura* (Florence: Società editrice fiorentina, 2008); and Luca Degl'Innocenti, *"Al suon di questa cetra": Ricerche sulla poesia orale del Rinascimento* (Florence: Società editrice fiorentina, 2016). An important role in stimulating this recent interdisciplinary interest in the topic was played by the research project *Italian Voices: Oral Culture, Manuscript and Print in Early Modern Italy 1450–1700*, carried out under the leadership of Brian Richardson at the University of Leeds between 2011 and 2015, which gave rise to a number of important publications, including the edited volumes Luca Degl'Innocenti, Brian Richardson, and Chiara Sbordoni, eds., *Interactions Between Orality and Writing in Early Modern Italian Culture* (Abingdon, UK: Routledge, 2016); and Stefano Dall'Aglio, Brian Richardson, and Massimo Rospocher, eds., *Voices and Texts in Early Modern Italian Society* (Abingdon, UK: Routledge,

2017); a special issue of *The Italianist* 34, no. 3 (2014), "Oral Culture in Early Modern Italy: Performance, Language, Religion," edited by Stefano Dall'Aglio, Luca Degl'Innocenti, Brian Richardson, Massimo Rospocher, and Chiara Sbordoni; a special issue of *Italian Studies* 71, no. 2 (May 2016), "The Cantastorie in Renaissance Italy: Street Singers Between Oral and Literate Cultures," edited by Luca Degl'Innocenti, Massimo Rospocher, and Rosa Salzberg; and a special issue of *Renaissance Studies* 33, no. 1 (February 2019), "Street Singers in Renaissance Europe," edited by Luca Degl'Innocenti and Massimo Rospocher.

5 See, in addition to the works cited in the preceding note, James Hankins, "Humanism and Music in Italy," in *The Cambridge History of Fifteenth-Century Music*, ed. Anna Maria Busse Berger and Jesse Rodin (Cambridge: Cambridge University Press, 2015), 231–62; and Rosa Salzberg and Massimo Rospocher, "Street Singers in Italian Renaissance Urban Culture and Communication," *Cultural and Social History* 9 (2015): 9–26.

6 Musicologist Blake Wilson's extensive work on orality and music in Renaissance Italy has culminated in the recent publication of his book *Singing to the Lyre in Renaissance Italy: Memory, Performance, and Oral Poetry* (Cambridge: Cambridge University Press, 2019), which reconstructs the musical activities and cultural world of Italy's *canterini* from the thirteenth to the sixteenth century. While Wilson's study was published after the first version of this book's manuscript was complete, my subsequent revisions have provided an opportunity to incorporate some of Wilson's new findings. Other extremely important contributions by musicologists include James Haar, *Essays on Italian Poetry and Music in the Renaissance, 1350–1600* (Berkeley: University of California Press, 1986); Timothy J. McGee, *The Ceremonial Musicians of Late Medieval Florence* (Bloomington: Indiana University Press, 2009); and Philippe Canguilhem, "Improvisation as Concept and Musical Practice in the Fifteenth Century," in Busse Berger and Rodin, *Cambridge History of Fifteenth-Century Music*, 149–63.

7 "Audivi ego quondam Antonium, in vico Martini, bella Orlandi canentem tanta eloquentia ut Petrarcham audire viderer, ut agi, non referri, bella putares. Legi post carmina eius, inculta ut alia crederes." Latin text from Armando F. Verde and Raffaella Maria Zaccaria, *Lo studio fiorentino, 1473–1503: Ricerche e documenti* (Florence: L.S. Olschki, 1973), 3:689.

8 See Paola Ventrone, *Gli araldi della commedia: Teatro a Firenze nel Rinascimento* (Pisa: Pacine, 1993), 108–14. Paul Zumthor has written extensively on the textual mobility ("mouvance") that characterizes many forms of oral poetry, whereby different instantiations of a poetic work reflect an ongoing interaction between written culture and orality at each stage of transmission. See Paul Zumthor, *Oral Poetry: An Introduction*, trans. Kathryn Murphy-Judy (Minneapolis: University of Minnesota Press, 1990).

9 Luca Degl'Innocenti discusses this episode in Luca Degl'Innocenti, "Paladini e canterini: Appunti sull'oralità nella tradizione cavalleresca italiana del Quattrocento e Cinquecento," in *Carlo Magno in Italia e la fortuna dei libri di cavalleria*, ed. Johannes Bartuschat and Franca Strologo (Ravenna: Longo Editore, 2016), 307.

10 See Luca Degl'Innocenti, "Verba manent: Precisazioni e supplementi d'indagine sulla trascrizione dell'oralità nei cantari dell'Altissimo," *Rassegna europea di letteratura italiana* 39 (2012): 109–34.

11 Brian Richardson, *Manuscript Culture in Renaissance Italy* (Cambridge: Cambridge University Press, 2009), 256.

12 See Thomas Christensen, "The Improvisatory Moment," in *Studies in Historical Improvisation: From Cantare Super Librum to Partimenti*, ed. Massimiliano Guido (New York: Routledge, 2017), 9–24. On composition in performance as practiced by the oral bards of the former Yugoslavia, see Albert Bates Lord, *The Singer of Tales*, edited by Stephen A. Mitchell and Gregory Nagy (Cambridge, MA: Harvard University Press, 2000).

13 Wilson, *Singing to the Lyre*, 6.

14 "Feci abito alquanto nel celebrato suono de la predicta lira e, asuefacta la lingua al poetico materno stile, mi trovai più volte, certando, esser vincitore e, coronato per prezio de Victoria de laureati serti, como concedea lo academico costume, mi condussi a più alte palestre. E accadendo con alcuni, io per via de diporto, alternando cantar versi impremeditati, datosi l'uno a l'altro la materia diversa." Italian text from Niccolò da Correggio, *Opere*, edited by Antonia Tissoni Benvenuti (Bari: Laterza, 1969), 4.

15 "Non multos ante hos dies a Leone X iussus cum Marone certare in Medicorum Cosmiana sollemnitate victus cessit … Andreas Maro … in Cosmiano Leonis X convivio ceteros qui multi aderant poetas proposita materia quam referrent ex tempore obmutescere quasi elingues fecerit, inter quos lippus." L.G. Giraldi, *Modern Poets*, trans. J.N. Grant (Cambridge, MA: Harvard University Press, 2011), 80–3. Cited in Anthony M. Cummings, "Informal Academies and Music in Pope Leo X's Rome," *Italica* 86, no. 4 (2009): 597.

16 "Perché i suggetti non paressero pensati, aprivano a sorte libri d'antiche poesie, sì come sono le Trasformationi d'Ovidio; & secondo il suggetto venuto a caso, così eglino cantavano all'improviso." Italian text from Antonio Corsaro, "Intorno a un'ottava (ignorata) forse di Niccolò Machiavelli," *Interpres* 28 (2009): 272. See also Giuseppe Crimi, "Il presto legittimato: La poesia all'improvviso," in *Festina lente: Il tempo della scrittura nella letteratura del Cinquecento*, ed. Chiara Cassiani and Maria Cristina Figorilli (Rome: Edizioni di storia e letteratura, 2014), 215.

17 "Avvenne un giorno fra gli altri, che volendo udire Nicolò Machiavelli, uno de' detti gentil'huomini, gli venne per sorte aperto il libro nella favola di Venere, & di Marte: & havendo egli brevemente raccontato ne' primi sei versi, come

Vulcano accortosi dell'adulterio della moglie, & volendo ciò vendicare, fabricasse la sottilissima rete di ferro, per pigliare con essa amendue gli amanti, mentre prendevano insieme amoroso diletto; conchiuse in quella guisa, dicendo:

> Stese la rete, pigliando a quel gitto
> Venere ignuda.

Et fermatosi qui, continuando però tuttavia di sonar la lira, quasi che pensasse a ritrovare il rimanente del verso, che mancava; una di quelle gentildonne a lui più domestica, gli prese a dire; finite tosto, M. Nicolò, perché pensandoci voi tanto, non sarà poi d'improviso. Onde subito Niccolò, senza più indugiare, ripigliando da capo la chiusa della stanza, disse:

> Vulcano tirò la rete, & prese a gitto
> Venere ignuda, et Marte a … ritto.

O nella malhora, dissero quelle gentildonne, fatte rosse per la vergogna, che è quello, che voi dite, M. Nicolò? Alle quale egli rispose; questa Madonna m'ha con le sue parole tanto solecitato, che io non ho considerato quello, che poco honestamente m'è uscito di bocca."

Italian text from Corsaro, "Intorno a un'ottava (ignorata) forse di Niccolò Machiavelli," 273. On Machiavelli as improvisor see also Richardson, *Manuscript Culture in Renaissance Italy*, 252–3; and Luca Degl'Innocenti, "Machiavelli canterino?," *Nuova rivista di letteratura italiana* 18, no. 1 (2015): 11–67.

18 On the social world of the itinerant street singers of Renaissance Italy, see Salzberg and Rospocher, "Street Singers in Italian Renaissance Urban Culture and Communication."

19 For a recent collection of studies on traditions of sung performance of *ottava rima* poetry in different historical periods, see Maurizio Agamennone, ed., *Cantar ottave: Per una storia culturale dell'intonazione cantata in ottava rima* (Lucca: Libreria musicale italiana, 2017).

20 Luca Degl'Innocenti's work on Cristoforo Fiorentino l'Altissimo has revealed numerous examples of intertextual connections between the poet's chivalric poems and his lyric *strambotti*, suggesting that the poet deployed the same improvisational techniques across both genres. See Degl'Innocenti, *I Reali dell'Altissimo*, 39. On the *cantari*, see Michelangelo Picone and Maria Bendinelli Predelli, eds., *I cantari: Struttura e tradizione; Atti del convegno internazionale di Montreal: 19–20 marzo 1981* (Florence: Leo S. Olschki, 1984); Michelangelo Picone and Luisa Rubini, eds., *Il cantare italiano fra folklore e letteratura: Atti del Convegno internazionale di Zurigo (Landesmuseum, 23–25 giugno 2005)* (Florence: Olschki, 2007); and Maria Cristina Cabani, *Le forme del cantare epico-cavalleresco* (Lucca: Maria Pacini Fazzi Editore, 1988).

21 Blake Wilson, "The Cantastorie/Canterino/Cantimbanco as Musician," *Italian Studies* 71 (2016): 157–8. See also Timothy J. McGee, "Cantare

all'improvviso: Improvising to Poetry in Late Medieval Italy," in *Improvisation in the Arts of the Middle Ages and Renaissance*, ed. Timothy J. McGee (Kalamazoo: Medieval Institute Publications, Western Michigan University, 2003), 31–70.

22 On the lira da braccio and its predecessors, see McGee, *Ceremonial Musicians of Late Medieval Florence*, 81–3.

23 Wilson, "The Cantastorie/Canterino/Cantimbanco as Musician," 159–60.

24   "Vedevasi poi l'Unico Aretino,
         un nuovo Orfeo, dir colla cetra in collo
         all'improvviso, in stil tanto divino
         che invidia gli ebbe non pochi anni Apollo."
    Italian text from Francesco Gavagni, *L'Unico Aretino (Bernardo Accolti) e la corte dei duchi d'Urbino* (Arezzo: Cagliani, 1906), 6.

25 See Chriscinda Henry, "*Alter Orpheus*: Masks of Virtuosity in Renaissance Portraits of Musical Improvisers," *Italian Studies* 71, no. 2 (2016): 238–58.

26 Giuseppe Scavizzi, "The Myth of Orpheus in Italian Renaissance Art, 1400–1600," in *Orpheus, the Metamorphoses of a Myth*, ed. John Warden (Toronto: University of Toronto Press, 1982), 123–4.

27 Jerzy Miziolek, "*Orpheus and Eurydice*: Three *Spalliera* Panels by Jacopo Del Sellaio," *I Tatti Studies in the Italian Renaissance* 12 (2009): 143.

28 D.P. Walker, *Spiritual and Demonic Magic: From Ficino to Campanella* (Notre Dame, IN: University of Notre Dame Press, 1975), 3–29.

29 See Luca Degl'Innocenti, "Il poeta, la viola e l'incanto: Per l'iconografia del canterino nel primo Cinquecento," *Paragone* 62, no. 93–5 (2011): 148.

30 Lodovico Frati, ed., *Rimatori bolognesi del Quattrocento* (Bologna: Romagnoli dall'Acqua, 1908), 281.

31   "Unde tra i docti par che non se stima
         Materia dicta in versi a l' improvista."
    Frati, *Rimatori bolognesi del Quattrocento*, 324.

32   "Ma l' improviso dir talvolta impetra
         Più gratia assai ch' un ben stillato inchiostro."
    Frati, *Rimatori bolognesi del Quattrocento*, 325.

33   "L'amante Orpheo col canto e cum la cetra
         Già il furor tolse a ogni tartareo mostro."
    Frati, *Rimatori bolognesi del Quattrocento*, 325.

34   "Questo è quel' Aretin Bernardo Accolti,
         Ch' in voce e cum la penna ognun confonde,
         Cum non pensate rime a lui tal vena
         Che Phebo se ne ammira e ogni Camena."
    Frati, *Rimatori bolognesi del Quattrocento*, 326.

35   "Quel onorato divo e excelso lauro,
         Gloria de l'Arno anzi d' Etruria tutta …

> Cum una eburnea lira e un plectro d' auro
> Sua musa in cotal stil spesso hebbe indutta."

Frati, *Rimatori bolognesi del Quattrocento*, 325–6.

36   "Et oltra ancor questo è firmo argumento
> Quando il furor d' Apol presto lavora."

Frati, *Rimatori bolognesi del Quattrocento*, 326.

1 The Uses of Oral Poetry in Quattrocento Florence

1 On Antonio di Guido, see Wilson, *Singing to the Lyre*, 123–42.

2 "Dopo el disnare [...] reductome in una camera con tutta la compagnia ò 'ldito cantare con la citara uno maestro Antonio, che credo che V. Exc.tia debba, se non cognoscere, almanco havere oldito nominare, quale, princip-iato da le prime cose, che V. E. fece, et venuto non solo al fine di quelli ... ma poi, disceso in commendatione mia, narrò ogni cosa con tanta dignità et modo, che 'l magiore poeta né oratore che sia al mundo, se l'avesse avuto a fare tale acto, forse non ne saria uscito con tanta commendatione da ogni canto del dire suo, che in vero fu tale che fece signare de maraviglia et max-ime quilli che più docti sono, vedendo loro, ultra arte comparatione che 'l fece, de quale non so se Lucano né Dante ne facessero mai alcuna più bella, miscolare tante historie antiche, nome de romani vechi innumerabili, fabule, poeti et il nome de tutte quante le muse." Italian text from Paolo Orvieto, *Pulci medievale: Studio sulla poesia volgare fiorentina del Quattrocento* (Rome: Salerno, 1978), 181. On this performance, see also Wilson, *Singing to the Lyre*, 124–7.

3 See Bianca Becherini, "Un canta in panca fiorentino, Antonio di Guido," *Rivista musicale italiana* 50 (1948): 241–7.

4 Dale Kent, *Cosimo De' Medici and the Florentine Renaissance: The Patron's Oeuvre* (New Haven, CT: Yale University Press, 2000), 53.

5   "Ad Fabianum, de Antonio tusco extemporali poeta.
> Tuscus ab othrysio, Fabiane, Antonius Orpheo
> Hoc differt: homines hic trahit, ille feras."

Latin text from Angelo Poliziano, *Prose volgari inedite e poesie latine e greche edite e inedite*, ed. Isidoro Del Lungo (Florence: Barbera, 1867), 121. Cited in Marco Villoresi, "Panoramica sui poeti performativi d'età laurenziana," *Rassegna europea di letteratura italiana* 34 (2009): 21.

6 This is documented by Ficino in a letter, where he refers to an oration that Giuliano had delivered to this *compagnia di notte*, an exhortation to penitence that had a powerful impact on the listeners, and especially on Antonio di Guido: "That moral discourse you gave some time ago at an evening gathering brought your friends to tears and repentance for their sins; some cried out, whilst others struck their chests with their hands. It is

said that Antonio, the Tuscan poet, went pale and fell, as if struck dead."
Marsilio Ficino, *The Letters of Marsilio Ficino: Translated from the Latin by Members of the Language Department of the School of Economic Science, London,* 10 vols. (London: Shepheard-Walwyn, 1975), 1:118. Antonio's integration into Medicean circles was ultimately cemented when Lorenzo's own oral poetic pursuits led him to seek out Antonio's poetic and performative collaboration, as we will see in chapter 4.

7 In an important study focusing on the activities of Venetian *canterini,* Massimo Rospocher and Rosa Salzberg have argued that these street singers exerted a significant political function. See Massimo Rospocher and Rosa Salzberg, "An Evanescent Public Sphere: Voices, Spaces, and Publics in Venice During the Italian Wars," in *Beyond the Public Sphere: Opinions, Publics, Spaces in Early Modern Europe,* ed. Massimo Rospocher (Bologna: Il Mulino, 2012), 93–114.

8 One notable exception is the work of Dale Kent and in particular *Cosimo De' Medici and the Florentine Renaissance.*

9 See Kent, *Cosimo De' Medici and the Florentine Renaissance,* 20.

10 Kent, *Cosimo De' Medici and the Florentine Renaissance,* 53–4.

11   "Fia prima arato e seminato il mare
                e per montagne e per la piana terra
                e pesci si vedranno a passi andare

                prima ch'io scioglier possa chi mi serra:
                quest'è d'atar la tua gentil figura,
                la qual dà a Lombardia o pace o guerra.

                E prima muterà il corso suo natura …
                prima ch'io possi mai lasciar d'atarti
                o ch'io prometta mai d'atare altrui.

                Le tenebre saran per tutte parti
                chiare di luce, e sarà scuro il sole
                e spenti fian e l'ingegni e l'arti …
                e a rovescio andrà prima ogni cosa
                che io non ami continovo e sempre

                Francesco Sforza sopra ogni altra cosa."
       Italian text from *Lirici toscani del Quattrocento,* vol. 2, ed. Antonio Lanza (Rome: Bulzoni, 1975), 55–6.

12 "la mia 'ntenzione, assai chiaro si vede / Ch' i' 'l vo' remunerar di tanta fede." Text from Francesco Flamini, *La lirica toscana del Rinascimento anteriore ai tempi del Magnifico* (Pisa: P. Nistri, 1891), 232.

13 "m'allunga il viver che sarebbe corto." Text from Flamini, *La lirica toscana del Rinascimento,* 232.

14 Suzanne Branciforte, "Ars Poetica Rei Publicae: The Herald of the Florentine Signoria" (PhD diss., University of California, Los Angeles, 1990), 149.

15 *Lirici toscani del Quattrocento*, 2:111.

16 See Timothy J. McGee, "Dinner Music for the Florentine Signoria, 1350–1450," *Speculum* 74, no. 1 (1999): 95–114; McGee, *Ceremonial Musicians of Late Medieval Florence*, Branciforte, "Ars Poetica Rei Publicae"; and Flamini, *La lirica toscana del Rinascimento.*

17 "ad recitandum coram dominis Prioribus et Vexillifero ad mensam et prout est consuetum cantilenas morales et similia." Latin text from Branciforte, "Ars Poetica Rei Publicae," 18. The translation is from McGee, "Dinner Music for the Florentine Signoria," 97.

18 "[*Araldi*] had to be able to perform and sing compositions that had either been previously prepared or were 'improvised,' demonstrating perfect technical mastery of the use of the voice." Paola Ventrone, "'Civic Performance' in Renaissance Florence," in Dall'Aglio, Richardson, and Rospocher, *Voices and Texts in Early Modern Italian Society*, 156. See also McGee, *Ceremonial Musicians of Late Medieval Florence*, 90.

19 Kent, *Cosimo De' Medici and the Florentine Renaissance*, 49. Blake Wilson observes that specific cases of individual performers moving between these two performance contexts have yet to be clearly documented in the existing literature, while arguing that some repertoire, at least, was likely shared between these spaces; see Wilson, *Singing to the Lyre*, 152.

20 Among Antonio's works praising Sforza are a *capitolo*, "Viva viva oramai viva l'onore," that Antonio probably performed in his presence when Sforza visited Florence in 1435 (Branciforte, "Ars Poetica Rei Publicae," 143); a *canzone*, "Il gran famoso Publio Scipione," which according to a manuscript rubric was performed on 12 April 1437 (Flamini, *La lirica toscana del Rinascimento*, 235); and two sonnets, "O Conte illustre, l'avere e la vita" and "Vittrice illustre Conte e gran signore," performed for Sforza by Antonio's son Giovan Matteo, which appear in *Lirici toscani del Quattrocento*, 2:139–40; see Flamini, *La lirica toscana del Rinascimento*, 235.

21 The text of the poem quoted here is from *Lirici toscani del Quattrocento*, vol. 1, ed. Antonio Lanza (Rome: Bulzoni, 1973), 346–8. Fighting with Piccinino in the conflict were the Florentine exiles led by Rinaldo degli Albizzi, bitter enemies of the Medici. Piccinino and the Albizzi exiles were defeated in 1440 at the Battle of Anghiari, where the Florentine forces were directed by Neri Capponi and Bernardo de' Medici, Cosimo's distant cousin; see Branciforte, "Ars Poetica Rei Publicae," 193–4; and John Najemy, *A History of Florence, 1200–1575* (Oxford: Blackwell, 2008), 289. Calderoni's poem praises Bernardo de' Medici for carrying the Florentine standard in the battle.

22 Dale Kent, "Michele del Giogante's House of Memory," in *Society and Individual in Renaissance Florence*, ed. William J. Connell (Berkeley: University of California Press, 1973), 115.

23 Blake Wilson, "Sound Patrons: The Medici and Florentine Musical Life," in *The Medici: Citizens and Masters*, ed. Robert Black and John Law (Cambridge, MA: Harvard University Press, 2015), 273.

24 On Michele del Giogante and Niccolò Cieco, see Wilson, *Singing to the Lyre*, 102–23.

25 "Dii boni, quam audientiam Nicolaus coecus habebat, cum festis diebus, etruscis numeris, aut sacras historias aut annales rerum antiquarum e suggestu decantabat! Qui doctorum hominum, qui Florentiae permulti tunc erant, concursus ad eum fiebat!" Latin text from Ezio Levi, "I cantari leggendari del popolo italiano nei secoli XIV e XV," *Giornale storico della letteratura italiana* suppl. 16 (1914): 3.

26   "Quel che 'l mal fato a sua natura tolse,
                        virtù visiva et extrinseca luce,
                        ristrecta all' intellecto suo riluce,
                        ché tutta insieme con lui si racholse.

                        Non cecho adunque, come 'l fato volse;
                        ma sí gran lume il suo ingegno produce,
                        ch' a molti fu col suo poema duce."

Italian text from Flamini, *La lirica toscana del Rinascimento*, 191–2.

27 "Cicierone in artis oratorie ... nuovo Tito Livio ad alt'istorie." Italian text from Flamini, *La lirica toscana del Rinascimento*, 186.

28 *Lirici toscani del Quattrocento*, 2:189.

29 *Lirici toscani del Quattrocento*, 2:95.

30 Flamini, *La lirica toscana del Rinascimento*, 185–6.

31 "Simone di Grazia ... quel fanciullo, che io già missi in San Martino in panca a cantare inproviso, di buono ingiegno et fantasia, proprio da natura dotato a quella fachultà." Italian text from Flamini, *La lirica toscana del Rinascimento*, 600. Part of this letter has been translated by Dale Kent in *Cosimo De' Medici and the Florentine Renaissance*, 48.

32 See Flamini, *La lirica toscana del Rinascimento*, 161; and Kent, *Cosimo De' Medici and the Florentine Renaissance*, 53.

33 "un fanciullo ch'aveva una gientil pronunzia." Flamini, *La lirica toscana del Rinascimento*, 162.

34 "ché sai sognando di servirti bramo." *Lirici toscani del Quattrocento*, 1:672. See Kent, *Cosimo De' Medici and the Florentine Renaissance*, 73.

35 "da doversi per senpre tener scolpita nel core." Flamini, *La lirica toscana del Rinascimento*, 136.

36 "Magnifica Madonna mia, Io vi rimando per Tommaso quelle vostre laude e sonetti e ternarii che mi prestasti quando fui costà. Presonne quelle donne un piacere estremo; e madonna Lucrezia, o vero Lucrezia, aveva apparato a mente tutta la Lucrezia." Italian text from Poliziano, *Prose volgari inedite*, 72.

37 "Rimangomi solo, e quando sono restucco dello studio, mi do a razolare tra
   morìe e guerre, e dolore del passato e paura dell'avvenire; nè ho con chi
   crivellare queste mie fantasie. Non truovo qui la mia madonna Lucrezia in
   camera, colla quale io possi sfogarmi; e muoio di tedio." Italian text from
   Poliziano, *Prose volgari inedite*, 68.

38 "Ebbe questa nobilissima Dama particolare inclinazione alla Volgar Poesia;
   e tanto innanzi vi si portò con la felicità del suo ingegno, che certamente
   si lasciò indietro la più parte de' Poeti del suo tempo, per non dir tutti."
   Italian text from Giovanni Mario Crescimbeni, *L'istoria della volgar poesia*
   (Venice: Basegio, 1731), 3:277.

39 The most important twentieth-century editions and studies of Lucrezia's
   poetry are Fulvio Pezzarossa, *I poemetti sacri di Lucrezia Tornabuoni* (Florence:
   L.S. Olschki, 1978); Lucrezia Tornabuoni, *La istoria della casta Susanna*, ed.
   Paolo Orvieto (Bergamo: Moretti and Vitali, 1992); and Mario Martelli,
   "Lucrezia Tornabuoni," in *Les femmes écrivains en Italie au Moyen Âge et à la
   Renaissance* (Aix-en-Provence: Université de Provence, 1994), 51–86.

40 Lucrezia Tornabuoni de' Medici, *Sacred Narratives*, ed. and trans. Jane Tylus
   (Chicago: University of Chicago Press, 2001).

41 See Luca Mazzoni, "Lucrezia Tornabuoni fra Lorenzo, Poliziano e Pulci," in
   Memoria poetica: Questioni filologiche e problemi di metodo, ed. Giuseppe Alvino,
   Marco Berisso, and Irene Falini (Genoa: Genova University Press, 2019),
   121–32.

42 Tornabuoni de' Medici, *Sacred Narratives*, 40–3.

43 Pezzarossa, *I poemetti sacri di Lucrezia Tornabuoni*, 83.

44 Tylus notes that a similar address is found in Cicerchia's *cantare The
   Resurrection*. Tornabuoni de' Medici, *Sacred Narratives*, 42.

45 "per aver la corona, i' l'ho sentito, / e massime improvviso, in dir polito."
   Villoresi, "Panoramica sui poeti performativi d'età laurenziana," 24.

46 A letter by Francesco Cranchidino of 1485 remarks that Bellincioni "ha
   adoperata la sua viola et armonie che avessero potuto fare Lino, Orpheo,
   Amphion, Daphnis el Patareo Apollo." See Villoresi, "Panoramica sui poeti
   performativi d'età laurenziana," 24.

47 Pezzarossa, *I poemetti sacri di Lucrezia Tornabuoni*, 40.

48 Felicità Giulia Mondino, *Lucrezia Tornabuoni* (Turin: Tipografia Eredi Botta,
   1900), 42–3.

49   "E nel principio sonar la ribeca
                     mi dilettai, perch'avea fantasia
                     cantar di Troia e d'Ettore e d'Achille,
                     non una volta già, ma mille e mille."
   Luigi Pulci, *Morgante* 18.118. Italian text from Luigi Pulci, *Morgante
   e lettere*, ed. Domenico De Robertis (Florence: Sansoni, 1962), 448–9;
   translation from Luigi Pulci, *Morgante: The Epic Adventures of Orlando and*

His Giant Friend Morgante, trans. Joseph Tusiani (Bloomington: Indiana University Press, 1998), 365.

50 Orvieto, *Pulci medievale*, 176–86.

51 Villoresi, "Panoramica sui poeti performativi d'età laurenziana," 15.

52 Luigi Pulci, *Morgante* 28.144. Italian text from Pulci, *Morgante e lettere*, 916–17. Translation from Pulci, *Morgante: The Epic Adventures of Orlando and His Giant Friend Morgante*, 759.

53 Pezzarossa, *I poemetti sacri di Lucrezia Tornabuoni*, 40–3.

54 On this text, see Gerry Milligan, "Unlikely Heroines in Lucrezia Tornabuoni's 'Judith' and 'Esther,'" *Italica* 88, no. 4 (2011): 538–64.

55 Pulci describes the *padiglione* of Luciana in *Morgante* 14.43–86. See Tornabuoni, *La istoria della casta Susanna*, 25.

56 Orvieto, *Pulci medievale*, 154–70.

57 "in burla come la *Nencia* di Lorenzo de' Medici e la *Beca* di Luigi Pulci." Italian text from Lorenzo de' Medici, *Tutte le opere*, ed. Paolo Orvieto (Rome: Salerno, 1992), 676.

58 The most forceful advocate for Lorenzo's role as original author of the text has been Mario Fubini, who has argued that the original text is the version known as redaction A (preserved in a manuscript in Lorenzo's own handwriting); see Mario Fubini, "I tre testi della 'Nencia da Barberino' e la questione della paternità del poemetto," in *Studi sulla letteratura del Rinascimento* (Florence: La nuova Italia, 1971), 62–125. Fubini's intervention was intended to counter a series of articles by Federico Patetta, which sought to deny Lorenzo's authorship of the text. See Arnaldo Di Benedetto, "Federico Patetta e la 'Nencia da Barberino,'" *Critica letteraria* 178 (2018): 3–8. Fubini's work did not end the debate, however, which was repeatedly reignited by new textual discoveries.

59 "La *Nencia* rientra o, almeno, ha tutti gli attributi per rientrare in questo tipo di produzione del canto 'all' improvviso.'" Medici, *Tutte le opere*, 681.

60 "Con ogni probabilità al canto (perché in effetti sono ottave recitate e cantate prima che scritte) delle ottave nenciali si alternavano indistintamente tanto Lorenzo, quanto Pulci e Poliziano (e, perché no, anche Alessandro Braccesi, del quale si conoscono due sonetti dedicati alla Nencia)." Medici, *Tutte le opere*, 682.

61 Mario Fubini's arguments in favour of Lorenzo's primary role in the composition of the work have proven convincing. See Mario Fubini, *Studi sulla letteratura italiana del Rinascimento* (Florence: Sansoni, 1947), 119–21.

62 "E cosí passa, o compar, lieto il tempo,
    e con mille rime a zucchero e a tempo."
    Text from Medici, *Tutte le opere*, 670. Translation from Lorenzo de' Medici, *Selected Poems and Prose*, ed. and trans. Jon Thiem (University Park: Pennsylvania State University Press, 1991), 41.

63 Paolo Orvieto, "Angelo Poliziano 'compare' della brigata laurenziana," *Lettere Italiane* 25, no. 3 (1973): 303.

64 See Orvieto, "Angelo Poliziano 'compare' della brigata laurenziana." Orvieto's intuition may well be correct – certainly Poliziano was an active participant, together with Lorenzo, in performances of poetry to music – but many scholars regard the identity of this mysterious "compare" as still an open question.

65 Lorenzo de Medici, *Opere*, ed. Tiziano Zanato (Turin: G. Einaudi, 1992), 230. Zanato asserts that there are only limited connections between Lorenzo's poem and the musical-poetic genre of the "caccia" that flourished in the fourteenth century; one connection that Zanato does note is the frequency, in these texts, of short interjections, epanalepsis, and onomatopoeia. Such effects serve to enhance the text's impact as a simulation or re-creation of orality. For a study of related phenomena of orality within fifteenth- and sixteenth-century *novelle*, see Enrico Testa, *Simulazione di parlato: Fenomeni dell'oralità nelle novelle del Quattro-Cinquecento* (Florence: Accademia della Crusca, 1991).

66 "eserciti la bocca equal che 'l culo." Italian text from *Lirici toscani del Quattrocento*, 1:324.

67 See Michelangelo Zaccarello, "The *Tenzone* Between Matteo Franco and Luigi Pulci in the Context of Renaissance *Vituperium*: Notes on Language and Intertextuality," in *Luigi Pulci in Renaissance Florence and Beyond*, ed. James K. Coleman and Andrea Moudarres (Turnhout: Brepols, 2017), 51–72.

68 Numbers 12, 73, 74, and 310 in Angelo Poliziano, *Detti piacevoli*, ed. Tiziano Zanato (Rome: Istituto della Enciclopedia Italiana, 1983).

69 See Claudia Tripodi, "Guglielmo de' Pazzi," in *Dizionario Biografico degli Italiani*, vol. 82 (Rome: Istituto della Enciclopedia Italiana, 2015).

70   "Luigi Pulci anco rimaso fia:
            e' se n'andò là oggi in un boschetto,
            ch' aveva il capo pien di fantasia:
            vorrà fantasticar qualche sonetto;
            guarti, Corona, per la fede mia,
            che borbottòe staman molto nel letto,
            e' ricordava ogni volta il Corona,
            e l'ha a cacciar in frottola o in canzona."
   Italian text from Medici, *Tutte le opere*, 669.

71   "Non prese mai il Corona uno starnone,
            se per disgrazia non l'ha preso o a caso;
            e più sparvier' ha morti già meschini
            ch'Orlando non uccise Saracini."
   Italian text from Medici, *Tutte le opere*, 668.

72   "Poi, fatto cerchio a uno infrescatoio,
            truovansi tutti co' bicchieri a galla.
            Quivi si fa un altro uccellatoio,
            quivi si dice un gru d'ogni farfalla …
            chi d'una cosa e chi d'altra favella;
            ciascuno al suo sparvier dava l'onore,
            cercando d'una scusa pronta e bella;
            e chi molto non fe' col suo sparviere,
            si sfoga or qui col ragionare e 'l bere."
       Italian text from Medici, *Tutte le opere*, 669.

73 See Ingeborg Walter, *Lorenzo il Magnifico e il suo tempo*, trans. Roberto
    Zapperi (Rome: Donzelli Editore, 2005), 65; and John Considine, *Small
    Dictionaries and Curiosity: Lexicography and Fieldwork in Post-Medieval Europe*
    (Oxford: Oxford University Press, 2017), 43–4.

74 Italian text from Luigi Pulci, *Lettere di Luigi Pulci a Lorenzo il Magnifico e ad
    altri* (Lucca: Giusti, 1886), 58.

75 This example and others are discussed in Guglielmo Gorni, "Su Lorenzo
    poeta: Parodia, diletti e noie della caccia," in *Lorenzo il Magnifico e il suo
    mondo: Convegno internazionale di studi (Firenze, 9–13 giugno 1992)*, ed. Gian
    C. Garfagnini (Florence: L.S. Olschki, 1994), 221.

76 Italian text from Lorenzo de' Medici, *Opere*, ed. Attilio Simioni (Bari:
    Laterza, 1913), 4.

77 "Essendo la sacra opera di questo celebratissimo poeta dopo la sua morte
    per molti e vari luoghi della Grecia dissipata e quasi dimembrata, Pisistrato,
    ateniese principe, uomo per molte virtú e d'animo e di corpo prestantis-
    simo, proposti amplissimi premi a chi alcuni de' versi omerici gli apportassi,
    con somma diligenzia ed esamine tutto il corpo del santissimo poeta
    insieme raccolse." Italian text from Medici, *Opere* (1913), 4.

78 Wilson, "Dominion of the Ear," 286.

2 "Inspired and Possessed": Marsilio Ficino and Oral Poetry

 1 "Vale et veni non absque Orphica lyra." Latin text from Marsilio Ficino,
    Lettere, vol. 1, ed. Sebastiano Gentile (Florence: Olschki, 1990), 6; trans-
    lation from Ficino, *Letters of Marsilio Ficino*, 1:32. Since the letter was pub-
    lished by Ficino, the extent to which the text accurately reflects whatever
    Cosimo actually wrote to Ficino on this occasion is unknown. See James
    Hankins, *Plato in the Italian Renaissance* (Leiden: Brill, 1990), 268.

 2 See Michael J.B. Allen, "Summoning Plotinus: Ficino, Smoke and the
    Strangled Chickens," in *Reconsidering the Renaissance: Papers from the Twenty-First
    Annual Conference Medieval & Renaissance Texts & Studies*, ed. Mario A. Di
    Cesare (Binghamton, NY: Medieval & Renaissance Texts & Studies, 1992), 86.

3 The early impact of the renewed circulation of the *Orphic Hymns* on vernacular poetry in Italy has been studied by Stefano Carrai; see "Appunti sulla prima fortuna volgare degli *Inni orfici*," in *Dotti bizantini e libri greci nell'Italia del secolo XV: Atti del convegno internazionale, Trento 22–23 ottobre 1990*, ed. Mariarosa Cortesi and Enrico V. Maltese (Naples: M. D'Auria, 1992), 193–200.

4 See D.P. Walker, "Orpheus the Theologian and Renaissance Platonists," *Journal of the Warburg and Courtauld Institutes* 16 (1953): 100–20; D.P. Walker, *The Ancient Theology: Studies in Christian Platonism from the Fifteenth to the Eighteenth Century* (London: Duckworth, 1972); Walker, *Spiritual and Demonic Magic: From Ficino to Campanella*; and Angela Voss, "Orpheus redivivus: The Musical Magic of Marsilio Ficino," in *Marsilio Ficino: His Theology, His Philosophy, His Legacy*, ed. Michael J.B. Allen, Valery Rees, and Martin Davies (Leiden: Brill, 2002), 227–41.

5 Fabio Falugiani, "Un codice ficiniano nella tradizione manoscritta delle Argonautiche Orfiche," *Giornale italiano di filologia* 47 (1995): 158.

6 Vatican Library MS Vat. Lat. 3251 contains a marginal note by Filelfo with a Latin translation of vv. 806–8 of the *Orphic Argonautica*. Filelfo's translation of the first four verses of the *Orphic Argonautica* also survives. See Falugiani, "Un codice ficiniano," 171–2.

7 See N.G. Wilson, *From Byzantium to Italy: Greek Studies in the Italian Renaissance* (London: Bloomsbury Academic, 2017), 136–8.

8 See Francis Vian, "Leodrisio Crivelli traducteur des Argonautiques orphiques," *Revue d'histoire des textes* 16, no. 1986 (1988): 63–82, and Falugiani, "Un codice ficiniano," 169. Only six verses of Ficino's translation survive, preserved in Florence's Biblioteca Riccardiana MS Ricc. 62.

9 "Argonautica et hymnos Orphei, et Homeri et Proculi, Theologiamque Hesiodi, quae adolescens, nescio quomodo, ad uerbum mihi soli transtuli, quemadmodum tu nuper hospes apud me uidisti, edere nunquam placuit, ne forte lectores ad priscum deorum daemonumque cultum iamdiu merito reprobatum, reuocare uiderer." Latin text from Marsilio Ficino, *Opera omnia* (Basel, Switzerland: Henricus Petrus, 1576), 933; translation from Ficino, *Letters of Marsilio Ficino*, 10:27.

10 The remark appears in Ficino's epitome to Plato's *Second Alcibiades*, in Ficino, *Opera omnia*, 1134. See Paul Oskar Kristeller, "Marsilio Ficino as a Beginning Student of Plato," *Scriptorium* 20, no. 1 (1966): 41–54.

11 "Hoc enim saeculum tamquam aureum liberales disciplinas ferme iam exstinctas reduxit in lucem, grammaticam, poesim, oratoriam, picturam, sculpturam, architecturam, musicam, antiquum ad Orphicam lyram carminum cantum. Idque Florentiae." Latin text from Ficino, *Opera omnia*, 944. English translation from Ficino, *Letters of Marsilio Ficino*, 10:51.

12 Text and translation from James Hankins, "Cosimo De' Medici and the 'Platonic Academy,'" *Journal of the Warburg and Courtauld Institutes* 53 (1990): 149, 159.

13　See Walker, *Ancient Theology*.

14　The manuscript in question is now held at Florence's Biblioteca Laurenziana, as MS Laur. LXXXV, 9. See Hankins, "Cosimo De' Medici and the 'Platonic Academy,'" 157.

15　Along with the *Orphic Hymns*, the other translations from Greek that Ficino is known to have carried out prior to 1462 are the *Argonautica* attributed to Orpheus, the hymns of Zoroaster, the Homeric and Hesiodic Hymns, Hesiod's *Theogony*, and the hymns of Proclus. These are all poems originally conceived for oral performance, and Ficino's early interest in these Greek poems is linked to his desire to revive what he took to be ancient practices of performing poetry to the accompaniment of music. Sebastiano Gentile, "Sulle prime traduzioni dal greco di Marsilio Ficino," *Rinascimento* 30 (1990): 72.

16　"Antiquum cytharae sonum et cantum et carmina Orphica oblivioni prius tradita luci restituisses." Ficino, *Opera omnia*, 871. See also John Warden, "Orpheus and Ficino," in *Orpheus, the Metamorphoses of a Myth*, ed. John Warden (Toronto: University of Toronto Press, 1982), 87.

17　　　　　　"Verum, ubi pulsa fames, vates consurgit Etruscus
　　　　　　Marsilius pulsatque lyram. Tum voce canora
　　　　　　Concordat versus, quales Rhodopeius Orpheus
　　　　　　Euridice amissa lachrymans apud impia frustra
　　　　　　Tartara deflevit cytharam mirantibus umbris:
　　　　　　Quis maris et terrae, caeli quis terminus extet,
　　　　　　Quae rerum causae, quis spiritus, unde creati
　　　　　　Quorsum homines celeresque animi, qui corpore functi
　　　　　　Quo volitent, caelumne petant Stygiamque paludem,
　　　　　　Lydius haec docto cantabat pectine vates" (15.282–91).
　　　Ugolino Verino, *Carlias: Ein Epos Des 15. Jahrhunderts* (Munich: Fink, 1995), 410–11. See James K. Coleman, "Boccaccio's Demogorgon and Renaissance Platonism," *Italian Studies* 74, no. 1 (2019): 2–6.

18　"Marsilius donec divina e sorte daretur induerat cuius membra pudica libens. Hinc rigidas cythara quercus et carmine mulcet atque feris iterum mollia corda facit." Latin text from Marsilio Ficino, *Supplementum ficinianum*, ed. Paul Oskar Kristeller (Florence: Olschki, 1973), 2:262]. See Warden, "Orpheus and Ficino," 86.

19　"Orpheus hic ego sum, movi qui carmine silvas." Latin text from Ficino, *Supplementum ficinianum*, 2:262. See Warden, "Orpheus and Ficino," 87.

20　"Orphea sed verum faciet te barbara vestis / Cum tibi sit cantus illius atque lyra." Latin text from Ficino, *Supplementum ficinianum*, 2:225. See Warden, "Orpheus and Ficino," 87.

21　　　　　　"Marsilii cithuram crispus si tentet Apollo,
　　　　　　Et dextra et cantu victus Apollo cadit.

Et furor est, cum cantat amans cantante puella
Ad flexum, ad nutum percutit ille lyram.
Tunc ardent oculi, tunc planta exsurgit utraque,
Et quos non didicit, comperit ille modos."
     Latin text from Arnaldo Della Torre, *Storia dell'Accademia Platonica di Firenze* (Florence: G. Carnesecchi, 1902), 791. The translation is from Voss, "Orpheus redivivus," 234.

22 See Allen, "Summoning Plotinus," 75.

23 *Phaedrus*, 245A. Translation from Plato, *Euthyphro, Apology, Crito, Phaedo, Phaedrus*, trans. H.N. Fowler (New York: G.P. Putnam's Sons, 1919), 469.

24 See Sebastiano Gentile, "In margine all'epistola 'De divino furore' di Marsilio Ficino," *Rinascimento* 23 (1983): 33–77. For an illuminating perspective on Bruni's and Ficino's approaches to translating Plato, focusing on their treatments of the homoerotic dimensions of the Platonic corpus, see Todd W. Reeser, *Setting Plato Straight: Translating Ancient Sexuality in the Renaissance* (Chicago: University of Chicago Press, 2016), chaps. 2–4.

25 "Non enim omne opus poema est, ne si versibus quidem constet: sed illud praestans, illud hac honorata nuncupatione dignum, quod afflatu quodam divino emittitur. Itaque quanto vaticinium conjectioni dignitate praestat, tanto poema, quod ex furore sit, sanorum hominum artificio est anteponendum … Poetae quoque tunc demum boni existunt, cum suo illo corripiuntur furore. Qua de causa vates eos nuncupamus, quasi furore quodam correptos. Qui vero absque furore Musarum poeticas ad fores, ut inquit Plato, accedit sperans quasi arte quadam poetam se bonum evasurum, inanis ipse, atque ejus poesis prae illa, quae ex furore est, haec, quae ex prudentia, disperditur." Latin text from Leonardo Bruni, *Epistolarum libri VIII*, ed. Lorenzo Mehus and James Hankins (Rome: Edizioni di storia e letteratura, 2007), 2:37–40.

26 "Di questa seconda spetie fu Dante, per che per studio di philosophia et di teologia et astrologia, aritmetica et geometria, per letione di storie, per revolutione di molti et varii libri, vigilando et sudando nelli studi, acquistò la scienza, la quale doveva ornare et explicare co' li suoi versi." Italian text from Leonardo Bruni and Paolo Viti, *Opere letterarie e politiche* (Turin: UTET, 1996), 548–9.

27 Gentile, "In margine all'epistola 'De divino furore' di Marsilio Ficino," 60.

28 "Oriri vero poeticum hunc furorem a Musis existimat; qui autem absque Musarum instinctu poeticas ad fores accedit, sperans quasi arte quadam poetam se bonum evasurum, inanem illum quidem atque eius poesim esse censet, eosque poetas qui celesti inspiratione ac vi rapiuntur adeo divinos sepenumero Musis aflatos sensus expromere, ut ipsimet postmodum extra furorem positi que protulerint minus intelligant." Latin text from Ficino, *Lettere*, 24–5; translation from Ficino, *Letters of Marsilio Ficino*, 1:17–18.

29 "Quatuor ergo divini furoris sunt speties. Primus quidem poeticus furor, alter mysterialis, tertius vaticinium, amatorius affectus est quartus … Poetico

ergo furore primum opus est, qui per musicos tonos que torpent suscitet, per harmonicam suavitatem que turbantur mulceat, per diversorum denique consonantiam dissonantem pellat discordiam et varias partes animi temperet ... Omnibus iis furoribus occupatum fuisse Orpheum libri eius testimonio esse possunt." The passage is in Speech VII, chapter 14. Latin text from Marsilio Ficino, *Commentaire Sur Le Banquet De Platon* (Paris: Les Belles Lettres, 2002), 259–60; translation from Marsilio Ficino, *Commentary on Plato's Symposium on Love*, trans. Sears Reynolds Jayne (Dallas: Spring Publications, 1985), 170–1.

30 "Quicunque numine quomodolibet occupatur, profecto propter ipsam impulsus divini vehementiam virtutisque plenitudinem exuberat, concitatur, exultat, finesque et mores humanos excedit. Itaque occupatio haec sive raptus furor quidam et alienatio non iniuria nominatur. Furens autem nullus est simplici sermone contentus, sed in clamorem prorumpit et cantus et carmina. Quamobrem furor quilibet, sive fatidicus sive mysterialis seu amatorius, dum in cantus procedit et carmina, merito in furorem poeticum videtur absolvi." Latin text and translation from Marsilio Ficino, *Commentaries on Plato: Phaedrus and Ion*, ed. and trans. Michael J.B. Allen (Cambridge, MA: Harvard University Press, 2008), 52–3.

31 "Id vero non arti modo ac studio, sed, et multo magis, divino illi furori, sine quo quenquam magnum unquam fuisse virum Democritus ac Plato negant, ascribo; quo te afflari, ut ita dixerim, ac penitus corripi, concitatiores quidam motus affectusque ardentissimi, quos scripta tua exprimunt, argumento esse possunt. Atque hanc ipsam, que externis moribus fit, concitationem, potissimum philosophi veteres argumentum esse voluerunt, vim quandam in animis nostris esse divinam." Latin text from Ficino, *Lettere*, 19–20; translation from Ficino, *Letters of Marsilio Ficino*, 1:14.

32 "Ceterum in eo furore qui ad amorem divinum poesimque pertinet describendo, duabus de causis longior esse malui, quod videlicet utroque te affici vehementer agnovi, et ut memineris que a te scribuntur ab Iove Musisque, quarum spiritu ac divinitate compleris, non abs te proficisci. Quapropter, o mi Peregrine, iuste pieque feceris, si, ut hactenus te egisse arbitror, maximarum optimarumque rerum nec te nec alium omnino quenquam hominum, sed immortalem potius Deum auctorem ac principium esse cognoveris." Latin text from Ficino, *Lettere*, 1:28; translation from Ficino, *Letters of Marsilio Ficino*, 1:20.

33 "Ergo posthac mitte, precor, amice, mortales et, quandoquidem aspirante Deo canis, cane Deum. Quod quidem non Moyses solum et David ceterique Hebreorum prophete, verum etiam Zoroaster, Linus, Orpheus, Museus, Moscus, Empedocles, Parmenides, Heraclitus, Xenophanes manifeste nos religiosis carminibus suis admonuerunt; admonuere insuper Pythagoras atque Plato, qui Homerum Hesiodumque – quod partim tanquam ingrati

divina ad homines, partim tanquam impii humana ad deos transtulerint – , ex hominum cetu ad inferos expulerunt. Proinde si – quod absit – forte quasi Deo ingratus solos cantabis homines, ingratos ut plurimum mutosque cantabis; quotiens vero Deum canes – quod potius te spero facturum – , totiens tuum cantum suaviter et feliciter comitabitur Echo." Latin text from Ficino, *Lettere*, 238–9; translation from Ficino, *Letters of Marsilio Ficino*, 1:170–1.

34 How much the translation predates the manuscript (1465–75) is not known. See Albinia de la Mare, "The Library of F. Sassetti (1421–90)," in *Cultural Aspects of the Italian Renaissance*, ed. Cecil Clough (Manchester: Manchester University Press, 1976), 188.

35 "instictu potius afflatuque diuino effusa, quam humano studio elaborata uideantur." Biblioteca Laurenziana MS Plut. 65.52, f. 3r.

36 "sine calore, uique mentis qui diuinus appellatur furor nihil egregium scribere posse." Biblioteca Laurenziana MS Plut. 65.52, f. 3v.

37 One piece of evidence regarding the effects of Ficino's promotion of poetic frenzy is the fact that Lorenzo Lippi undertook a translation of Plato's *Ion* into Latin between 1464 and 1469: see Ficino, *Commentaries on Plato*, 225. In the letter dedicating the translation to Piero de' Medici, Lippi recounts that the idea for the translation was born from a conversation he had with two of his schoolmates about the true nature of poetic frenzy. James Hankins has described it as "a poor piece of work," which was ultimately rendered obsolete by Ficino's translation of the *Ion*. See Hankins, *Plato in the Italian Renaissance*, 488.

38 See Kristeller cited in Michael J.B. Allen and Marsilio Ficino, *Icastes: Marsilio Ficino's Interpretation of Plato's Sophist: Five Studies and a Critical Edition with Translation* (Berkeley: University of California Press, 1989), 15–17.

39 "Linum rapuit idem qui et te iam nunc exagitat, Phoebus, optime Laurenti, Pheobus, inquam, qui avo tuo Cosmo vaticinium dedit, parenti autem Petro arcum atque medelas, tibi denique lyram et carmina." Latin text and translation from Ficino, *Commentaries on Plato*, 206–7.

40 Plato, *The Statesman, Philebus, Ion*, trans. Harold N. Fowler and W.R.M. Lamb (New York: G.P. Putnam's Sons, 1925), 421.

41 Plato, *The Dialogues of Plato*, vol. 3, *Ion, Hippias Minor, Laches, Protagoras*, trans. R.E. Allen (New Haven, CT: Yale University Press, 1996), 7. On the history of interpretations of the *Ion*, see E.N. Tigerstedt, "Plato's Idea of Poetical Inspiration," *Commentationes Humanarum Litterarum (Societas Scientiarum Fennica)* 44, no. 2 (1969): 18–19; John D. Moore, "The Dating of Plato's *Ion*," *Greek, Roman and Byzantine Studies* 15, no. 4 (1974): 421–4; Plato, *Plato on Poetry*, ed. Penelope Murray (Cambridge: Cambridge University Press, 1996), 96; Albert Rijksbaron, *Plato: Ion*, Amsterdam Studies in Classical Philology (Leiden: Brill, 2007), 1–8; and Rana Saadi

Liebert, "Fact and Fiction in Plato's *Ion*," *American Journal of Philology* 131, no. 2 (2010): 179–80.

42 Michael Allen discusses the distance between the content of Plato's dialogue and Ficino's interpretation of it in "The Soul as Rhapsode: Marsilio Ficino's Interpretation of Plato's Ion," in *Plato's Third Eye: Studies in Marsilio Ficino's Metaphysics and Its Sources* (Brookfield, VT: Variorum, 1995), XV:125–48.

43 "'Rhapsodus' autem hoc in libro significat recitatorem interpretemque et cantorem carminum. Interpretabatur Ion Homeri carmina et coram populo ad lyram canebat atque ita era affectus ut alium poetam nullum praeter Homerum exponeret ... interpres poetae Ion et alii multi, qui similiter affecti sunt divino instinctu alienam poesim interpretantur; quod si ad percipiendam poesim iam traditam humanum ingenium non sufficit, multo minus ad inventionem sufficiet." Latin text and translation from Ficino, *Commentaries on Plato*, 200–3.

44 Translation from E.N. Tigerstedt, "The Poet as Creator: Origins of a Metaphor," *Comparative Literature Studies* 4 (1968): 458–9.

45 See Raymond Marcel, *Marsile Ficin, 1433–1499* (Paris: Société d'édition Les belles lettres, 1958), 732.

46 Walker, *Spiritual and Demonic Magic*, 19–20.

47 See Warden, "Orpheus and Ficino," 98.

48 See Carlo Dionisotti, *Gli umanisti e il volgare fra Quattro e Cinquecento* (Florence: F. Le Monnier, 1968), 73.

49 Latin text from Joannes Antonius Campanus, *Epistolae et poemata*, ed. Joannes Burchardus Menckenius (Leipzig: Gleditch, 1707), 339.

50 Nino Pirrotta and Elena Povoledo, *Li due Orfei: Da Poliziano a Monteverdi* (Turin: Einaudi, 1975), 45–6.

51 See Giovanni Zannoni, "Strambotti inediti del cod. Vat. Urb. 729," *Rendiconti dell'Accademia Nazionale dei Lincei, Ser. 5* 1 (1892): 371–87, 626.

52 See Raimondo Guarino, "Figures et mythes de la musique dans les spectacles de la Renaissance italienne," *Imago Musicae* 16–17 (1999): 12–13.

53 "Longa veniebat veste sacerdos / Treicius, Cythara qui Iovis arma movet / Demulcetque tigres." Guarino, "Figures et mythes," 12.

54   "Utque magis stupeas, residens in culmine montis
               Orpheus ille parens ratum modulamine prisco
               Omne epulum mensae, volucres animalia pisces
               Alliciens stygia demitti visus ab unda est.
               Is tamen Etrusca Romam de gente profectus
               Baccius an Bacchus, dubium, fuit alter ab illo
               Temporibus nostris vivens Eagrius heros ...
               ... Modulis nunc ille canoris

    Baccius exultat, cunctos ex tempore vates

    Ingenioque gravi superans."

Guarino, "Figures et mythes," 13.

55 Ficino, *Letters of Marsilio Ficino*, 10:34.

56 Ficino, *Letters of Marsilio Ficino*, 1:98–9.

57 On Quarquagli, see Della Torre, *Storia dell'Accademia Platonica di Firenze*, 795–7.

58   "Quarqualium vultu fusco, sed mente serena

    Phoebus amat: Phoebi pectore numen habet.

    Laeta canit, dulcique vocat Lebetrides ore,

    Pro quibus et dentes perdidit ille duos.

    Nam Cyrrham Nisae dum praefert, motus Hyacus

    Irata cyathum fregit in ora manus.

    Eripere at citharam nequiit."

Latin text from Campanus, *Epistolae et poemata*, 340.

59 See Ficino, *Letters of Marsilio Ficino*, 10:33–4.

60 "Sed dic amabo, putastine nunc e memoria nobis nostrum Quarqualium excidisse? Quisquis Quarqualii mei me putat oblitum, me quoque putet oblitum esse me." Latin text from Ficino, *Opera omnia*, 805; translation from Ficino, *Letters of Marsilio Ficino*, 4:61.

61 "Iubet Dauid Mercuriusque, quandoquidem Deo mouente canimus, canamus et Deum." Latin text from Ficino, *Opera omnia*, 744; translation from Ficino, *Letters of Marsilio Ficino*, 2:66.

62 Serafino Ciminelli, *Strambotti*, ed. Antonio Rossi (Parma: Ugo Guanda Editore, 2002), 195.

63 See Zannoni, "Strambotti inediti del cod. Vat. Urb. 729."

64 See Ficino, *Letters of Marsilio Ficino*, 1:123.

65 "Mi Foresi, quid agis hodie? Lyram pulsas? Cane ne hanc sine Marsilio tuo pulses. Alioquin si fidem fregeris, fides tibi penitus dissonabunt. Ego quotiens ad lyram cano, tecum concino, non est mihi suavis absque amico suavissimo melodia. Landino meo amico vero me commenda." Latin text from Ficino, *Opera omnia*, 725; translation from Ficino, *Letters of Marsilio Ficino*, 2:14.

66 "Nemo est ex omnibus familiaribus meis, quicum altius, dulciusque loquar, dulcissime mi Foresi, quam tecum. Caeteris enim lingua tantum, vel calamo loquor, tibi vero saepe plectroque lyraque; alioquin plectra sine te mihi silent, muta sine te mihi lyra. Age, amabo, mi Foresi, quotiens ad lyram canis, cane tu quoque mecum. At video te, dum alteram istam intentius fabricas citharam, interea cantum sonumque alterius praetermittere. Inter coelicolas, Bastiane, Phoebus pulsat quidem, non fabricat citharam; Mercurius autem fabricat, sed non pulsat. Nemo igitur confidat in terris utramque facultatem et fabricandae et pulsandae citharae pariter exercere." Latin text from Ficino, *Opera omnia*, 788. Quoted in Della Torre,

Storia dell'Accademia Platonica di Firenze, 793. Translation from Ficino, *Letters of Marsilio Ficino*, 4:16–17.

67 "Equidem, mi Foresi, postquam tibi modo scripsi Vale, surrexi properaui, sumpsi lyram. Incoepi lungum ab Orphei carmine cantum. Tu quoque uicissim, postquam legeris hic iterum Vale, (si sapis surge) protinus surge, libens sume lyram, laborum dulce lenimen." Latin text from Ficino, *Opera omnia*, 823; translation from Ficino, *Letters of Marsilio Ficino*, 6:38.

68 See Della Torre, *Storia dell'Accademia Platonica di Firenze*, 793.

69 On Michele del Giogante, see Degl'Innocenti, *I Reali dell'Altissimo*, 79–81; and Wilson, "Dominion of the Ear," 277, 285–6.

70 "Insanum te dicere vereor; nec tamen prius appellabo prophetam, quam ista videam, quae futura praenuntias. Iturus sum Romam, brevi rediturus. Quum rediero, ad te cum lyra protinus adventabo: ita me ista docebis." Latin text from Della Torre, *Storia dell'Accademia Platonica di Firenze*, 794.

71   "S'Anphïon col canto e con sua dolce lyra
    l'antica Tebe circundò di mura;
    s'Arion sopra un dalphin, sprezando l'ira
    di Neptun, solcò il mar senza paura;
    s'Orpheo del centro ov'ogni alma sospira
    trasse Euridice sua per strata obscura;
    tu sol col canto, Altissimo, fatto hai
    più che tutti costor non fecer mai."

Italian text from Degl'Innocenti, *I Reali dell'Altissimo*, 276. At the end of his *Ultimo e fine de tutti li libri de orlando inamorato* (6.7.96), Agostini claims to have composed the work "a l'improvista," "in dieci dì." See Degl'Innocenti, *I Reali dell'Altissimo*, 57.

72 Degl'Innocenti, "Verba manent."

73   "O vertù, che li egitii disser Mente,
    Mente divina, e i greci in alcun canto
    la chiamâr poi divin Furore ardente,
    perché questo furore infiamma tanto
    ch'egli alza l'alma a Dio; e ciò al presente
    appresso a noi si chiama Spirto Santo,
    che spira ai vati i secreti di Dio:
    questi s'infonda dentro al petto mio."

Italian text from Degl'Innocenti, *I Reali dell'Altissimo*, 109–10.

74 The other occurrences are at 9.1.7–8 and 39.1.5–6. See Degl'Innocenti, *I Reali dell'Altissimo*, 109.

75 Degl'Innocenti, *I Reali dell'Altissimo*, 179.

76 "Dum apud Ferdinandum primum Neapolitanarum Regem ... adornatos heroicas laudes extemporali carmine celebraret, plurimum et laudis et gratiae reportarit ... apud plerosque regni proceres summo et

animo et ingenio adomatos heroicas laudes extemporali carmine celebraret." Text and translation from Raffaele Lippo Brandolini, *On Music
and Poetry* [*De musica et poetica, 1513*], trans. Ann E. Moyer and Marc
Laureys (Tempe: Arizona Center for Medieval and Renaissance Studies,
2001), 111.

77 "Permansitque Florentiae integrum annum, ubi Laurentii Medices Florenti-
nae tunc rei publicae principis beneficentia non destitutus, acutissimis licet
Politiani iaculis appeteretur." Text and translation from Brandolini, *On Music and Poetry*, 112–13.

78   "Ipse para calamum, scriptor amice, tuum.
                            Non poteris mea verba sequi: velocius ibo,
                            non poteris nostros scribere versiculos."
    Text and translation from F. Alberto Gallo, *Music in the Castle:
    Troubadours, Books, and Orators in Italian Courts of the Thirteenth, Fourteenth,
    and Fifteenth Centuries*, trans. Anna Herklotz (Chicago: University of Chicago
    Press, 1995), 79.

79 "Si quos invenisti versus minus bonos, id erroris ascribito iis qui Lyppo
fiorentino caeco canente scriptitarunt." Text and translation from Gallo,
Music in the Castle, 79.

80 "Maiorem deinde fidem admirationemque improvisum quam elaboratum
poema procul dubio comparare." Text and translation from Brandolini,
On Music and Poetry, 80–3.

81 "An tu illam contemnere audebis, ad quam non arte instituti, sed natura
sumus imbuti, et quam nos non humani doctoris alicuius adminiculo
didicimus, accepimus, legimus, sed divino nutu atque instinctu arripuimus,
hausimus, effudimus, et quae non a turpitudine aliqua et nequitia, sed a
divino culto, a pietate, a physicis quaestionibus, ab astrorum rationibus, ab
humanae vitae institutis profecta est?" Text and translation from Brandolini,
On Music and Poetry, 44–5.

82 "Maiorem dico vel certe parem extemporaneum quam diu multumque
lucubratum oratorium poeticumque dicendi genus commendationem
promerere." Text and translation from Brandolini, *On Music and
Poetry*, 85.

83 "An non audisti poetas quo tanguntur furore divinitus esse afflatos et
poeticam spiritalem quandam esse virtutem, quae et figmenta et verba
rebus accommodata et res verbis aptissimas, utrisque affectus, affectibus
dignitatem venustatemque inspiret? Eoque et Plato poetarum genus esse
divinum dixit et poetas ipsos divino instinctu concitatos eundem interpre-
tibus (quos rapsodos appellat) furorem infundere imitarique magnetis
lapidis naturam, qui non solum ferreos anulos trahit, sed eandem trahendi
vim ipsis anulis latenter insinuat." Text and translation from Brandolini, *On
Music and Poetry*, 40–3.

3 "Secret Frenzies": Angelo Poliziano and Invention

1 From Poliziano's preface to the Manto:
> "Stabat adhuc rudibus Pagaseo in litore remis
> quae ratis undosum prima cucurrit iter.
> Dum tamen extremis haerent succinta ceruchis
> lintea, dum nautas flamina nulla vocant,
> conveniunt Minyae gemini Chironis ad antrum …
> Finis erat dapibus; citharam pius excitat Orpheus
> et movet ad doctas verba canora manus …
> Et iam materno permulserat omnia cantu,
> cum tacuit querulam deposuitque fidem.
> Occupat hanc audax digitosque affringit Achilles
> indoctumque rudi personat ore puer."

Text and translation from Angelo Poliziano, *Silvae*, trans. Charles Fantazzi (Cambridge, MA: Harvard University Press, 2004), 4–5. Useful information for contextualizing the ambitious opening lectures that Poliziano prepared for his courses at Florence's *Studio* (including the *Silvae*) is found in Christopher S. Celenza, "Poliziano's *Lamia* in Context," in *Angelo Poliziano's Lamia: Text, Translation, and Introductory Studies*, ed. Christopher S. Celenza (Leiden: Brill, 2010), 1–45.

2 See Cynthia Munro Pyle, "Il tema di Orfeo, la musica e le favole mitologiche del tardo Quattrocento," in *Ecumenismo della cultura*, vol. 2, ed. Giovannangiola Tarugi (Florence: L.S. Olschki, 1981), 123. Other important intertexts include the *Argonautica* of Apollonius Rhodius and that of Valerius Flaccus; see Francesco Bausi, "Orfeo e Achille: La prefazione alla 'Manto' di Angelo Poliziano," *Schede umanistiche* 1 (1992): 31–59.

3
> "Saepe graves pellit docta testudine curas,
> Et vocem argutis suggerit articulis,
> Qualis Apollinei modulator carminis Orpheus
> Dicitur Odrysias allicuisse feras.
> Marmaricos posset cantu mulcere leones."

Latin text from Ida Maïer, *Ange Politien: La formation d'un poète humaniste, 1469–1480* (Geneva: Droz, 1966), 75.

4 On Fonzio's reliance on Ficino's theory, see Charles Trinkaus, "The Unknown Quattrocento Poetics of Bartolommeo Della Fonte," *Studies in the Renaissance* 13 (1966): 40–95.

5 "SUBITO CALORE. Quasi χαρακτηρισμός silvae est. Nam, ut dictum a Fabio est, qui sylvam componunt calorem atque impetum sequentes ex tempore scribunt. CALORE. Ergo omnino videtur hic poeta concitatioris ingenii fervidiorisque fuisse et quod impetus magis ac celeritate polleret, quam robore et viribus; quapropter in his libellis vivit illa incitatio et eminet. Natura enim

operi impar non erat fervorque ille animi ad finem usque perseverabat. Quales enim sensus haberet, tales quoque hos libellos componebat, qui nimirum vel granditate heroica, vel sensibus, vel ipsa gratia etiam Thebaida elimatissimum opus longe antecellunt, quod in illa a natura destitutus, quippe quae ultra primos impetus deferbuerat, artis praesidium necessario exigebat. Verum nulla tanta ars est, quae afflationem illam mentis, quam ἐνθυσιασμόν Graeci dicunt, imitari possit, unde existit Platonis illa atque ante ipsum Democriti opinio: 'poetam bonum neminem sine inflammatione animorum existere posse et sine quodam afflatu quasi furoris.'" Latin text from Angelo Poliziano, *Commento inedito alle "Selve" di Stazio*, ed. Lucia Cesarini Martinelli (Florence: Sansoni, 1978), 29.

6 For an important study of the aesthetic ideals that Poliziano developed through his studies of Statius, see Attilio Bettinzoli, "Le 'Sylvae': Questioni di poetica," in *Daedaleum iter: Studi sulla poesia e la poetica di Angelo Poliziano* (Florence: Leo S. Olschki, 1995), 67–151.

7 "ignorantissimum omnium viventium." Antonio Manfredi, "I papi e gli umanisti: Libri, biblioteche e studi; Il concilio di Costanza tra medioevo ed età moderna," *Archivio storico lodigiano* 136, no. 2 (2017): 30. See L.D. Reynolds and Peter K. Marshall, *Texts and Transmission: A Survey of the Latin Classics* (Oxford: Clarendon Press, 1983), 397–8.

8 Reynolds and Marshall, *Texts and Transmission*, 333–4.

9 "Nam si parti utrilibet omnino alteram detrahas, natura etiam sine doctrina multum valebit, doctrina nulla esse sine natura poterit" (2.19.2). Text and translation from Quintilian, *The Orator's Education*, vol. 1: *Books 1–2*, ed. and trans. Donald A. Russell (Cambridge, MA: Harvard University Press, 2002), 398–9.

10 "Qua via in ceteris rebus ingenii bonitas imitatur saepe doctrinam, ars porro naturae commoda confirmat et auget." Text and translation from Marcus Tullius Cicero, *Rhetorica Ad Herennium*, trans. Harry Caplan (Cambridge, MA: Harvard University Press, 1954), 206–7.

11 "Et hercule ut illi naturae caelesti atque inmortali cesserimus, ita curae et diligentiae vel ideo in hoc plus est, quod ei fuit magis laborandum." *Institutio Oratoria*, 10.1.86. Text and translation from Quintilian, *The Orator's Education*, vol. 4, *Books 9–10*, ed. and trans. Donald A. Russell (Cambridge, MA: Harvard University Press, 2002), 292–7. Cited in Anthony Welch, *The Renaissance Epic and the Oral Past* (New Haven, CT: Yale University Press, 2012), 209.

12 "Itaque dum se 'diu multumque dubitasse' ait, an eos libellos de integro collectos emitteret, facile ad id viam sternit quo sibi perveniendum destinaverat, ut tumultuaria scilicet esse illos 'subitoque calore' effusos persuaderet ... saepe evenit, sive id morositate quadam ingenii, sive iudicii nimia severitate, atque adeo tristissima censura, ut nihil interim absolutum

putemus nisi in quo vehementissime laboratum sit. Contra vero saepe usu venit ut scripta nostra nimia cura vel peiora fiant, neque tam lima poliantur quam exterantur." Latin text from Poliziano's *Oratio super Fabio Quintiliano et Statii Sylvis*, cited in Eugenio Garin, *Prosatori latini del Quattrocento* (Milan: Riccardo Ricciardi Editore, 1952), 874–5.

13 "Quamlibet enim multis neque fucosis ornamentis abundarent, minime tamen homini de omni sua existimatione sollicito vel haec ipsa celeritatis commendatio fuerat negligenda, quippe cui et indulgentia liberior et venia proclivior et admiratio maior deberetur." Latin text from Poliziano's *Oratio super Fabio Quintiliano et Statii Sylvis*, cited in Garin, *Prosatori latini del Quattrocento*, 874–5.

14 "Cum singulae ipsae quae Sylvae inscribuntur singula a se invicem disiuncta argumenta continerent, earumque fines haud ita multos intra versus includerentur, nihil profecto sibi reliqui facere ad industriam circumspectionemque poeta debuit, cum et tantae rerum de quibus ageretur varietati respondendum videret, et haud longo in opere somnum obrepere sibi nefas existimaret. Itaque ut omnem facillime culpam praestari ab eo intelligas, nihil in illis non sagacissime inventum, non prudentissime dispositum est, nullus non tentatus locus atque excussus, unde aliqua modo voluptas eliceretur. Elocutionis autem ornamenta atque lumina tot tantaque exposuit, ita sententiis popularis, verbis nitidus, figuris iucundus, tralationibus magnificus, grandis resonansque carminibus esse studuit, ut omnia illi facta compositaque ad pompam, omnia ad celebritatem comparata videantur." Latin text from Garin, *Prosatori latini del Quattrocento*, 872–3.

15 Angelo Poliziano, *Opera omnia* (Basel, Switzerland: Nicolaus Episcopus, 1553), 216.

16 "Cogis tu quidem me, Laurenti, carmen edere inconditum, inemendatum, et quod in publico semel pronuntiatum, nimis fuisse impudens visum sit. Satis profecto fuerat vixisse unum diem quod tam foret imperfectum animal, ac posse etiam inter insecta illa quae vocentur ephemera connumerari. Namque ego id ad praesentem dumtaxat celebritatem ... concinnaveram." Text and translation from Poliziano, *Silvae*, 2–3.

17 "En tibi quam flagitabas Elegiam, pene illam quidem extemporaneam; siquidem mane, dum se rei divinae sacerdos parat, inchoatam, absolvi dein post meridiem, dum rediens carrucae adequito." Latin text from Antonia Tissoni Benvenuti, *L'Orfeo del Poliziano: Con il testo critico dell'originale e delle successive forme teatrali* (Padua: Editrice Antenore, 1986), 4–5.

18 "Et nunc, quae magnum longe testentur amorem, / scripta repentino fusa calore damus." Latin text from Tissoni Benvenuti, *L'Orfeo del Poliziano*, 4.

19 Lucia Cesarini Martinelli, "In margine al commento di Angelo Poliziano alle 'Selve' di Stazio," *Interpres* 1 (1978): 98.

20 On Poliziano and music, see Elisa Curti, "'Udii cantar improviso': Alcune osservazioni su Poliziano e la musica," in *L'attore del Parnaso: Profili di*

attori-musici e drammaturgie d'occasione, ed. Francesca Bortoletti (Milan: Mimesis, 2012), 211–23.

21 Poliziano, *Prose volgari inedite*, 75.

22 See Orvieto, "Angelo Poliziano 'compare' della brigata laurenziana."

23 Charles Dempsey has written that "despite the claim in Orvieto's title, the identity of the particular compare in question is still far from settled, and it is complicated by the fact that Lorenzo de' Medici certainly had many accompanists in his employ during his lifetime." Charles Dempsey, *The Portrayal of Love: Botticelli's Primavera and Humanist Culture at the Time of Lorenzo the Magnificent* (Princeton, NJ: Princeton University Press, 1992), 97.

24 The passage from Giovio's *Elogia doctorum virorum* is cited in Pyle, "Il tema di Orfeo," 128.

25 Luigi Castagna, "Il 'Politiani tumulus' di Pietro Bembo (Carminum XXVI)," *Aevum* 69, no. 3 (1995): 539–40.

26 Angelo Poliziano, *Rime*, ed. Daniela Delcorno Branca (Venice: Marsilio Editori, 1990), 14.

27 Antonia Tissoni Benvenuti, "La ricezione delle *Silvae* di Stazio e la poesia all'improvviso nel Rinascimento," in *Gli antichi e i moderni: Studi in onore di Roberto Cardini*, ed. L Bertolini and Donatella Coppini (Florence: Polistampa, 2010), 1301.

28 Tissoni Benvenuti, "La ricezione delle *Silvae* di Stazio," 1298.

29 On the theme of song within Poliziano's *rispetti*, see Daniela Delcorno Branca, "Il laboratorio del Poliziano: Per una lettura delle 'Rime,'" *Lettere Italiane* 29 (1987): 168.

30 The date of the composition of Poliziano's *Orfeo* has not been determined with certainty. The long-prevailing view that the text was composed in 1480 was challenged by Antonia Tissoni Benvenuti, who, in her critical edition of the text, proposed 1478 as the *terminus ante quem* for the text's composition. Many though not all scholars have found her arguments convincing. See Tissoni Benvenuti, *L'Orfeo del Poliziano*, 58–70; and Angelo Poliziano, *Poesie*, ed. Francesco Bausi (Turin: UTET, 2006), 20.

31 "Quid postremo carminibus illis sive quae ad citharam canit ex tempore, sive quae per otium componit, dulcius, mundius, limatius, venustius?" Latin text from Angelo Poliziano, *Opera omnia* (Venice: Aldo Manuzio, 1498), 58v.

32 Pirrotta and Povoledo, *Li due Orfei*, 13–47.

33 *Orfeo*, vv. 108–9. Italian text from Tissoni Benvenuti, *L'Orfeo del Poliziano*, 146.

34   "Orpheos atque lyram curva de valle secutas
in caput isse retro liquido pede fluminis undas."
    Nutricia, vv. 285–6. Text and translation from Poliziano, *Silvae*, 128–9. The similarity between the two passages has been noted by Tissoni Benvenuti in *L'Orfeo del Poliziano*, 146.

35 *Rispetti*, 7.7–8. Italian text from Poliziano, *Rime*, 55.

36   "Che maraviglia è s'i' son fatto vago
d'un sì bel canto e s'i' ne sono ingordo?
Costei farebbe inamorare un drago,
un bavalischio, anz'un aspido sordo!
I' mi calai, e or la pena pago,
ch'i' mi truovo impaniato com'un tordo.
Ognun fugga costei quand'ella ride:
col canto piglia e poi col riso uccide."
Italian text from Poliziano, *Rime*, 54.

37 Italian text from Tissoni Benvenuti, *L'Orfeo del Poliziano*, 136.

38 Nino Pirrotta and Elena Povoledo, *Music and Theatre from Poliziano to Monteverdi*, trans. Karen Eales (Cambridge: Cambridge University Press, 1981), 25.

39   "El non è tanto el mormorio piacevole
delle fresche acque che d'un saxo piombano,
né quando soffia un ventolino agevole
fra le cime de' pini e quelle trombano,
quanto le rime tue son sollazzevole,
le rime tue che per tutto rimbombano:
s'ella l'ode, verrà com'una cucciola.
Ma ecco Tyrsi che del monte sdrucciola."
Italian text from Tissoni Benvenuti, *L'Orfeo del Poliziano*, 145.

40 Pirrotta and Povoledo, *Li due Orfei*, 30.

41 Italian text from Tissoni Benvenuti, *L'Orfeo del Poliziano*, 136.

42 "nullum enim ex illis biduo longius tractum." Statius, *Silvae*, trans. D.R. Shackleton Bailey (Cambridge, MA: Harvard University Press, 2003), 26–7.

43 "Syluam hic dicimus poema calore quodam ingenii et subito furore ac poetico spiritu fusum." Nicolas Bérauld, *"Praelectio" et commentaire à la "Silve Rusticus" d'Ange Politien (1518)*, ed. Perrine Galand (Geneva: Droz, 2015), 86. See Jean Lecointe, *L'Idéal et la Différence: La perception de la personnalité littéraire à la Renaissance* (Geneva: Droz, 1993), 318.

44 "Quotiens haec lego, totiens audire uideor Politianum ipsum, diuino quodam furore percitum, subito atque ex tempore fundentem hos uersus, ac suo illo ore rotundo, canoraque ac plus quam cygnea uoce modulantem." Latin text from Bérauld, *"Praelectio" et commentaire à la "Silve Rusticus" d'Ange Politien*, 112.

45 See Terence Cave, *The Cornucopian Text* (Oxford: Oxford University Press, 1985), 135.

46   "Quo me, pietas temeraria, cogis
attonitum? quinam hic animo trepidante tumultus?
Fallor, an ipsa aptum dominae praecordia munus
parturiunt ultro vocemque et verba canoro
concipiunt sensim numero inlibataque fundunt

carmina numquam ullis Parcarum obnoxia pensis?
Sic eat. En agedum, qua se furor incitat ardens,
qua mens, qua pietas, qua ducunt vota, sequamur."
Text and translation from Poliziano, *Silvae*, 112–15.

47   "Nitidos vatum defaecatosque sonori
informant flammantque animos modulamina caeli.
Is rapit euantem fervor fluctuque furoris
mens prior it pessum. Tum clausus inaestuat alto
corde deus, toto lymphatos pectore sensus
exstimulans sociumque hominem indignatus, ad imas
cunctantem absterret latebras; vacua ipse potitus
sede, per obsessos semet tandem egerit artus
inque suos humana ciet praecordia cantus."
Text and translation from Poliziano, *Silvae*, 122–3.

48 *Nutricia*, vv. 127–31. Poliziano, *Silvae*, 120–1.

49 *Nutricia*, vv. 285–317. "Lyra divulsum caput a cervice cruenta heu! medium veheret resonans lugubre per Hebrum." Poliziano, *Silvae*, 128–31.

50   "Lustris nondum tribus ecce peractis,
iam tamen in Latium Graiae monimenta senectae
evocat et dulci detornat carmina plectro."
Nutricia, vv. 776–84. Poliziano, *Silvae*, 158–61.

51 Plato, *Ion* 536A, in Plato, *Ion*, trans. W.R.M. Lamb (New York: G.P. Putnam's Sons, 1925), 427–9.

52 Donatella Coppini has discussed the significance of Poliziano's modification of this metaphor, in "L'ispirazione per contagio: 'Furor' e 'remota lectio' nella poesia latina di Angelo Poliziano," in *Agnolo Poliziano: Poeta, scrittore, filologo; Atti del Convegno internazionale di studi, Montepulciano, 3–6 novembre 1994*, ed. Vincenzo Fera and Mario Martelli (Florence: Le Lettere, 1998), 127–64.

53   "Ipsaque Niliacis longum mandata papyris
carmina Phoebeos videas afflare furores
et caeli spirare fidem; quin sancta legentem
concutiunt parili turbam contagia moto
deque aliis alios idem proseminat ardor
pectoris instinctu vates, ceu ferreus olim
anulus, arcana quem vi Magnesia cautes
sustulerat, longam nexu pendente catenam
implicat et caecis inter se conserit hamis."
Nutricia, vv. 188–96. Text and translation from Poliziano, *Silvae*, 122–5.

54   "Cur non totum in praeconia solvam
Maeonidae magni, cuius de gurgite vivo
combibit arcanos vatum omnis turba furores?
Utque laboriferi ferrum lapis Herculis alte

erigit et longos Chalybum procul implicat orbes
vimque suam aspirat cunctis, ita prorsus ab uno
impetus ille sacer vatum dependet Homero.
Ille, Iovis mensae accumbens, dat pocula nobis
Iliaca porrecta manu, quae triste repellant
annorum senium vitamque in saecla propagent."
   Ambra, vv. 11–20. Text and translation from Poliziano, *Silvae*, 70–1.

55 On what is known of the life and career of Petreio, see Petreio, *Un commento inedito all'"Ambra" del Poliziano*, ed. Alessandro Perosa (Rome: Bulzoni, 1994), xxvi–xxxvi.

56 "De eodem Marsilius noster Ficinus in *Epistolis.*" Petreio, *Un commento inedito all'"Ambra" del Poliziano*, 8.

57 "Comparatio sumpta ex Platone in rem diversam. Ille enim ait bonos poetas ita omnes furore divino attrahi, ut ferrum a magnete lapide; Policianus autem per licentiam, quae poetae conceditur, dicit ex uno Homero ceteros poetas pendere, veluti ex lapide magnete dependent complures annuli ferrei. 'Herculeum' autem 'lapidem' magnetem appellat; sic enim dictum ab Euripide eum esse Plato auctor est, quod vi quadam herculea, idest heroica, in attrahendo utatur. Hoc apud Latinos, ni fallor, alibi nusquam reperies." Petreio, *Un commento inedito all'"Ambra" del Poliziano*, 8–9.

58 "Neque vero non et illud in poeta hoc caelestis plane immortalisque naturae lumen effulget quod pulcherrima illa carmina, quae iure aetas omnis mirata est, illaborata ipsi atque extemporanea fluebant vivoque – ut ita dixerim – gurgite exundabant, cum e diverso mantuanum poetam paucissimos die composuisse versus auctor sit Varus." Angelo Poliziano, *Praelectiones 2*, ed. Giorgia Zollino (Florence: L.S. Olschki, 2016), 88.

59 "Extantque adhuc non pauca canente illo excepta poemata quae, prout a quoque bene maleque acceptus fuerat, continuo in eum subito quodam re-pentinoque instinctu et ferente – ut aiunt – flatu proferebantur, ut facile intel-ligantur non quasi sub incudem venisse humanae fabricae, sed divino quodam impulsu instinctuque velut e cortina atque adyto sacris esse escussa praecor-diis, ut iam dubitandum nullo pacto sit quin vere de illo Democritus naturae rerum conscius praedicaverit: Ὅμηρος φύσεως λαχὼν θεαζοίσης ἐπέων κόσμον ἐτεκτήνατο παντοίων." Poliziano, *Praelectiones 2*, 88. Paola Megna discusses the significance of this passage in Angelo Poliziano, *Oratio in expositione Homeri*, ed. Paola Megna (Rome: Edizioni di storia e letteratura, 2007), lxxvi–lxxvii.

60 An English translation of the pseudo-Herodotean *Life of Homer* can be found in Homer, *The Odyssey of Homer, with the Hymns, Epigrams, and Battle of the Frogs and Mice*, trans. Theodore Alois Buckley (New York: Harper and Bros., 1895), v–xxxii.

61 See Lucia Cesarini Martinelli, "Poliziano professore allo Studio fiorentino," in *La Toscana al tempo di Lorenzo il Magnifico: Politica, economia, cultura, arte;*

Convegno di studi promosso dalle Università di Firenze, Pisa e Siena: 5–8 novembre 1992, ed. Luigi Beschi (Pisa: Pacini editore, 1996).

62 See Lord, *Singer of Tales.*

63 Landino explicitly states that Homer's poems contained the same allegorical meanings that his own teaching and writings identified in the *Aeneid.* See, for instance, Cristoforo Landino, *Disputationes Camaldulenses,* ed. Peter Lohe (Florence: Sansoni, 1980), 118–19.

64 For a detailed and nuanced analysis of Poliziano's evolving stance towards Neoplatonic approaches to philosophical interpretation of texts, see Denis J.-J. Robichaud, "Angelo Poliziano's *Lamia*: Neoplatonic Commentaries and the Plotinian Dichotomy Between the Philologist and the Philosopher," in *Angelo Poliziano's Lamia: Text, Translation, and Introductory Studies,* ed. Christopher S. Celenza (Leiden: Brill, 2010), 131–89.

65 "Venus in manu vulneratur quoniam celestis illa venus platonis cum in sensu tangendi polluitur vulgaris evadit." The manuscript note is published in Alice Levine Rubenstein, "The Notes to Poliziano's 'Iliad,'" *Italia medioevale e umanistica* 25 (1982): 205–39. Rubenstein notes the connection to Ficino's *De amore.*

66 Paola Megna, in her edition of the *Oratio in expositione Homeri,* notes the lack of interest that Poliziano, in this and subsequent works, shows towards allegorical interpretation of Homer: Poliziano, *Oratio in expositione Homeri,* lxxiv–lxxv. On Poliziano's Homeric studies, see also Léon Dorez, "L'hellénisme d'Ange Politien," *Mélanges d'archéologie et d'histoire* 15 (1895): 24–8; Innocente Toppani, "Poliziano e Omero," in *Studi triestini di antichità in onore di Luigia Achillea Stella* (Trieste: Università degli studi di Trieste, 1975), 470–80; and Perrine Galand-Hallyn, *Les yeux de l'éloquence: Poétiques humanistes de l'évidence* (Orléans: Paradigme, 1995).

67 See Isidoro Del Lungo, *Florentia: Uomini e cose del Quattrocento* (Florence: G. Barbèra, 1897), 311.

68   "Seu numeros Phoebi modulataque carmina mavis
    Vocali junxisse lyrae, plectroque sonantes
    Impellis nervos, auritas ducere quercus
    Cantando rabidasque potes mulcere leaenas."
  Latin text from Poliziano, *Prose volgari inedite,* 432. See Stephen Murphy, *The Gift of Immortality: Myths of Power and Humanist Poetics* (Madison, NJ: Fairleigh Dickinson University Press, 1997), 177.

69   "Solus tu carmina nobis
    Ismarium possis afferre aequantia plectrum;
    Te duce, vel priscis ausim certare poetis."
  Latin text from Poliziano, *Prose volgari inedite,* 434.

70 Rubenstein, "Notes to Poliziano's 'Iliad,'" 210–11. See also Perrine Galand, "L''enargia' chez Politien," *Bibliothèque d'Humanisme et Renaissance* 49, no. 1

(1987): 25–53. For a broad perspective on *enargeia*, see Heinrich F. Plett, *Enargeia in Classical Antiquity and the Early Modern Age: The Aesthetics of Evidence* (Leiden: Brill, 2012).

71 "In Homeri poesi ... omnium rerum humanarum simulacra effigiesque intueamur ipsaque illa nobis expressa expromptaque ante oculos constituerit quae ipsemet profecto numquam suis oculis usurpaverat." Latin text from Poliziano, *Praelectiones 2*, 88.

72 "Quas φαντασίας Graeci vocant (nos sane visiones appellemus), per quas imagines rerum absentium ita repraesentantur animo ut eas cernere oculis ac praesentes habere videamur, has quisquis bene ceperit is erit in adfectibus potentissimus." Quintilian, *Institutio Oratoria*, 6.2.29–30; text and translation from Quintilian, *The Orator's Education*, vol. 3, *Books 6–8*, ed. and trans. Donald A. Russell (Cambridge, MA: Harvard University Press, 2002), 58–61.

73 "Insequitur ἐνάργεια, quae a Cicerone inlustratio et evidentia nominatur, quae non tam dicere videtur quam ostendere, et adfectus non aliter quam si rebus ipsis intersimus sequentur." Quintilian, *Institutio Oratoria*, 6.2.32; text and translation from Quintilian, *Orator's Education*, vol. 3, 60–1.

74 "Si calor ac spiritus tulit, frequenter accidit ut successum extemporalem consequi cura non possit. Deum tunc adfuisse cum id evenisset veteres oratores, ut Cicero dicit, aiebant, sed ratio manifesta est. Nam bene concepti adfectus et recentes rerum imagines continuo impetu feruntur, quae nonnumquam mora stili refrigescunt et dilatae non revertuntur ... Quare capiendae sunt illae de quibus dixi rerum imagines, quas vocari φαντασίας indicavimus, omniaque de quibus dicturi erimus, personae, quaestiones, spes, metus, habenda in oculis, in adfectus recipienda: pectus est enim quod disertos facit et vis mentis." Quintilian, *Institutio Oratoria*, 10.7.13–14; text and translation from Quintilian, *Orator's Education*, vol. 4, 378–81.

75   "Nec solum quae facta sint aut fiant sed etiam quae futura sint
            aut futura fuerint imaginamur
            ... tralatio temporum, quae proprie μετάστασις dicitur."
    Istitutio Oratoria, 9.2.41–2. Text and translation from Quintilian, *Orator's Education*, vol. 4, 56–7.

76 *Istitutio Oratoria*, 10.7.1; text and translation from Quintilian, *Orator's Education*, vol. 4, 372–3.

77 Ed Sarath, "A Consciousness-Based Look at Spontaneous Creativity," in *The Oxford Handbook of Critical Improvisation Studies*, ed. George E. Lewis and Benjamin Piekut, vol. 2 (Oxford: Oxford University Press, 2016), 135.

78   "El tempo fugge e tu fuggir lo lassi,
            che non ha el mondo la più cara cosa;
            e se tu aspetti che 'l maggio trapassi,
            invan cercherai poi di côr la rosa.

> Quel che non si fa presto, mai poi fassi:
> or che tu puoi, non istar più pensosa.
> Piglia el tempo che fugge pel ciuffetto,
> prima che nasca qualche stran sospetto."

    Italian text from Poliziano, *Rime*, 64.

79 On the distinction between *kairos* and *chronos*, see Phillip Sipiora and
    James S. Baumlin, *Rhetoric and* Kairos: *Essays in History, Theory, and Praxis*
    (Albany: State University of New York Press, 2002); Silvia Mattiacci, "Da
    'Kairos' a Occasio: Un percorso tra letteratura e iconografia," in *Il calamo
    della memoria: Riuso di testi e mestiere letterario nella tarda antichità*, vol. 4,
    ed. Lucio Cristante and Simona Ravalico (Trieste: EUT Edizioni, 2011);
    Simona Cohen, *Transformations of Time and Temporality in Medieval and
    Renaissance Art* (Leiden: Brill, 2014); Erwin Panofsky, *Studies in Iconology:
    Humanistic Themes in the Art of the Renaissance* (Boulder, CO: Westview Press,
    1972), 69–93; Paula Philippson, "Il concetto greco di tempo nelle parole
    aion, chronos, kairos, eniautos," *Rivista di Storia della Filosofia* 4, no. 2
    (1949): 81–97; Frank Kermode, *The Sense of an Ending: Studies in the Theory
    of Fiction* (Oxford: Oxford University Press, 2000), 46–50; and Panofsky,
    Studies in Iconology, 71–4.

80 "Occasio autem est pars temporis habens in se alicuius rei idoneam faci-
    endi aut non faciendi opportunitatem. Quare cum tempore hoc differt:
    nam genere quidem utrumque idem esse intelligitur, verum in tempore
    spatium quodam modo declaratur quod in annis aut in anno aut in aliqua
    anni parte spectatur, in occasione ad spatium temporis faciendi quaedam
    opportunitas intelligitur adiuncta." *De inventione*, 1.27. Text and translation
    from Marcus Tullius Cicero, *Cicero: De Inventione, De Optimo Genere Oratorum,
    Topica*, trans. H.M. Hubbell (Cambridge, MA: Harvard University Press,
    1968), 78–9.

81 Vasari writes, "E perché Mariotto non era tanto fondato nel disegno …
    si diede allo studio di quelle anticaglie che erano allora in Fiorenza, la
    maggior parte e le migliori delle quali erano in casa Medici: e disegnò
    assai volte alcuni quadretti di mezzo rilievo che erano sotto la loggia nel
    giardino di verso San Lorenzo … in uno dei quali sono due putti che por-
    tano il fulmine di Giove, nell'altro è uno ignudo vecchio, fatto per l'Occa-
    sione, che ha le ali sopra le spalle ed a' piedi ponderando con le mani un
    par di bilance." The text, from Vasari's biography of Mariotto Albertinelli,
    is cited in Beatrice Paolozzi Strozzi and Erkinger Schwarzenberg, "Un
    Kairos mediceo," *Mitteilungen des Kunsthistorischen Institutes in Florenz* 35,
    no. 2/3 (1991): 308.

82 It is important to note that, while the rediscovery of Ausonius's epigram
    certainly helped to stimulate interest in the iconography of Kairos/Occasio
    on the part of Poliziano and others, Occasio had been a familiar figure

to Latin-educated readers throughout the Middle Ages, appearing in the popular teaching text known as the *Disticha Catonis* (2.26), in the *Fabulae* of Phaedrus (5.8), and in the *Carmina Burana.* Works by Ausonius did circulate during the Middle Ages but mostly anonymously; see Decimus Magnus Ausonius, *Ausonius: Moselle, Epigrams, and Other Poems*, trans. Deborah Warren (Abingdon, UK: Routledge, 2017), 13. The publication of the *editio princeps* of Ausonius's poetry in Venice in 1472 marked an important turning point in the revival of interest in this poet; see Cohen, *Transformations of Time and Temporality in Medieval and Renaissance Art*, 222.

83 "Cuius opus? Phidiae: qui signum Pallados, eius / quique Iovem fecit; tertia palma ego sum. / sum dea quae rara et paucis Occasio nota." Ausonius, *Epigram* 33, vv. 1–3. Text and translation from Ausonius, *Ausonius*, trans. Hugh G. Evelyn White (Cambridge, MA: Harvard University Press, 1985), 174–5.

84 Greek Anthology, 16.275. Translation from *The Greek Anthology*, vol. 5, trans. W.R. Paton (Cambridge, MA: Harvard University Press, 1918), 325; cited in Cohen, *Transformations of Time and Temporality in Medieval and Renaissance Art*, 200.

85 Poliziano, *Commento inedito alle "Selve" di Stazio*, 49–50; chapter 49 of the *Miscellanea* I. See Mattiacci, "Da 'Kairos' a Occasio," 148.

86 It is possible, though not certain, that the Kairos relief held today in the State Hermitage Museum in St. Petersburg may be that which was once part of the Medici collection, heavily damaged and altered. See Cohen, *Transformations of Time and Temporality in Medieval and Renaissance Art*, 216.

87 Strozzi and Schwarzenberg, "Un Kairos mediceo," 309–11.

88 Pliny, *Natural History in Ten Volumes*, trans. H. Rackham (Cambridge, MA: Harvard University Press, 1967), XXXVI, 17.

89 See Strozzi and Schwarzenberg, "Un Kairos mediceo," 311. Before publishing the *Miscellaneorum centuria prima* in 1489, Poliziano had previously written about this issue in his commentary on Statius's *Silvae*, which he did not publish. The relevant passage can now be read in Poliziano, *Commento inedito alle "Selve" di Stazio*, 49–50.

90 Cited in A.F. Stewart, "Lysippan Studies: 1. The Only Creator of Beauty," *American Journal of Archaeology* 82, no. 2 (1978): 165.

91 In the British Library MS Add. 16436 (at c. 68r), the poem bears the title "Serenata over lettera in istrambotti." The text could be considered a "lettera" of sorts in that the singer-poet (the lyric "I") is imagined as bearing a message from the lover to the beloved. However, no reference is made to a written letter within the text, whereas references to a sung performance are frequent.

92 Walter J. Ong, *Orality and Literacy: The Technologizing of the Word* (New York: Routledge, 2005), 10–11.

4 "The Power to Stir Up Others": Lorenzo de' Medici and Improvisation

1 "In collibus Ambre Agnanaeque vallis Laurens ille Phoebeus Dionysio
nectare passim ebrius debacchatur. Tum vero afflatus ex alto coelestia
super hominem carmina fundit ore rotundo, profunda quorum sensa nullis
unquam penetrare fas est, nisi ingeniis simili quodam furore correptis.
Rapit vero secum noster ille patronus, nonnullos interdum attentius atque
felicius audientes; in eos uidelicet prae caeteris ubertate furoris exuberans."
Latin text from Ficino, *Opera omnia*, 927; translation from Ficino, *Letters of
Marsilio Ficino*, 10:10.

2 Niccolò Valori, *Laurentii Medicei vita a Nicolao Valorio scripta ex cod. Mediceo
Laurentiano nunc primum latine in lucem eruta*, ed. Lorenzo Mehus (Florence:
Giovannelli, 1749), 46. On Lorenzo's cultivation of music, see Frank
A. D'Accone, "Lorenzo the Magnificent and Music," in *Lorenzo il Magnifico
e il suo mondo: Convegno internazionale di studi (Firenze, 9–13 giugno 1992)*,
ed. Gian Carlo Garfagnini (Florence: Leo S. Olschki, 1994), 271–8; Emile
Haraszti, "La technique des Improvisateurs de langue vulgaire et de latin
au quattrocento," *Revue belge de Musicologie / Belgisch Tijdschrift voor Muziekwetenschap* 9 (1955): 19; Francesco Bausi, "Lorenzo de' Medici tra pubblico
e privato: In margine al XII volume delle Lettere del Magnifico," *Schede
umanistiche* 22 (2008), 119–20; McGee, *Ceremonial Musicians of Late Medieval
Florence*, 178–89; and Luigi Parigi, *Laurentiana: Lorenzo dei Medici cultore della
musica* (Florence: L.S. Olschki, 1954).

3 Mario Martelli, *Studi laurenziani* (Florence: Leo S. Olschki, 1965), 122.

4 "Tornatevene el più presto potete, perché ogni ora arèi bisogno di voi: la
viuola e l'altre cose aspetto, e a ogni modo fate di portarnele con voi." Martelli, *Studi laurenziani*, 181.

5 Franca Brambilla Ageno, "Una nuova lettera di Luigi Pulci a Lorenzo de'
Medici," *Giornale Storico della Letteratura Italiana* 141 (1964): 107.

6 Martelli, *Studi laurenziani*, 122.

7 Martelli, *Studi laurenziani*, 122–3.

8 Martelli, *Studi laurenziani*, 123.

9 Della Torre, *Storia dell'Accademia Platonica di Firenze*, 799.

10 Del Lungo, *Florentia: Uomini e cose del Quattrocento*, 307.

11 "Quam eleganter ex tempore Laurentius canat" – a gloss on *Nutricia*,
vv. 736–44. See Bausi, "Lorenzo de' Medici tra pubblico e privato," 120.

12 Medici, *Tutte le opere*, 605–6.

13 On the mutual antipathy and polemics between Pulci and Ficino, see
chapters 6 and 7 of Orvieto, *Pulci medievale*.

14   "Se son nimici capital' del vino,
                    el vino è poi lor capital nimico,
                    ch'al capo drizza el suo furor di-vino."

Il Simposio, VI, 94–6. Italian text from Medici, *Tutte le opere*, translation from Lorenzo de' Medici, *The Complete Literary Works of Lorenzo De' Medici*, trans. Guido A. Guarino (New York: Italica Press, 2016), 308.

15 "Tres enim illas opto Gratias Medici nostro propitias fore, que ab Orpheo describuntur: Ἀγλαίη τε Θάλεια καὶ Εὐφροσύνη πολύολβε, scilicet Splendorem, Letitiam, Viriditatem; splendorem, inquam, mentis, letitiam voluntatis, viriditatem corporis et fortune. Aspirant iam ex alto he Gratie Laurentio, ac tandiu aspirabunt, quandiu agnoscet gratias a Deo solo se accepisse." Latin text from Ficino, *Lettere*, 1:56; translation from Ficino, *Letters of Marsilio Ficino*, 1:67.

16 "Ego forsitan, Nicholae, nisi que Laurentii sunt mea quoque essent, non possem tot, tanta, tam senilia bona adolescenti non invidere ... Cessistis iampridem Lauro poete, cessistis oratores modo, iamiam philosophi cedamus." Latin text from Ficino, *Lettere*, 1:55; translation from Ficino, *Letters of Marsilio Ficino*, 1:66–7.

17 "Audivi quandoque Laurentium Medicem nostrum nonnulla horum similia ad lyram canentem furore quodam divino, ut arbitror, concitum." Latin text from Ficino, *Lettere*, 1:211; translation from Ficino, *Letters of Marsilio Ficino*, 1:179.

18 A letter sent to Lorenzo on 26 September 1466 from his tutor Gentile Becchi demonstrates that this problem was beginning to become a preoccupation among the regime several years before Lorenzo became head of his family: "Parebbe a questi tua amici che tu tornassi. Vorrebbero anchora, tornato che tu fussi, che tu veghiassi um pocho più lo stato tuo ... et che in re venerea tu havessi riguardo in dua luoghi da bene dove t'importa la vita. Vogliono che io metta a scotto la mia gratia techo in ricordarti queste chose, parendo loro mi debbi prestare fede ... Perdonami se chostoro me hanno cavato del mio ordinario, che è solo d'ubidire." The letter is quoted in Mario Martelli, "Il 'Giacoppo' di Lorenzo," *Interpres* 7 (1987): 104. On Lorenzo's reputation for sexual indiscretion, see also Francis W. Kent, "Lorenzo De' Medici and the Love of Women," in *Princely Citizen: Lorenzo De' Medici and Renaissance Florence*, ed. Carolyn James (Turnhout: Brepols, 2013), 41–66.

19   "Erano gli orecchi alle parole intesi,
        quando una nuova voce a sé gli trasse,
        da piú dolce armonia legati et presi.

        Pensai che Orpheo al mondo ritornasse
        o quel che chiuse Thebe col suon degno,
        sí dolce lyra mi parea suonasse.

        "Forse caduta è dal superno regno
        la lira ch'era tra•lle stelle fisse?
        – diss'io –, il ciel sarà senza il suo segno,

o forse, come quello antico disse,
l'alma d'alcun di questi trasmutata
nel suonatore per suo destino si misse!"

Et mentre che tra fronde et fronde guata
et segue l'occhio ove l'orecchio tira,
per veder tal dolcezza onde è causata,

ecco in un puncto sente, intende et mira
l'occhio, la mente nobile e l'orecchio
chi suona, sua doctrina et la sua lyra:

Marsilio, habitatore del Montevecchio."
    De summo bono, II, 1–19. Text from Medici, *Tutte le opere*, 933–4; translation
from Medici, *Selected Poems and Prose*, 69–70.

20   "Apollo, se ami ancor le caste chiome
della tua tanto disiata Damne,
soccorri a chi ritiene il suo bel nome;

et tanto del tuo sacro furor danne,
non quanto a me conviensi, ma al suggiecto
di che debbo cantare, bisogno fanne.

Tua gratia abondi piú, se è piú il difecto,
acciò che quello che soggiunse Marsilio
ne' versi chiuga come è nel concetto."
    De summo bono, IV, 37–45. Italian text from Medici, *Tutte le opere*, 952–3;
translation from Medici, *Selected Poems and Prose*, 79.

21 See in particular Ficino's letters to the poets Pellegrino Agli and Alessandro
Braccesi, discussed above.

22   "Cosí ciascun tornossi al proprio albergo,
et me acceso della sancta fiamma,
mentre che drieto al pensier dolce pergo,

mosse ad cantar l'Amor che 'l tucto infiamma."
    De summo bono, V, 178–81. Italian text from Medici, *Tutte le opere*, 967;
translation from Medici, *Selected Poems and Prose*, 86. It is worth noting that
these lines echo the final three verses of Dante's *Paradiso*.

23 Ficino, *Lettere*, 1:211.

24 "Qui c'è piuttosto un non interrotto saltare di palo in frasca, aggrovigliando
gli argomenti ed omettendo non di rado di sottolineare i convenienti pas-
saggi dall'uno all'altro, a tal punto che, a lettura ultimata, lo studioso resta
profondamente perplesso sul senso preciso da attribuire ad un'opera come
questa." Martelli, *Studi laurenziani*, 148.

25 In her 1986 critical edition, Raffaella Castagnola rejected most of these hypotheses by Martelli. See Lorenzo de' Medici, *Stanze* (Florence: L.S. Olschki, 1986), lxx–lxxxvii.

26 Castagnola, in her critical edition, has made a case for replacing the traditional title *Selve* with *Stanze*. While Castagnola's work succeeds in illustrating the impossibility of establishing with certainty that any of the titles found in the manuscript tradition originated with the author, her conclusion that *Stanze* should be preferred to *Selve* has not been widely accepted by scholars. See the reviews of her critical edition by Stefano Carrai, *Rivista di letteratura italiana* 5, no. 1 (1987): 181–99; and by Emilio Bigi, *Giornale storico della letteratura italiana* 165 (1988): 307–11. In support of the title *Stanze*, Castagnola has also argued that Lorenzo's work is influenced more deeply by Poliziano's *Stanze* than by his *Silvae* or those of Statius; see Raffaella Castagnola, "Lorenzo classico: Considerazioni sulle 'Stanze,'" in *Lorenzo De' Medici: New Perspectives: Proceedings of the International Conference Held at Brooklyn College and the Graduate Center of the City University of New York, April 30–May 2, 1992*, ed. Bernard Toscani (New York: P. Lang, 1993), 64–6. Lorenzo was demonstrably familiar with all of the texts in question, and they all constitute important models for his work.

27 Martelli, *Studi laurenziani*, 146.

28 "Trovandosi il magnifico Lorenzo de' Medici, padre di papa Leone e gran poeta, in buona compagnia e divisandosi della natura dell'uomo, chi una cosa e chi un'altra dicea. Onde egli pregato di dirne la sua opinione, la descrisse all'improviso graziatamente in questa guisa, dicendo:

> Teme, spera, rallegrasi e contrista,
> ben mille volte il dì nostra natura.
> Spesso il mal la fa lieta e 'l ben l'attrista,
> spera il suo danno e del ben ha paura,
> tanta ha il viver mortal corta la vista.
> Al fin vano è ogni pensier e cura."

Quoted in Brian Richardson, "Improvising Lyric Verse in the Renaissance: Contexts, Sources and Imitation," in *Cultural Reception, Translation and Transformation from Medieval to Modern Italy: Essays in Honour of Martin McLaughlin*, ed. Guido Bonsaver, Brian Richardson, and Giuseppe Stellardi (Cambridge: Legenda, 2017), 101. The translation of the verses is from Medici, *Complete Literary Works of Lorenzo De' Medici*, 14; the translation of the prose is my own.

29 Richardson, "Improvising Lyric Verse in the Renaissance," 102.

30 Daniela Delcorno Branca, "Da Poliziano a Serafino," in *Miscellanea di studi in onore di Vittore Branca* (Florence: L.S. Olschki, 1983), 439–40.

31 Paul Oskar Kristeller, *Early Florentine Woodcuts: With an Annotated List of Florentine Illustrated Books* (London: Kegan Paul, Trench, Trübner, and Co., 1897), 109.

32   "Spesso soliva a la dolce ombra tangere
                      col plectro aurato la sonora cetera,
                      che facea per dolceza i saxi frangere,

                      cantando come l'età prima vetera
                      amasse il legno e despregiasse l'auro,
                      che il mondo brama più quanto più invetera."

    Italian text from Anna Ceruti Burgio, "La cultura fiorentina ai tempi del Magnifico: Echi della poesia di Lorenzo nelle rime di Jacopo Corsi," *Lettere Italiane* 26 (1974): 340–1.

33 "Il Corso, quale stava col reverendissimo cardinale Sanseverino et diceva in proviso et in sonetti, è stato morto de mezzo giorno apresso Monte Iordano da tre che erano a cavallo, vestiti a la spagnuola, incogniti. Si ha opinione che sia facto fare del cardinale San Pietro in Vincoli [Giuliano della Rovere], el quale aveva facto fare doglianze al papa chel doveva havere cantato improviso alcune cose poco honorevole de luy." ("Jacopo Corsi, who was a guest of the most reverend cardinal Sanseverino, and who used to perform improvised poetry and sonnets, was killed around noon near Monte Giordano by three unknown men on horseback, dressed in the Spanish style. The prevailing opinion is that this was ordered by the cardinal of San Pietro in Vincoli [Giuliano della Rovere], who had complained to the pope that Corsi had improvised some verses that were damaging to the cardinal's honor.") Text from Giovanni Parenti, "Corsi, Jacopo," in *Dizionario Biografico degli Italiani*, vol. 29 (Rome: Istituto della Enciclopedia Italiana, 1983).

34 "Mirificeque etiam voluptas ex his hominibus capi honesta potest qui ex tempore dicuntur plebeio sermone canere solere ad lyram. Quo ex genere, ut nuper B. Ugolinus et Jacobus Corsus in Italia sunt laudari soliti, sic hodie maxime debet Bernardus Accoltus celebrari." ("Marvellously, we can get honest enjoyment from these men who are said to be in the habit of singing extemporaneously to the lyre in the vernacular. Up until recently Baccio Ugolini and Jacopo Corsi have generally been praised as the greatest of this sort in Italy, but now Bernardo Accolti should be most celebrated.") The passage is quoted in Dionisotti, *Gli umanisti e il volgare fra Quattro e Cinquecento*, 73.

35 Vincenzo Calmeta, *Prose e lettere edite e inedite* (Bologna: Commissione per i testi di lingua, 1959), 11. Cited in Vittore Branca, *Poliziano e l'umanesimo della parola* (Turin: G. Einaudi, 1983), 446.

36 This is the most complete set of subtitles, which appears in MS XIII. D. 2 of the Biblioteca Nazionale di Napoli and MS Palatino 206 of the Biblioteca Nazionale Centrale di Firenze. Other manuscripts contain variations of these subtitles, in some cases including only a subset of them. In some manuscripts the subtitles are in vernacular Tuscan rather than Latin. See

Elisa Curti, *Tra due secoli: Per il tirocinio letterario di Pietro Bembo* (Bologna: Gedit Edizioni, 2006), 69–70.

37 *Selva I*, 102.7–8. Italian text from Medici, *Tutte le opere*, 574; translation from Medici, *Selected Poems and Prose*, 152.

38   "Così, pien di fatica e luce, il giorno
                pallida e rossa l'aurora caccia;
                lei poi la notte; qual fuggendo intorno
                convien che 'l giorno alfin sua preda faccia:
                e mentre suona il cacciatore il corno,
                vinto rimane in questa eterna caccia."

   Selva I, 97.1–6. Translation from Medici, *Selected Poems and Prose*, 150.

39 *Selva I*, 35.5–6. Italian text from Medici, *Tutte le opere*, 552.

40   "Nel primo tempo che Caòs antico
                partorí il figlio suo diletto Amore,
                nacque questa maligna dea ch'io dico:
                nel medesimo parto venne fore.
                Giove, padre benigno, al mondo amico,
                la relegò tra l'ombre inferiore
                con Pluton, con le Furie; e stiè con loro
                mentre regnò Saturno e l'età d'oro."

   Selva 1, 40.1–8. Italian text from Medici, *Tutte le opere*, 553–4; translation from Medici, *Selected Poems and Prose*, 143–4.

41 Tiziano Zanato's commentary on Lorenzo's *Selva I* attentively notes the major Hesiodic intertexts at play within the poem: see Medici, *Opere* (1992), 440 and following.

42 The Homeric Hymns and the hymns of Proclus are also among the works that Ficino mentions having translated in this early phase. See Ficino's letter to Martin Prenninger in Ficino, *The Letters of Marsilio Ficino*, 10:27.

43 *Theogony*, 115 and following; Hesiod, *Hesiod, the Homeric Hymns, and Homerica*, trans. Hugh G. Evelyn-White (Cambridge, MA: Harvard University Press, 1914), 86–7.

44 "Orfeo nell' Argonautica, imitando la teologia di Mercurio Trismegisto, quando cantò de' principii delle cose alla presentia di Chirone e degli Heroi, cioè huomini angelici, pose el chaos innanzi al mondo e dinanzi a Saturno, Giove e gli altri iddii. Nel seno d'esso chaos collocò l'Amore, dicendo Amore essere antiquissimo, per sé medesimo perfecto, di gran consiglio." *El libro dell'amore*, 1.3.1. Italian text from Marsilio Ficino, *El libro dell'amore*, ed. Sandra Niccoli (Florence: L.S. Olschki, 1987), 10; translation from Ficino, *Commentary on Plato's Symposium on Love*, 37–8.

45 Ficino, *Letters of Marsilio Ficino*, 1:98.

46 "Quod autem de Venere in Theologia tractat Hesiodus, cum dicit Saturnum castrasse coelium testiculosque in mare iecisse ex quibus et spuma

agitata nata sit Venus, intelligendum est forte de foecunditate rerum omnium procreandarum." Text and translation from Michael J.B. Allen, *Marsilio Ficino: The Philebus Commentary* (Tempe: Arizona Center for Medieval and Renaissance Studies Press, 2000), 139. Ficino is referring to *Theogony*, 178–206.

47 Translation from Hesiod, *Theogony, Works and Days, Testimonia*, ed. and trans. Glenn W. Most (Cambridge, MA: Harvard University Press, 2018), 4–5.

48 Translation from Hesiod, *Theogony, Works and Days, Testimonia*, 4–5.

49 Translation from Hesiod, *Theogony, Works and Days, Testimonia*, 4–5.

50 See letter 1.17 of Ficino's collected correspondence.

51 See Poliziano, *Stanze*, 1.97–9, in *Poesie*.

52 Cf. *Works and Days*, 232–3.

53 Janet Cox-Rearick, "Themes of Time and Rule at Poggio a Caiano: The Portico Frieze of Lorenzo Il Magnifico," *Mitteilungen des Kunsthistorischen Institutes in Florenz* 26 (1982): 183.

54   "E nel suo bel vexillo si vedea
         di sopra un sole e poi l'arcobaleno,
         dove a lettere d'oro si leggea:
         'Le tems revient,' che si può interpetrarsi
         tornare il tempo e 'l secol rinnovarsi."

    64.4–8. Italian text from Luigi Pulci, *Opere minori*, ed. Paolo Orvieto (Milan: Mursia, 1986), 86.

55 Text and translation from Dante Alighieri, *Purgatorio*, ed. Robert M. Durling and Ronald L. Martinez, trans. Robert M. Durling (Oxford: Oxford University Press, 2003), 386–7.

56 E.H. Gombrich, "Renaissance and Golden Age," *Journal of the Warburg and Courtauld Institutes* 24 (1961): 308.

57 "Hic sacros coluit vates, hic aurea nobis / Caesaris Augusti saecla redire dedit." Latin text from Ugolino Verino, *Flametta*, ed. Luciano Mencaraglia (Florence: L.S. Olschki, 1940), 107.

58 "Iam mihi, iam, Medices, te consultore redibant / Aurea Saturni saecla benigna senis." vv. 349–50. Latin text from Naldo Naldi, *Elegiarum libri III*, ed. László Juhász (Leipzig: B.G. Teubner, 1934), 89.

59   "Pria che venissi al figlio di Iapeto
         del tristo furto il dannoso pensiero,
         reggeva nel tempo aureo quieto
         Saturno il mondo sotto il giusto impero."

    Selve, 1.84.1–4. Italian text from Medici, *Tutte le opere*, 568; translation from Medici, *Selected Poems and Prose*, 147.

60 "Ergo ipsius boni radius quamquam in se unus hac tamen in mente triplice resultat et triplex: dum ad bonum quod coelium aliqui dicunt nititur, Saturnus; dum in se reflectitur, Jupiter; dum vertit ad inferiora,

Prometheus, hoc est, providentia." Text and translation from Allen, *Marsilio Ficino: The Philebus Commentary*, 240–1.

61 "Quo quidem gubernatore et quondam fuisse aurea secula perhibentur, et reditura quandoque uaticinatus est Plato, quando in eundem animum potestas sapientiaque concurrent." Text from Ficino, *Opera omnia*, 762–3; translation from Ficino, *Letters of Marsilio Ficino*, 3:31.

62 "In collibus Ambre Agnanaeque vallis Laurens ille Phoebeus Dionysio nectare passim ebrius debacchatur. Tum vero afflatus ex alto coelestia super hominem carmina fundit ore rotundo, profunda quorum sensa nullis unquam penetrare fas est, nisi ingeniis simili quodam furore correptis. Rapit vero secum noster ille patronus, nonnullos interdum attentius atque felicius audientes; in eos uidelicet prae caeteris ubertate furoris exuberans." Latin text from Ficino, *Opera omnia*, 927; translation from Ficino, *Letters of Marsilio Ficino*, 10:10.

63 "Qualem Gentes Orpheum, qualem nostri Dauidem fuisse t<r>adunt. Cognouimus et nos ingenium nostro seculo felicissimum, quatuor has aeque furorem dotes a quatuor numinibus consecutum." Latin text from Ficino, *Opera omnia*, 927; translation from Ficino, *Letters of Marsilio Ficino*, 10:10.

64 "Dicono che [Orfeo] col suono della sua cythera ragunava a sé le fiere, et muoveva e monti, et fermava e fiumi. Il che non è altro se non che chon la sua eloquentia tirava alla vita civile gli huomini efferati, et commovea alla virtù gl'huomini stupidi et rozzi, et acquietava l'impeto de' furiosi." Italian text from Cristoforo Landino, *Comento sopra la Comedia*, ed. Paolo Procaccioli (Rome: Salerno, 2001), 1:440.

5 The Improvisor and the World of the Courts

1 See Lucia Bertolini, "Michele di Nofri del Giogante e il Certame Coronario," *Rivista di letteratura italiana* 5 (1987): 467–77.

2 See McGee, *Ceremonial Musicians of Late Medieval Florence*, 84.

3 Robert Black, *Benedetto Accolti and the Florentine Renaissance* (Cambridge: Cambridge University Press, 1985), 215.

4 On Accolti, see Jonathan Unglaub, "Bernardo Accolti, Raphael's 'Parnassus' and a New Portrait by Andrea Del Sarto," *Burlington Magazine* 149, no. 1246 (2007): 14–22; Jonathan Unglaub, "Bernardo Accolti, Raphael, and the Sistine Madonna: The Poetics of Desire and Pictorial Generation," in *Ut Pictura Amor: The Reflexive Imagery of Love in Artistic Theory and Practice, 1500–1700*, ed. Walter S. Melion, Joanna Woodall, and Michael Zell (Boston and Leiden: Brill, 2017), 612–45; and Wilson, *Singing to the Lyre*, 295–303.

5 Anton Francesco Doni, *I Marmi*, ed. E. Chiòboli (Bari: G. Laterza, 1928), 2:46.

6 "Nè altrimenti che nei dì festivi, si serravano le botteghe, correndo ognuno in Castello tosto che si sapeva che il celebre Bernardo Accolti doveva

improvvisare al cospetto di infiniti grandi maestri e prelati." Italian text
from Gavagni, *L'Unico Aretino (Bernardo Accolti) e la corte dei duchi d'Urbino*,
7. See Danilo Romei, "Dalla Toscana a Roma: Pietro Aretino 'erede' di
Bernardo Accolti," in *Pietro Aretino nel cinquecentenario della nascita* (Rome:
Salerno, 1995), 183.

7 Blake Wilson, "*Canterino* and *Improvvisatore*: Oral Poetry and Performance,"
   in Busse Berger and Rodin, *Cambridge History of Fifteenth-Century Music*, 300–1.

8 "Sive coelestem Platonem audis, agnoscis protinus eius stylum, ut
   Aristoteles inquit, inter solutam orationem et carmen medium fluere.
   Agnoscis orationem Platonicam, ut Quintilianus ait, multum supra prosam
   pedestremque orationem surgere, ut non humano ingenio Plato noster,
   sed Delphico quodam oraculo videatur instinctus." Latin text from Ficino,
   Opera omnia, 724; translation from Ficino, *Letters of Marsilio Ficino*, 2:9. The
   passage is cited in Marsilio Ficino, *Marsilio Ficino and the Phaedran Charioteer:
   Introduction, Texts, Translations*, ed. Michael J.B. Allen (Berkeley: University
   of California Press, 1981), 12, 40.

9 Ficino, *Commentaries on Plato*, 4–5.

10 For an important study of the gender dimensions of performance practices
   in Quattrocento Florence, see Judith Bryce, "Performing for Strangers:
   Women, Dance, and Music in Quattrocento Florence," *Renaissance Quarterly*
   54, no. 4 (2001): 1074–107.

11 *Orlando furioso*, 46.10.

12 "Mirificeque etiam voluptas ex his hominibus capi honesta potest qui ex
   tempore dicuntur plebeio sermone canere solere ad lyram. Quo ex genere,
   ut nuper B. Ugolinus et Jacobus Corsus in Italia sunt laudari soliti, sic
   hodie maxime debet Bernardus Accoltus celebrari, qui, quanquam versus
   ex tempore dicat, ita tamen apte sententiis verba concinna iungit, ut, cum
   celeritati semper parata sit venia, magis in eo sint laudanda quae fundat
   quam ignoscendum quod ex tempore et partu repentino dicat." Latin text
   from Dionisotti, *Gli umanisti e il volgare fra Quattro e Cinquecento*, 73.

13 "At uero carminum modi hi numerari solent qui maxime octasticorum aut
   trinariorum ratione constant ... Quare iure affirmari potest uehementius
   in hoc genere editis carminibus animorum solere sedari et incitari motus.
   Nam cum uerborum sentantiarumque numeri cum modorum suauitate
   coniunguntur, nihil cause esse potest quin propter aurium uim animique
   similitudinem maxima permotio in audiendo fiat. Idque tum fere saepe
   euenire solet cum uersibus aut turbidi canendo repraesentantur motus aut
   animi morum disciplinaeque institutione admonentur, in qua sita foelicitas
   humana sit." Text and translation from Nino Pirrotta, "Music and Cultural
   Tendencies in 15th-Century Italy," *Journal of the American Musicological Society*
   19 (1966): 151–5. On the intellectual context of Cortesi's *De cardinalatu*, see
   Hankins, "Humanism and Music in Italy," 248–51.

14 "Multa eius variis modis descripta carmina circumferuntur, sed in eo maxime unicus et insignis semper fuit cum Polyxenam ad aram pereuntem et
quartum Virgilii librum de Didonis amoribus ab se incomparabili felicitate
translatum ad lyram magnis principibus recitaret." Latin text from Paolo
Giovio, *Notable Men and Women of Our Time*, ed. and trans. Kenneth Gouwens
(Cambridge, MA: Harvard University Press, 2013), 262–3.

15 This initial section of *capitoli* is followed by a collection of *strambotti* attributed
to Accolti, and the last section consists mainly of *sonetti*, with some additional
strambotti. On this manuscript, see Maria Pia Mussini Sacchi, "Le ottave epigrammatiche di Bernardo Accolti nel ms. Rossiano 680: Per la storia dell'epigramma in volgare tra Quattro e Cinquecento," *Interpres* 15 (1995):
219–301; and Raffaella Ianuale, "Prima ricognizione del manoscritto Rossiano 680 della Biblioteca Apostolica Vaticana," *Filologia e critica* 19 (1994):
275–96. The work by Mussini Sacchi and Ianuale on texts attributed to Accolti in this manuscript has focused on the shorter lyric poems (*strambotti* and
sonetti) and not on the *capitoli* that are analysed in the present chapter.

16 "l'ordine della lor testura […] è tanto noto, fino al volgo, che ancora all'improviso si truovan molti, che ne compongono, et ancora perfettamente."
Text and translation from Richardson, *Manuscript Culture in Renaissance
Italy*, 252–3.

17 "Sì come fra molti s'ha memoria di M. Nicolò Macchiavelli, il quale
aprendo qual si voglia poeta Latino, et mettendoselo avanti sopr'una tavola
egli sonando la lira veniva improvisamente cantando, et volgarizando, ò
traducendo quei versi di quel poeta, et facendone stanze d'Ottava Rima,
con tanta leggiadria di stile, et con tanta agevolezza serbando i veri modi
del tradurre, che il mio M. Francesco del Nero, il quale fu molto suo
domestico, mi raccontava in Napoli, che egli con molt'altri in Fiorenza
fecero ogni pruova per chiarirsi, che il detto Macchiavelli ciò facesse
improvisamente, parendo a ciascuno impossibile, che all'improviso egli
potesse far quello, che molti dotti, et di sublime ingegno confessavano, che
haverebbono penato à far con qualche convenevole spatio di tempo." Text
and translation from Richardson, *Manuscript Culture in Renaissance Italy*,
252–3. See also Degl'Innocenti, "Machiavelli canterino?"

18 Virgil, *Eclogues, Georgics, Aeneid 1–6*, trans. H. Rushton Fairclough and
G.P. Goold (Cambridge, MA: Harvard University Press, 1999), 442–3.

19 "Quid moror? an mea Pygmalion dum moenia frater / destruat aut captam
ducat Gaetulus Iarbas?" Text and translation from Virgil, *Eclogues, Georgics,
Aeneid 1–6*, 444–5.

20 "Ogni hor mi par mio fratel crudo / Veder nel regno mio con fiamma
infesta. / Parmi vedere ogni hora el ferro nudo / Di Iarba re, qual con
fronte sicura / Per te exclusi; hor me di vita excluda." Italian text from
Vatican Library (BAV) manuscript Ross. 680, f. 6v.

21 "Con dextra feroce / fa sopra a me de' Greci la vendetta." Italian text from
    BAV MS Ross. 680, f. 7r.
22 Italian text from BAV MS Ross. 680, f. 7r.
23 See Marjorie Curry Woods, *Weeping for Dido: The Classics in the Medieval Class-
    room* (Princeton, NJ: Princeton University Press, 2019), 139–40.
24 See, for example, the passage by Cassio da Narni quoted in the introduction
    and in Gavagni, *L'Unico Aretino (Bernardo Accolti) e la corte dei duchi d'Urbino*, 6.
25 Italian text from BAV MS Ross. 680, f. 26r.
26 Italian text from BAV MS Ross. 680, f. 26r.
27   "iamque iterum moriens non est de coniuge quicquam
                questa suo (quid enim nisi se quereretur amatam?)
                supremumque 'vale,' quod iam vix auribus ille
                acciperet, dixit revolutaque rursus eodem est."
    Text and translation from Ovid, *Metamorphoses*, vol. 2, trans. Frank Justus
    Miler and G.P. Goold (Cambridge, MA: Harvard University Press, 1916),
    68–9.
28 Degl'Innocenti, "Verba manent," 110–11. On this text, see also Paolo
    Orvieto, "Boccaccio mediatore di generi o dell'allegoria dell'amore,"
    Interpres 2 (1978): 68.
29 "E accadendo con alcuni, io per via de diporto, alternando cantar versi
    impremeditati, datosi l'uno a l'altro la materia diversa, a me tocò per sorte
    tractare de un figmento amoroso, se non vero, non del tutto falso." Italian
    text from da Correggio, *Opere*, 4.
30 "Alcune stanzie, non lo sapendo io, furno da certi astanti … in quel punto
    raccolte; che certo a me ne dolse." Italian text from da Correggio, *Opere*, 4.
31 "de l'ornamento de la lira private." Italian text from da Correggio, *Opere*, 4.
32 "cantata nel passato carnevale." Italian text from da Correggio, *Opere*, 500.
33 Tissoni Benvenuti, "La ricezione delle *Silvae* di Stazio e la poesia all'improv-
    viso nel Rinascimento," 1304–5.
34 This exchange is discussed in Richardson, *Manuscript Culture in Renaissance
    Italy*, 249.
35 Alessandro Luzio and Rodolfo Renier, "Niccolò da Correggio," *Giornale
    storico della letteratura italiana* 21 (1893): 247.
36 James Haar, *The Science and Art of Renaissance Music*, ed. Paul E. Corneilson
    (Princeton, NJ: Princeton University Press, 1998), 26.
37 "quelle non solo iudicando ma perfectamente componendo e
    perfectamente in viola o leuto recitandole." Text and translation from
    William F. Prizer, "Una 'Virtù Molto Conveniente a Madonne': Isabella
    D'Este as a Musician," *Journal of Musicology* 17, no. 1 (1999): 33.
38 See Ciminelli, *Strambotti*, 300–1.
39 "Per la qual ragione e auttorità par quasi poter affermare che senza lettere
    un poeta volgare possa a qualche parte di perfezione nella profession

poetica aggiungere, purché da natura sia di poetica vena dotato e da divino furor mosso." Italian text from Calmeta, *Prose e lettere edite e inedite*, 8–9.

40 "Che maggior instinto di natura si potria trovare di quel che hanno avuto Luigi Pulci, il Corso e 'l Serafino e molti altri? Ne' quali, per la inequalità dell'opere loro, massime in composizion lunga, si discerne apertamente, in molti luoghi, dove l'arte, della quale erano ignari, sarebbe stata necessaria loro." Italian text from Calmeta, *Prose e lettere edite e inedite*, 11.

41 Calmeta, *Prose e lettere edite e inedite*, 11.

42 "Nulla est enim tanta ubertas ingenii, quam sine huius artis ratione bene disposta ac praeclare inventa possit effingere." Latin text from Giacomo Ferrau, "Il 'De hominibus doctis' di Paolo Cortesi," in *Umanità e storia: Studi in onore di Adelchi Attisani* (Naples: Giannini, 1971), 286.

43 "Nam, cum poeta vi naturae inflammetur, numquam desperat quod optimum est: et propterea multos decipit illa P. Maronis blanda, sui concil- iatrix, Musa quum dulci tantummodo sono deliniti, reconditum artificium non agnoscant." Latin text from Ferrau, "Il 'De hominibus doctis' di Paolo Cortesi," 287.

44 Wilson discusses *Il Cortegiano* in relation to the art of the *improvvisatori* in Wilson, *Singing to the Lyre*, 287–95.

45 Haar, *Science and Art of Renaissance Music*, 26.

46 "Ma sopra tutto parmi gratissimo il cantare alla viola per recitare; il che tanto di venustà ed efficacia aggiunge alle parole, che è gran maraviglia." *Cortegiano*, 2.13. Italian text from Baldesar Castiglione, *Il libro del cortegiano*, ed. Bruno Maier (Turin: UTET, 1981), 213; translation from Baldesar Castiglione, *The Book of the Courtier*, ed. Daniel Javitch, trans. Charles Singleton (New York: W.W. Norton, 2002), 76.

47 Haar, *Science and Art of Renaissance Music*, 26.

48 Gavagni, *L'Unico Aretino (Bernardo Accolti) e la corte dei duchi d'Urbino*, 5–6.

49 Unglaub, "Bernardo Accolti, Raphael, and the Sistine Madonna," 631.

50 "Heri sera l'Unico Aretino disse a l'improviso inanti al Papa, per tre hore, con grandissima audientia: secondo il suo consueto mirabelmente." Italian text from Castiglione, *Le Lettere I (1497–Marzo 1521)*, ed. Guido La Rocca (Milan: Mondadori, 1978), 711. The letter is cited in Anthony M. Cummings, *The Maecenas and the Madrigalist: Patrons, Patronage, and the Origins of the Italian Madrigal* (Philadelphia: American Philosophical Society, 2004), 83, 239.

51 "L'Unico, avendo tacciuto alquanto ed essendogli pur replicato che dicesse, in ultimo disse un sonetto sopra la materia predetta, dechiarando ciò che significava quella lettera S; che da molti fu estimato fatto all'improvviso, ma, per esser ingenioso e culto più che non parve che comportasse la brevità del tempo, si pensò pur che fosse pensato." Italian text from Castiglione, *Il libro del cortegiano*, 98; translation from Castiglione, *Book of the Courtier*, 17.

52 Italian text from Castiglione, *Il libro del cortegiano*, 98.

53 *Cortegiano*, 1.9. Italian text from Castiglione, *Il libro del cortegiano*, 97.

54   "Carmina, quae subito tibi sunt effusa calore,

                          Vel quae sunt lima saepe polita tua

                          Qui legit, haud cernit quid differat impetus arte

                          Et procusa pari cuncta labore putat,

                          Atque ait: haec si est ars, nihil hac est cultius arte:

                          Si furor, est ars hoc culta furore minus."

    Latin text from Giovanni Matteo Toscano, *Peplus Italiae* (Paris: Morelli,
    1578), 58.

55 "Vedete adunque come il mostrar l'arte ed un così intento studio levi la
    grazia d'ogni cosa." *Cortegiano*, 1.26. Italian text from Castiglione, *Il libro del
    cortegiano*, 128; translation from Castiglione, *Book of the Courtier*, 32.

56 "usar in ogni cosa una certa sprezzatura, che nasconda l'arte e dimostri ciò
    che si fa e dice venir fatto senza fatica e quasi senza pensarvi. Da questo
    credo io che derivi assai la grazia; perché delle cose rare e ben fatte ognun
    sa la difficultà, onde in esse la facilità genera grandissima maraviglia."
    Cortegiano, 1.26. Italian text from Castiglione, *Il libro del cortegiano*, 127–8;
    translation from Castiglione, *Book of the Courtier*, 32.

57 "Quamlibet enim multis neque fucosis ornamentis abundarent, minime
    tamen homini de omni sua existimatione sollicito vel haec ipsa celeritatis
    commendatio fuerat negligenda, quippe cui et indulgentia liberior et venia
    proclivior et admiratio maior deberetur." *Oratio super Fabio Quintiliano et
    Statii Sylvis*. Latin text from Garin, *Prosatori latini del Quattrocento*, 874–5.

Conclusion

1 "A ben conoscere l'entusiasmo di Corilla basta averla udita alcuna volta cantare, e dagli effetti sperimentati in noi stessi argomentare qual sia la natura
   e l'impeto di quel fuoco, che accende i sensi, incanta l'anima, e l'inebria, e
   l'innamora, e l'inonda di un'intima soavissima voluttà … Chi allora di voi
   non conobbe i manifesti segni dell'entusiasmo, che è uno stato dell'anima
   non ordinario? Chi non la vide star cheta prima e svogliata, incominciar
   languida e incerta, indi in un punto accendersi, ravvivarsi, levarsi sull'ale,
   affrettare il gesto e la voce … alzarsi ad una sfera più alta, e spirando
   un'aria più pura allontanarsi in certa guisa dalla condizion di mortale."
   Italian text from Evangelista Ferrari, Domenico Cagnoni, and Giambattista
   Bodoni, *Atti della solenne coronazione fatta in Campidoglio della insigne poetessa
   D[on]na Maria Maddalena Morelli Fernandez, pistojese tra gli Arcadi Corilla
   Olimpica* (Parma: Stamperia reale di Parma, 1779), 47–9.

2 Benedetto Croce, *Conversazioni critiche* (Bari: G. Laterza and Figli, 1918),
   219. On the effects Croce's negative judgments had in slowing the

development of scholarly work on the *improvvisatori*, see also Françoise Waquet, *Rhétorique et poétique chrétiennes: Bernardino Perfetti et la poésie improvisée dans l'Italie du XVIIIe siècle* (Florence: L.S. Olschki, 1992), 44–5.

3 "La nuova estetica aveva messo in primo piano, accanto o sopra del gusto, il genio, e aveva insistito su questo concetto come proprio della poesia e delle altre arti … l'ideale rapporto tra genio estetico e creazione artistica fu tradotto nell'altro, materialmente concepito, del poetare rapido e immediato o, come si diceva, all'improvviso." Benedetto Croce, "Gl'improvvisatori," in *La letteratura italiana del Settecento: Note critiche* (Bari: Laterza, 1949), 301.

4 "non solo la moda ma la genìa stessa degli improvvisatori spari dall'Italia." Croce, "Gl'improvvisatori," 305–6.

5 Croce, *Conversazioni critiche*, 219.

6 Alessandra Di Ricco noted this shortcoming, observing that Gentili "ends up contemplating 'the precise and surprising correspondence' between the extemporaneous poetry of the eighteenth century and the oral poetry of the ancient rhapsodes without offering an explanation for this apparent continuity" ("[Gentili] finisce col contemplare la 'puntuale e sorprendente rispondenza' tra la poesia estemporanea del Settecento e quella orale degli antichi aedi greci senza dar spiegazione di questa apparente continuità"). Alessandra Di Ricco, *L'inutile e maraviglioso mestiere: Poeti improvvisatori di fine Settecento* (Milan: Franco Angeli, 1990), 8.

7 Carlo Caruso, "Pietro Giordani e la poesia all'improvviso," in *Giordani Leopardi 1998: Convegno nazionale di studi, Piacenza, Palazzo Farnese, 2–4 aprile 1998*, ed. Roberto Tissoni (Piacenza: Tip.Le.Co., 2000), 164–71; Fabio Finotti, "Il canto delle Muse: Improvvisazione e poetica della voce," in *Corilla Olimpica e la poesia del Settecento europeo*, ed. Moreno Fabbri (Pistoia: Artout, 2002), 32–4.

8 Degl'Innocenti, *I Reali dell'Altissimo*, 236–9.

9 McGee, *Ceremonial Musicians of Late Medieval Florence*, 83.

10 "Nè altrimenti che nei dì festivi, si serravano le botteghe, correndo ognuno in Castello tosto che si sapeva che il celebre Bernardo Accolti doveva improvvisare al cospetto di infiniti grandi maestri e prelati." Gavagni, *L'Unico Aretino (Bernardo Accolti) e la corte dei duchi d'Urbino*, 7.

11 While Croce fails to acknowledge the importance of the phenomenon of poetic improvisation in the Renaissance, he does recognize that Renaissance theories of poetic frenzies influenced the later theories of inspiration and genius that shaped eighteenth- and nineteenth-century discussions of the *improvvisatori*. Croce, "Gl'improvvisatori," 301.

12 Crescimbeni, *L'istoria della volgar poesia*, 1:220–1. See Finotti, "Il canto delle Muse," 31–2.

13 Pier Francesco Versari, "Dialogo pastorale," in *I giuochi olimpici celebrati in Arcadia nell'ingresso dell'olimpiade DCXXXIII: In onore degli Arcadi illustri defunti* (Rome: Monaldini, 1754), 48–9.

14 "la più celebre donna del nostro secolo, a cui Natura fè dono del vero estro
e di quell'entusiasmo, che vantavano già la illustre Saffo, e 'l gran Pindaro,
ma che in lor parve tale, perché coll'arte emularono la natura, ed ispirati
si fecer credere, perché il perfetto studio e lavoro giunse a nascondere, ed
a sopprimere i replicati sforzi dell'arte?" *Adunanza tenuta dagli Arcadi per la
coronazione della celebre pastorella Corilla Olimpica* (Rome: Salomoni, 1775),
xxiv–xxv. The passage is quoted in Raimondo Guarino, "L'incoronazione di
Corilla Olimpica e l'improvvisazione in Arcadia nel Settecento," *Atti e memorie dell'Arcadia* 5 (2016): 182.

15 "Poeta, che tale è nato, e che animato da un fuoco elettrico interno si desta,
si anima, e si solleva, sopra la mortal condizione, e canta senza preparazi-
one, e canta nobili cose, e accende a nobili imprese, e adopera il linguaggio
vero de' Numi, e fa vedere gli oggetti vivi e presenti, e seduce la fantasia,
v'ispira i suoi sentimenti, v'incanta il cuore, si fa padrone di voi." *Adunanza
tenuta dagli Arcadi per la coronazione della celebre pastorella Corilla Olimpica*,
xxiv–xxv. The passage is quoted in Guarino, "L'incoronazione di Corilla
Olimpica e l'improvvisazione in Arcadia nel Settecento," 182.

16 "Diceva però, che quasi nulla intendeva cosa dicesse, quando era
nell'apice del suo furore: ed infatti Ella non riconosceva mai per sue certe
cose vibrate, ed entusiastiche, che restavano impresse nello stupefatto
uditorio, e che le si ripetevano dopo l'improviso, benché provasse una
modesta compiacenza d'averle dette." Cristofano Amaduzzi, letter of 29
April 1777 to Aurelio de' Giorgi Bertola, in Carlo Grigioni, "Sedici anni
della vita di Corilla Olimpica in un carteggio inedito (1776–1792)," *La
Romagna* 17 (1928): 287–8. Cited in Paola Giuli, "'Monsters of Talent':
Fame and Reputation of Women Improvisers in Arcadia," in *Italy's Eight-
eenth Century: Gender and Culture in the Age of the Grand Tour*, ed. Paula
Findlen, Wendy Wassyng Roworth, and Catherine M. Sama (Stanford, CA:
Stanford University Press, 2009), 325.

17 "Se questi pregi sieno comuni a tutte le donne poetesse per la maggiore
sensibilità dei loro nervi, per la maggiore elasticità, e delicatezza delle loro
fibre, e per qualche stravagante prodigioso rapporto dell'utero colla loro
mente, io non so: ma so bene che Ella mi è sembrata sempre superiore,
ne' suoi voli, ne' suoi trasporti, nelle sue immagini, nelle sue idee a tutti gli
omini poeti, che ho sentito in suo confronto, e lungi da Lei." Italian text
from Guarino, "L'incoronazione di Corilla Olimpica e l'improvvisazione in
Arcadia nel Settecento," 186.

18 "Io non avrei mai avuto idea dell'entusiasmo estemporaneo, se non avessi
veduto il bel fuoco, e non avessi udito i bei trasporti di Corilla … Dirò solo,
e il dirò con verità, che la sola Corilla ha a me potuto dare qualche idea,
e convincermi della possibilità di certe donne entusiastiche, ed invasate
di spirito presago, che abbia un tempo avuto l'antichità." Italian text from

Guarino, "L'incoronazione di Corilla Olimpica e l'improvvisazione in Arcadia nel Settecento," 186.

19 On Bettinelli, see Walter Binni, "Tra illuminismo e romanticismo: Saverio Bettinelli," in *Preromanticismo italiano* (Florence: Sansoni, 1985), 45–66; and Philippe Audegean, "Poésie et philosophie dans l' 'Entusiasmo' de Saverio Bettinelli," *Revue des études italiennes* 55 (2009): 291–7.

20 "Non v'ha forse esempio più manifesto dell' Entusiasmo quasi visibile quanto nell'occasione d'improvvisare. Un eccellente poeta estemporaneo, allorchè veramente è caldo dell'estro suo fa conoscere tutti gli effetti sopraccennati mirabilmente. Ho posto mente attentissima a quell'azione più volte, e ognun può verificare, osservandone uno de' più eccellenti, cui m'ha dato la sorte di potere soventemente considerare." Italian text from Saverio Bettinelli, *Dell'entusiasmo delle belle arti* (Milan: Giuseppe Galeazzi, 1769), 48.

21 "Così pure in Toscana ed altrove furon cantori non solo improvvisando, ma cantando lor rime Marsilio Ficino a quel tempo, e l'Aquilano, come dicemmo, e Nicolò Cieco d'Arezzo, e l'Altissimo, e il Tibaldeo, e Bernardo Accolti." Italian text from Saverio Bettinelli, *Risorgimento d'Italia negli studi, nelle arti e ne' costumi dopo il mille, Saverio Bettinelli: A cui si aggiugne ora per la prima volta l'Elogio del Petrarca scritta ultimamente dal medesimo autore* (Bassano: Remondini, 1786), 142.

22 P.M.S. Dawson, "Shelley and the Improvvisatore Sgricci: An Unpublished Review," *Keats-Shelley Memorial Bulletin* 32 (1981): 20.

23 Dawson, "Shelley and the Improvvisatore Sgricci," 25.

24 Percy Bysshe Shelley, *Selected Prose Works of Shelley* (London: Watts and Co., 1915), 118.

25 Dawson, "Shelley and the Improvvisatore Sgricci," 22. Dawson notes connections between the *Ion*, Shelley's review of Sgricci's performance, and "Defence of Poetry."

26 James A. Notopoulos, *The Platonism of Shelley: A Study of Platonism and the Poetic Mind* (Durham, NC: Duke University Press, 1949), 346–56, 462. See also James Whitehead, *Madness and the Romantic Poet: A Critical History* (Oxford: Oxford University Press, 2017), 32–3.

27 This approach by Shelley has been documented in detail by Stephanie Nelson, who observes that "Shelley used the Bipontine edition of Plato, with an accompanying Latin translation by the Neo-Platonist Marsilio Ficino (1433–1499) and was deeply dependent on this translation, often translating Ficino rather than the Greek." Stephanie Nelson, "Shelley and Plato's Symposium: The Poet's Revenge," *International Journal of the Classical Tradition* 14, no. 1/2 (2007): 101.

28 Shelley, *Selected Prose Works of Shelley*, 111.

29 Shelley, *Selected Prose Works of Shelley*, 95–6.

30 Shelley, *Selected Prose Works of Shelley*, 105.

31 See Angela Esterhammer's discussion of Shelley's "Orpheus" in *Romanticism and Improvisation, 1750–1850* (New York: Cambridge University Press, 2008), 119–20.

32 Percy Bysshe Shelley, *Relics of Shelley* (London: Edward Moxon, 1862), 20.

33 This interpretation was advanced first by Shelley's editor Richard Garnet in Shelley, *Relics of Shelley*, 20. See also Dawson, "Shelley and the Improvvisatore Sgricci," 20.

34 Shelley, *Relics of Shelley*, 20.

35 See Caruso, "Pietro Giordani e la poesia all'improvviso."

36 "E qui vi repetiamo che una successione ordinata di buoni pensieri, che è proprietà d'ingegno non volgare, ed acquisto di molte fatiche, non potrà mai (checchè ne dicano i ciurmatori) ottenersi per un subitaneo furore, per una repentina ispirazione. Non v'è altro furore che l'ingegno, non altra ispirazione che dallo studio. Or quale ingegno, quale studio hanno comunemente gl'improvvisatori? E n'avessero quanto Omero e Dante: non v'è ingegno, non v'è studio, che possa operare senza tempo." Italian text from Pietro Giordani, *Opere di Pietro Giordani*, vol. 10, ed. Antonio Gussalli (Milan: Borroni e Scotti, 1854), 106.

37 See, for example, Whitehead, *Madness and the Romantic Poet*, 41–4.

38 Angela Esterhammer, "The Improvisation of Poetry, 1750–1850: Oral Performance, Print Culture, and the Modern Homer," in *The Oxford Handbook of Critical Improvisation Studies*, ed. George Lewis and Benjamin Piekut, vol. 1 (New York: Oxford University Press, 2016), 239–54.

39 Eric Alfred Havelock, *Preface to Plato* (Cambridge, MA: Belknap Press, Harvard University Press, 1963), 156.

40 Luca Degl'Innocenti, "Singing and Printing Chivalric Poems in Early Modern Italy," *Journal of Early Modern Studies* 7 (2018): 43–62; Marco Villoresi, "Zanobi della Barba, canterino ed editore del Rinascimento," in *Il cantare italiano fra folklore e letteratura: Atti del Convegno internazionale di Zurigo (Landesmuseum, 23–25 giugno 2005)*, ed. Michelangelo Picone and Luisa Rubini (Florence: Olschki, 2007), 461–73; Lorenz Böninger, "Ricerche sugli inizi della stampa fiorentina (1471–1473)," *La Bibliofilia* 105 (2003): 225–48; and Peter Burke, "Oral Culture and Print Culture in Renaissance Italy," *ARV: Nordic Yearbook of Folklore* 54 (1998): 7–18.

41 See, for instance, Lord, *Singer of Tales*, 26.

Bibliography

Adunanza tenuta dagli Arcadi per la coronazione della celebre pastorella Corilla Olimpica. Rome: Salomoni, 1775.

Agamennone, Maurizio, ed. *Cantar ottave: Per una storia culturale dell'intonazione cantata in ottava rima.* Lucca: Libreria musicale italiana, 2017.

Ageno, Franca Brambilla. "Una nuova lettera di Luigi Pulci a Lorenzo de' Medici." *Giornale Storico della Letteratura Italiana* 141 (1964): 103–10.

Alighieri, Dante. *Purgatorio.* Edited by Robert M. Durling and Ronald L. Martinez. Translated by Robert M. Durling. Oxford: Oxford University Press, 2003.

Allen, Michael J.B. *Marsilio Ficino: The Philebus Commentary.* Tempe: Arizona Center for Medieval and Renaissance Studies Press, 2000.

– "The Soul as Rhapsode: Marsilio Ficino's Interpretation of Plato's Ion." In *Plato's Third Eye: Studies in Marsilio Ficino's Metaphysics and Its Sources,* XV:125–48. Brookfield, VT: Variorum, 1995.

– "Summoning Plotinus: Ficino, Smoke and the Strangled Chickens." In *Reconsidering the Renaissance: Papers from the Twenty-First Annual Conference Medieval & Renaissance Texts & Studies,* edited by Mario A. Di Cesare, 63–88. Binghamton, NY: Medieval & Renaissance Texts & Studies, 1992.

Allen, Michael J.B., and Marsilio Ficino. *Icastes: Marsilio Ficino's Interpretation of Plato's Sophist: Five Studies and a Critical Edition with Translation.* Berkeley: University of California Press, 1989.

Audegean, Philippe. "Poésie et philosophie dans l' 'Entusiasmo' de Saverio Bettinelli." *Revue des études italiennes* 55 (2009): 291–7.

Ausonius. *Ausonius.* Translated by Hugh G. Evelyn White. Cambridge, MA: Harvard University Press, 1985.

Ausonius, Decimus Magnus. *Ausonius: Moselle, Epigrams, and Other Poems.* Translated by Deborah Warren. Abingdon, UK: Routledge, 2017.

Bausi, Francesco. "Lorenzo de' Medici tra pubblico e privato: In margine al XII volume delle Lettere del Magnifico." *Schede umanistiche* 22 (2008): 91–121.

– "Orfeo e Achille: La prefazione alla 'Manto' di Angelo Poliziano." *Schede umanistiche* 1 (1992): 31–59.

Becherini, Bianca. "Un canta in panca fiorentino, Antonio di Guido." *Rivista musicale italiana* 50 (1948): 241–7.

Bérauld, Nicolas. *"Praelectio" et commentaire à la "Silve Rusticus" d'Ange Politien (1518)*. Edited by Perrine Galand. Geneva: Droz, 2015.

Bertolini, Lucia. "Michele di Nofri del Giogante e il Certame Coronario." *Rivista di letteratura italiana* 5 (1987): 467–77.

Bettinelli, Saverio. *Dell'entusiasmo delle belle arti*. Milan: Giuseppe Galeazzi, 1769.

– *Risorgimento d'Italia negli studi, nelle arti e ne' costumi dopo il mille, Saverio Bettinelli: A cui si aggiugne ora per la prima volta l'Elogio del Petrarca scritta ultimamente dal medesimo autore*. Bassano: Remondini, 1786.

Bettinzoli, Attilio. "Le 'Sylvae': Questioni di poetica." In *Daedaleum iter: Studi sulla poesia e la poetica di Angelo Poliziano*, 67–151. Florence: Leo S. Olschki, 1995.

Bigi, Emilio. "Recensione." *Giornale storico della letteratura italiana* 165 (1988): 307–11.

Binni, Walter. "Tra illuminismo e romanticismo: Saverio Bettinelli." In *Preromanticismo italiano*, 45–66. Florence: Sansoni, 1985.

Black, Robert. *Benedetto Accolti and the Florentine Renaissance*. Cambridge: Cambridge University Press, 1985.

Böninger, Lorenz. "Ricerche sugli inizi della stampa fiorentina (1471–1473)." *La Bibliofilia* 105 (2003): 225–48.

Bracciolini, Poggio. *Facezie*. Edited by Stefano Pittaluga. Milan: Garzanti, 1995.

Branca, Vittore. *Poliziano e l'umanesimo della parola*. Turin: G. Einaudi, 1983.

Branciforte, Suzanne. "Ars Poetica Rei Publicae: The Herald of the Florentine Signoria." PhD diss., University of California, Los Angeles, 1990.

Brandolini, Raffaele Lippo. *On Music and Poetry [De musica et poetica, 1513]*. Translated by Ann E. Moyer and Marc Laureys. Tempe: Arizona Center for Medieval and Renaissance Studies, 2001.

Bruni, Leonardo. *Epistolarum libri VIII*. 2 vols. Edited by Lorenzo Mehus and James Hankins. Rome: Edizioni di storia e letteratura, 2007.

Bruni, Leonardo, and Paolo Viti. *Opere letterarie e politiche*. Turin: UTET, 1996.

Bryce, Judith. "Performing for Strangers: Women, Dance, and Music in Quattrocento Florence." *Renaissance Quarterly* 54, no. 4 (2001): 1074–107.

Burgio, Anna Ceruti. "La cultura fiorentina ai tempi del Magnifico: Echi della poesia di Lorenzo nelle rime di Jacopo Corsi." *Lettere Italiane* 26 (1974): 338–48.

Burke, Peter. "Oral Culture and Print Culture in Renaissance Italy." *ARV: Nordic Yearbook of Folklore* 54 (1998): 7–18.

Cabani, Maria Cristina. *Le forme del cantare epico-cavalleresco*. Lucca: Maria Pacini Fazzi Editore, 1988.

Calmeta, Vincenzo. *Prose e lettere edite e inedite*. Bologna: Commissione per i testi di lingua, 1959.

Campanus, Joannes Antonius. *Epistolae et poemata*. Edited by Joannes Burchardus Menckenius. Leipzig: Gleditch, 1707.

Canguilhem, Philippe. "Improvisation as Concept and Musical Practice in the Fifteenth Century." In *The Cambridge History of Fifteenth-Century Music*, edited by Anna Maria Busse Berger and Jesse Rodin, 149–63. Cambridge: Cambridge University Press, 2015.

Carrai, Stefano. "Appunti sulla prima fortuna volgare degli *Inni orfici*." In *Dotti bizantini e libri greci nell'Italia del secolo XV: Atti del convegno internazionale, Trento 22–23 ottobre 1990*, edited by Mariarosa Cortesi and Enrico V. Maltese, 193–200. Naples: M. D'Auria, 1992.

– "Recensione." *Rivista di letteratura italiana* 5, no. 1 (1987): 181–99.

Caruso, Carlo. "Pietro Giordani e la poesia all'improvviso." In *Giordani Leopardi 1998: Convegno nazionale di studi, Piacenza, Palazzo Farnese, 2–4 aprile 1998*, edited by Roberto Tissoni, 161–83. Piacenza: Tip.Le.Co., 2000.

Castagna, Luigi. "Il 'Politiani tumulus' di Pietro Bembo (Carminum XXVI)." *Aevum* 69, no. 3 (1995): 533–53.

Castagnola, Raffaella. "Lorenzo classico: Considerazioni sulle 'Stanze.'" In *Lorenzo De' Medici: New Perspectives: Proceedings of the International Conference Held at Brooklyn College and the Graduate Center of the City University of New York, April 30–May 2, 1992*, edited by Bernard Toscani, 61–84. New York: P. Lang, 1993.

Castiglione, Baldesar. *The Book of the Courtier*. Edited by Daniel Javitch. Translated by Charles Singleton. New York: W.W. Norton, 2002.

– *Le Lettere I (1497–Marzo 1521)*. Edited by Guido La Rocca. Milan: Mondadori, 1978.

– *Il libro del cortegiano*. Edited by Bruno Maier. Turin: UTET, 1981.

Cave, Terence. *The Cornucopian Text*. Oxford: Oxford University Press, 1985.

Celenza, Christopher S. "Poliziano's *Lamia* in Context." In *Angelo Poliziano's Lamia: Text, Translation, and Introductory Studies*, edited by Christopher S. Celenza, 1–45. Leiden: Brill, 2010.

Christensen, Thomas. "The Improvisatory Moment." In *Studies in Historical Improvisation: From Cantare Super Librum to Partimenti*, edited by Massimiliano Guido, 9–24. New York: Routledge, 2017.

Cicero, Marcus Tullius. *Cicero: De Inventione, De Optimo Genere Oratorum, Topica*. Translated by H.M. Hubbell. Cambridge, MA: Harvard University Press, 1968.

– *Rhetorica Ad Herennium*. Translated by Harry Caplan. Cambridge, MA: Harvard University Press, 1954.

Ciminelli, Serafino. *Strambotti*. Edited by Antonio Rossi. Parma: Ugo Guanda Editore, 2002.

Cohen, Simona. *Transformations of Time and Temporality in Medieval and Renaissance Art*. Leiden: Brill, 2014.

Coleman, James K. "Boccaccio's Demogorgon and Renaissance Platonism." *Italian Studies* 74, no. 1 (2019): 1–9.

Considine, John. *Small Dictionaries and Curiosity: Lexicography and Fieldwork in Post-Medieval Europe*. Oxford: Oxford University Press, 2017.

Coppini, Donatella. "L'ispirazione per contagio: 'Furor' e 'remota lectio' nella poesia latina di Angelo Poliziano." In *Agnolo Poliziano: Poeta, scrittore, filologo; Atti del Convegno internazionale di studi, Montepulciano, 3–6 novembre 1994*, edited by Vincenzo Fera and Mario Martelli, 127–64. Florence: Le Lettere, 1998.

Corsaro, Antonio. "Intorno a un'ottava (ignorata) forse di Niccolò Machiavelli." *Interpres* 28 (2009): 268–74.

Cox-Rearick, Janet. "Themes of Time and Rule at Poggio a Caiano: The Portico Frieze of Lorenzo Il Magnifico." *Mitteilungen des Kunsthistorischen Institutes in Florenz* 26 (1982): 167–210.

Crescimbeni, Giovanni Mario. *L'istoria della volgar poesia*. 6 vols. Venice: Basegio, 1730–1.

Crimi, Giuseppe. "Il presto legittimato: La poesia all'improvviso." In *Festina lente: Il tempo della scrittura nella letteratura del Cinquecento*, edited by Chiara Cassiani and Maria Cristina Figorilli, 205–23. Rome: Edizioni di storia e letteratura, 2014.

Croce, Benedetto. *Conversazioni critiche*. Bari: G. Laterza and Figli, 1918.

– "Gl'improvvisatori." In *La letteratura italiana del Settecento: Note critiche*, 299–311. Bari: Laterza, 1949.

Cummings, Anthony M. "Informal Academies and Music in Pope Leo X's Rome." *Italica* 86, no. 4 (2009): 583–601.

– *The Maecenas and the Madrigalist: Patrons, Patronage, and the Origins of the Italian Madrigal*. Philadelphia: American Philosophical Society, 2004.

Curti, Elisa. *Tra due secoli: Per il tirocinio letterario di Pietro Bembo*. Bologna: Gedit Edizioni, 2006.

– "'Udii cantar improviso': Alcune osservazioni su Poliziano e la musica." In *L'attore del Parnaso: Profili di attori-musici e drammaturgie d'occasione*, edited by Francesca Bortoletti, 211–23. Milan: Mimesis, 2012.

da Correggio, Niccolò. *Opere*. Edited by Antonia Tissoni Benvenuti. Bari: Laterza, 1969.

D'Accone, Frank A. "Lorenzo the Magnificent and Music." In *Lorenzo il Magnifico e il suo mondo: Convegno internazionale di studi (Firenze, 9–13 giugno 1992)*, edited by Gian Carlo Garfagnini, 259–90. Florence: Leo S. Olschki, 1994.

Dall'Aglio, Stefano, Brian Richardson, and Massimo Rospocher, eds. *Voices and Texts in Early Modern Italian Society*. Abingdon, UK: Routledge, 2017.

Dawson, P.M.S. "Shelley and the Improvvisatore Sgricci: An Unpublished Review." *Keats-Shelley Memorial Bulletin* 32 (1981): 19–29.

de la Mare, Albinia. "The Library of F. Sassetti (1421–90)." In *Cultural Aspects of the Italian Renaissance*, edited by Cecil Clough, 160–201. Manchester: Manchester University Press, 1976.

Degl'Innocenti, Luca. *"Al suon di questa cetra": Ricerche sulla poesia orale del Rinascimento*. Florence: Società editrice fiorentina, 2016.

- "Il poeta, la viola e l'incanto: Per l'iconografia del canterino nel primo Cinquecento." *Paragone* 62, no. 93–5 (2011): 141–56.
- *I Reali dell'Altissimo: Un ciclo di cantari fra oralità e scrittura.* Florence: Società editrice fiorentina, 2008.
- "Machiavelli canterino?" *Nuova rivista di letteratura italiana* 18, no. 1 (2015): 11–67.
- "Paladini e canterini: Appunti sull'oralità nella tradizione cavalleresca italiana del Quattrocento e Cinquecento." In *Carlo Magno in Italia e la fortuna dei libri di cavalleria,* edited by Johannes Bartuschat and Franca Strologo, 301–23. Ravenna: Longo Editore, 2016.
- "Singing and Printing Chivalric Poems in Early Modern Italy." *Journal of Early Modern Studies* 7 (2018): 43–62.
- "Verba manent: Precisazioni e supplementi d'indagine sulla trascrizione dell'oralità nei cantari dell'Altissimo." *Rassegna europea di letteratura italiana* 39 (2012): 109–34.
Degl'Innocenti, Luca, Brian Richardson, and Chiara Sbordoni, eds. *Interactions Between Orality and Writing in Early Modern Italian Culture.* Abingdon, UK: Routledge, 2016.
Del Lungo, Isidoro. *Florentia: Uomini e cose del Quattrocento.* Florence: G. Barbèra, 1897.
Delcorno Branca, Daniela. "Da Poliziano a Serafino." In *Miscellanea di studi in onore di Vittore Branca,* 423–50. Florence: L.S. Olschki, 1983.
- "Il laboratorio del Poliziano: Per una lettura delle 'Rime.'" *Lettere Italiane* 29 (1987): 153–206.
Della Torre, Arnaldo. *Storia dell'Accademia Platonica di Firenze.* Florence: G. Carnesecchi, 1902.
Dempsey, Charles. *The Portrayal of Love: Botticelli's Primavera and Humanist Culture at the Time of Lorenzo the Magnificent.* Princeton, NJ: Princeton University Press, 1992.
Di Benedetto, Arnaldo. "Federico Patetta e la 'Nencia da Barberino.'" *Critica letteraria* 178 (2018): 3–8.
Di Ricco, Alessandra. *L'inutile e maraviglioso mestiere: Poeti improvvisatori di fine Settecento.* Milan: Franco Angeli, 1990.
Dionisotti, Carlo. *Gli umanisti e il volgare fra Quattro e Cinquecento.* Florence: F. Le Monnier, 1968.
Dizionario Biografico degli Italiani. Rome: Istituto della Enciclopedia Italiana, 1960.
Doni, Anton Francesco. *I Marmi.* 2 vols. Edited by E. Chiòboli. Bari: G. Laterza, 1928.
Dorez, Léon. "L'hellénisme d'Ange Politien." *Mélanges d'archéologie et d'histoire* 15 (1895): 3–32.
Esterhammer, Angela. "The Improvisation of Poetry, 1750–1850: Oral Performance, Print Culture, and the Modern Homer." In *The Oxford Handbook*

of Critical Improvisation Studies, edited by George E. Lewis and Benjamin Piekut, vol. 1, 239–54. New York: Oxford University Press, 2016.

– *Romanticism and Improvisation, 1750–1850*. New York: Cambridge University Press, 2008.

Falugiani, Fabio. "Un codice ficiniano nella tradizione manoscritta delle Argonautiche Orfiche." *Giornale italiano di filologia* 47 (1995): 155–73.

Ferrari, Evangelista, Domenico Cagnoni, and Giambattista Bodoni. *Atti della solenne coronazione fatta in Campidoglio della insigne poetessa D[on]na Maria Maddalena Morelli Fernandez, pistojese tra gli Arcadi Corilla Olimpica*. Parma: Stamperia reale di Parma, 1779.

Ferrau, Giacomo. "Il 'De hominibus doctis' di Paolo Cortesi." In *Umanità e storia: Studi in onore di Adelchi Attisani*, 261–90. Naples: Giannini, 1971.

Ficino, Marsilio. *Commentaire sur le Banquet de Platon*. Paris: Les Belles Lettres, 2002.

– *Commentaries on Plato: Phaedrus and Ion*. Edited and translated by Michael J.B. Allen. Cambridge, MA: Harvard University Press, 2008.

– *Commentary on Plato's Symposium on Love*. Translated by Sears Reynolds Jayne. Dallas: Spring Publications, 1985.

– *Lettere*. Vol. 1. Edited by Sebastiano Gentile. Florence: Olschki, 1990.

– *The Letters of Marsilio Ficino: Translated from the Latin by Members of the Language Department of the School of Economic Science, London*. 10 vols. London: Shepheard-Walwyn, 1975.

– *El libro dell'amore*. Edited by Sandra Niccoli. Florence: L.S. Olschki, 1987.

– *Marsilio Ficino and the Phaedran Charioteer: Introduction, Texts, Translations*. Edited by Michael J.B. Allen. Berkeley: University of California Press, 1981.

– *Opera omnia*. Basel, Switzerland: Henricus Petrus, 1576.

– *Supplementum ficinianum*. 2 vols. Edited by Paul Oskar Kristeller. Florence: Olschki, 1973.

Finotti, Fabio. "Il canto delle Muse: Improvvisazione e poetica della voce." In *Corilla Olimpica e la poesia del Settecento europeo*, edited by Moreno Fabbri, 31–42. Pistoia: Artout, 2002.

Flamini, Francesco. *La lirica toscana del Rinascimento anteriore ai tempi del Magnifico*. Pisa: P. Nistri, 1891.

Frati, Lodovico, ed. *Rimatori bolognesi del Quattrocento*. Bologna: Romagnoli dall'Acqua, 1908.

Fubini, Mario. *Studi sulla letteratura italiana del Rinascimento*. Florence: Sansoni, 1947.

– "I tre testi della 'Nencia da Barberino' e la questione della paternità del poemetto." In *Studi sulla letteratura del Rinascimento*, 62–125. Florence: La nuova Italia, 1971.

Galand, Perrine. "L''enargia' chez Politien." *Bibliothèque d'Humanisme et Renaissance* 49, no. 1 (1987): 25–53.

Galand-Hallyn, Perrine. *Les yeux de l'éloquence: Poétiques humanistes de l'évidence.* Orléans: Paradigme, 1995.

Gallo, F. Alberto. *Music in the Castle: Troubadours, Books, and Orators in Italian Courts of the Thirteenth, Fourteenth, and Fifteenth Centuries.* Translated by Anna Herklotz. Chicago: University of Chicago Press, 1995.

Garin, Eugenio. *Prosatori latini del Quattrocento.* Milan: Riccardo Ricciardi Editore, 1952.

Gavagni, Francesco. *L'Unico Aretino (Bernardo Accolti) e la corte dei duchi d'Urbino.* Arezzo: Cagliani, 1906.

Gentile, Sebastiano. "In margine all'epistola 'De divino furore' di Marsilio Ficino." *Rinascimento* 23 (1983): 33–77.

– "Sulle prime traduzioni dal greco di Marsilio Ficino." *Rinascimento* 30 (1990): 57–104.

Giordani, Pietro. *Opere di Pietro Giordani.* Vol. 10. Edited by Antonio Gussalli. Milan: Borroni e Scotti, 1854.

Giovio, Paolo. *Notable Men and Women of Our Time.* Edited and translated by Kenneth Gouwens. Cambridge, MA: Harvard University Press, 2013.

Giraldi, L.G. *Modern Poets.* Translated by J.N. Grant. Cambridge, MA: Harvard University Press, 2011.

Giuli, Paola. "'Monsters of Talent': Fame and Reputation of Women Improvisers in Arcadia." In *Italy's Eighteenth Century: Gender and Culture in the Age of the Grand Tour,* edited by Paula Findlen, Wendy Wassyng Roworth, and Catherine M. Sama, 303–30. Stanford, CA: Stanford University Press, 2009.

Gombrich, E.H. "Renaissance and Golden Age." *Journal of the Warburg and Courtauld Institutes* 24 (1961): 306–9.

Gorni, Guglielmo. "Su Lorenzo poeta: Parodia, diletti e noie della caccia." In *Lorenzo il Magnifico e il suo mondo: Convegno internazionale di studi (Firenze, 9–13 giugno 1992),* edited by Gian C. Garfagnini, 205–23. Florence: L.S. Olschki, 1994.

The Greek Anthology, vol. 5. Translated by W.R. Paton. Cambridge, MA: Harvard University Press, 1918.

Grigioni, Carlo. "Sedici anni della vita di Corilla Olimpica in un carteggio inedito (1776–1792)." *La Romagna* 17 (1928): 260–88.

Guarino, Raimondo. "Figures et mythes de la musique dans les spectacles de la Renaissance italienne." *Imago Musicae* 16–17 (1999): 11–24.

– "L'incoronazione di Corilla Olimpica e l'improvvisazione in Arcadia nel Settecento." *Atti e memorie dell'Arcadia* 5 (2016): 169–93.

Haar, James. *Essays on Italian Poetry and Music in the Renaissance, 1350–1600.* Berkeley: University of California Press, 1986.

– *The Science and Art of Renaissance Music.* Edited by Paul E. Corneilson. Princeton, NJ: Princeton University Press, 1998.

Hankins, James. "Cosimo De' Medici and the 'Platonic Academy.'" *Journal of the Warburg and Courtauld Institutes* 53 (1990): 144–62.

– "Humanism and Music in Italy." In *The Cambridge History of Fifteenth-Century Music*, edited by Anna Maria Busse Berger and Jesse Rodin, 231–62. Cambridge: Cambridge University Press, 2015.

– *Plato in the Italian Renaissance*. Leiden: Brill, 1990.

Haraszti, Emile. "La technique des Improvisateurs de langue vulgaire et de latin au quattrocento." *Revue belge de Musicologie / Belgisch Tijdschrift voor Muziekwetenschap* 9 (1955): 12–31.

Havelock, Eric Alfred. *Preface to Plato*. Cambridge, MA: Belknap Press, Harvard University Press, 1963.

Henry, Chriscinda. "*Alter Orpheus*: Masks of Virtuosity in Renaissance Portraits of Musical Improvisors." *Italian Studies* 71, no. 2 (2016): 238–58.

Hesiod. *Hesiod, the Homeric Hymns, and Homerica*. Translated by Hugh G. Evelyn-White. Cambridge, MA: Harvard University Press, 1914.

– *Theogony, Works and Days, Testimonia*. Edited and translated by Glenn W. Most. Cambridge, MA: Harvard University Press, 2018.

Homer. *The Odyssey of Homer, with the Hymns, Epigrams, and Battle of the Frogs and Mice*. Translated by Theodore Alois Buckley. New York: Harper and Bros., 1895.

Ianuale, Raffaella. "Prima ricognizione del manoscritto Rossiano 680 della Biblioteca Apostolica Vaticana." *Filologia e critica* 19 (1994): 275–96.

Kent, Dale. *Cosimo De' Medici and the Florentine Renaissance: The Patron's Oeuvre*. New Haven, CT: Yale University Press, 2000.

– "Michele del Giogante's House of Memory." In *Society and Individual in Renaissance Florence*, edited by William J. Connell, 110–36. Berkeley: University of California Press, 1973.

Kent, Francis W. "Lorenzo De' Medici and the Love of Women." In *Princely Citizen: Lorenzo De' Medici and Renaissance Florence*, edited by Carolyn James, 41–66. Turnhout: Brepols, 2013.

Kermode, Frank. *The Sense of an Ending: Studies in the Theory of Fiction*. Oxford: Oxford University Press, 2000.

Kristeller, Paul Oskar. *Early Florentine Woodcuts: With an Annotated List of Florentine Illustrated Books*. London: Kegan Paul, Trench, Trübner, and Co., 1897.

– "Marsilio Ficino as a Beginning Student of Plato." *Scriptorium* 20, no. 1 (1966): 41–54.

Landino, Cristoforo. *Comento sopra la Comedia*. Edited by Paolo Procaccioli. Rome: Salerno, 2001.

– *Disputationes Camaldulenses*. Edited by Peter Lohe. Florence: Sansoni, 1980.

Lecointe, Jean. *L'Idéal et la Différence: La perception de la personnalité littéraire à la Renaissance*. Geneva: Droz, 1993.

Levi, Ezio. "I cantari leggendari del popolo italiano nei secoli XIV e XV." *Giornale storico della letteratura italiana* suppl. 16 (1914): 1–159.

Liebert, Rana Saadi. "Fact and Fiction in Plato's *Ion*." *American Journal of Philology* 131, no. 2 (2010): 179–218.

Lirici toscani del Quattrocento. Vol. 1. Edited by Antonio Lanza. Rome: Bulzoni, 1973.

Lirici toscani del Quattrocento. Vol. 2. Edited by Antonio Lanza. Rome: Bulzoni, 1975.

Lord, Albert Bates. *The Singer of Tales.* Edited by Stephen A. Mitchell and Gregory Nagy. Cambridge, MA: Harvard University Press, 2000.

Luzio, Alessandro, and Rodolfo Renier. "Niccolò da Correggio." *Giornale storico della letteratura italiana* 21 (1893): 205–64.

Maïer, Ida. *Ange Politien: La formation d'un poète humaniste, 1469–1480.* Geneva: Droz, 1966.

Manfredi, Antonio. "I papi e gli umanisti: Libri, biblioteche e studi; Il concilio di Costanza tra medioevo ed età moderna." *Archivio storico lodigiano* 136, no. 2 (2017): 21–41.

Marcel, Raymond. *Marsile Ficin, 1433–1499.* Paris: Société d'édition Les belles lettres, 1958.

Martelli, Mario. "Il 'Giacoppo' di Lorenzo." *Interpres* 7 (1987): 103–24.

– "Lucrezia Tornabuoni." In *Les femmes écrivains en Italie au Moyen Âge et à la Renaissance,* 51–86. Aix-en-Provence: Université de Provence, 1994.

– *Studi laurenziani.* Florence: Leo S. Olschki, 1965.

Martinelli, Lucia Cesarini. "In margine al commento di Angelo Poliziano alle 'Selve' di Stazio." *Interpres* 1 (1978): 96–145.

– "Poliziano professore allo Studio fiorentino." In *La Toscana al tempo di Lorenzo il Magnifico: Politica, economia, cultura, arte; Convegno di studi promosso dalle Università di Firenze, Pisa e Siena: 5–8 novembre 1992,* edited by Luigi Beschi, 463–81. Pisa: Pacini editore, 1996.

Mattiacci, Silvia. "Da 'Kairos' a Occasio: Un percorso tra letteratura e iconografia." In *Il calamo della memoria: Riuso di testi e mestiere letterario nella tarda antichità,* vol. 4, edited by Lucio Cristante and Simona Ravalico, 127–54. Trieste: EUT Edizioni, 2011.

Mazzoni, Luca. "Lucrezia Tornabuoni fra Lorenzo, Poliziano e Pulci." In *Memoria poetica: Questioni filologiche e problemi di metodo,* edited by Giuseppe Alvino, Marco Berisso, and Irene Falini, 121–32. Genoa: Genova University Press, 2019.

McGee, Timothy J. "Cantare all'improvviso: Improvising to Poetry in Late Medieval Italy." In *Improvisation in the Arts of the Middle Ages and Renaissance,* edited by Timothy J. McGee, 31–70. Kalamazoo: Medieval Institute Publications, Western Michigan University, 2003.

– *The Ceremonial Musicians of Late Medieval Florence.* Bloomington: Indiana University Press, 2009.

– "Dinner Music for the Florentine Signoria, 1350–1450." *Speculum* 74, no. 1 (1999): 95–114.

Medici, Lorenzo de'. *The Complete Literary Works of Lorenzo De' Medici.* Translated by Guido A. Guarino. New York: Italica Press, 2016.

– *Opere.* Edited by Attilio Simioni. Bari: Laterza, 1913.

– *Opere.* Edited by Tiziano Zanato. Turin: G. Einaudi, 1992.

– *Selected Poems and Prose*. Edited and translated by Jon Thiem. University Park:
    Pennsylvania State University Press, 1991.
– *Stanze*. Edited by Raffaella Castagnola. Florence: L.S. Olschki, 1986.
– *Tutte le opere*. Edited by Paolo Orvieto. Rome: Salerno, 1992.
Milligan, Gerry. "Unlikely Heroines in Lucrezia Tornabuoni's 'Judith' and
    'Esther.'" *Italica* 88, no. 4 (2011): 538–64.
Miziolek, Jerzy. "*Orpheus and Eurydice*: Three *Spalliera* Panels by Jacopo Del Sellaio."
    I Tatti Studies in the Italian Renaissance 12 (2009): 117–48.
Mondino, Felicità Giulia. *Lucrezia Tornabuoni*. Turin: Tipografia Eredi Botta,
    1900.
Moore, John D. "The Dating of Plato's *Ion*." *Greek, Roman and Byzantine Studies*
    15, no. 4 (1974): 421–39.
Murphy, Stephen. *The Gift of Immortality: Myths of Power and Humanist Poetics*.
    Madison, NJ: Fairleigh Dickinson University Press, 1997.
Mussini Sacchi, Maria Pia. "Le ottave epigrammatiche di Bernardo Accolti
    nel ms. Rossiano 680: Per la storia dell'epigramma in volgare tra Quattro e
    Cinquecento." *Interpres* 15 (1995): 219–301.
Najemy, John. *A History of Florence, 1200–1575*. Oxford: Blackwell, 2008.
Naldi, Naldo. *Elegiarum libri III*. Edited by László Juhász. Leipzig: B.G. Teubner,
    1934.
Nelson, Stephanie. "Shelley and Plato's Symposium: The Poet's Revenge."
    International Journal of the Classical Tradition 14, no. 1/2 (2007): 100–29.
Notopoulos, James A. *The Platonism of Shelley: A Study of Platonism and the Poetic
    Mind*. Durham, NC: Duke University Press, 1949.
Ong, Walter J. *Orality and Literacy: The Technologizing of the Word*. New York:
    Routledge, 2005.
Orvieto, Paolo. "Angelo Poliziano 'compare' della brigata laurenziana." *Lettere
    Italiane* 25, no. 3 (1973): 301–18.
– "Boccaccio mediatore di generi o dell'allegoria dell'amore." *Interpres* 2 (1978):
    7–104.
– *Pulci medievale: Studio sulla poesia volgare fiorentina del Quattrocento*. Rome: Salerno,
    1978.
Ovid. *Metamorphoses*, vol. 2. Translated by Frank Justus Miller and G.P. Goold.
    Cambridge, MA: Harvard University Press, 1916.
Panofsky, Erwin. *Studies in Iconology: Humanistic Themes in the Art of the Renaissance*.
    Boulder, CO: Westview Press, 1972.
Parenti, Giovanni. "Corsi, Jacopo." In *Dizionario Biografico degli Italiani*, vol. 29.
    Rome: Istituto della Enciclopedia Italiana, 1983.
Parigi, Luigi. *Laurentiana: Lorenzo dei Medici cultore della musica*. Florence: L.S.
    Olschki, 1954.
Petreio. *Un commento inedito all'"Ambra" del Poliziano*. Edited by Alessandro
    Perosa. Rome: Bulzoni, 1994.

Pezzarossa, Fulvio. *I poemetti sacri di Lucrezia Tornabuoni.* Florence: L.S. Olschki, 1978.

Philippson, Paula. "Il concetto greco di tempo nelle parole aion, chronos, kairos, eniautos." *Rivista di Storia della Filosofia* 4, no. 2 (1949): 81–97.

Picone, Michelangelo, and Maria Bendinelli Predelli, eds. *I cantari: Struttura e tradizione; Atti del convegno internazionale di Montreal: 19–20 marzo 1981.* Florence: Leo S. Olschki, 1984.

Picone, Michelangelo, and Luisa Rubini, eds. *Il cantare italiano fra folklore e letteratura: Atti del convegno internazionale di Zurigo (Landesmuseum, 23–25 giugno 2005).* Florence: Olschki, 2007.

Pirrotta, Nino. "Music and Cultural Tendencies in 15th-Century Italy." *Journal of the American Musicological Society* 19 (1966): 127–61.

Pirrotta, Nino, and Elena Povoledo. *Li due Orfei: Da Poliziano a Monteverdi.* Turin: Einaudi, 1975.

– *Music and Theatre from Poliziano to Monteverdi.* Translated by Karen Eales. Cambridge: Cambridge University Press, 1981.

Plato. *The Dialogues of Plato.* Vol. 3, *Ion, Hippias Minor, Laches, Protagoras.* Translated by R.E. Allen. New Haven, CT: Yale University Press, 1996.

– *Euthyphro, Apology, Crito, Phaedo, Phaedrus.* Translated by H.N. Fowler. New York: G.P. Putnam's Sons, 1919.

– *Ion.* Translated by W.R.M. Lamb. New York: G.P. Putnam's Sons, 1925.

– *Plato on Poetry.* Edited by Penelope Murray. Cambridge: Cambridge University Press, 1996.

– *The Statesman, Philebus, Ion.* Translated by Harold N. Fowler and W.R.M. Lamb. New York: G.P. Putnam's Sons, 1925.

Plett, Heinrich F. *Enargeia in Classical Antiquity and the Early Modern Age: The Aesthetics of Evidence.* Leiden: Brill, 2012.

Pliny. *Natural History in Ten Volumes.* Translated by H. Rackham. Cambridge, MA: Harvard University Press, 1967.

Poliziano, Angelo. *Commento inedito alle "Selve" di Stazio.* Edited by Lucia Cesarini Martinelli. Florence: Sansoni, 1978.

– *Detti piacevoli.* Edited by Tiziano Zanato. Rome: Istituto della Enciclopedia Italiana, 1983.

– *Opera omnia.* Venice: Aldo Manuzio, 1498.

– *Opera omnia.* Basel, Switzerland: Nicolaus Episcopus, 1553.

– *Oratio in expositione Homeri.* Edited by Paola Megna. Rome: Edizioni di storia e letteratura, 2007.

– *Poesie.* Edited by Francesco Bausi. Turin: UTET, 2006.

– *Praelectiones 2.* Edited by Giorgia Zollino. Florence: L.S. Olschki, 2016.

– *Prose volgari inedite e poesie latine e greche edite e inedite.* Edited by Isidoro Del Lungo. Florence: Barbera, 1867.

– *Rime.* Edited by Daniela Delcorno Branca. Venice: Marsilio Editori, 1990.

– *Silvae*. Translated by Charles Fantazzi. Cambridge, MA: Harvard University Press, 2004.

Prizer, William F. "Una 'Virtù Molto Conveniente a Madonne': Isabella D'Este as a Musician." *Journal of Musicology* 17, no. 1 (1999): 10–49.

Pulci, Luigi. *Lettere di Luigi Pulci a Lorenzo il Magnifico e ad altri*. Lucca: Giusti, 1886.

– *Morgante: The Epic Adventures of Orlando and His Giant Friend Morgante*. Translated by Joseph Tusiani. Bloomington: Indiana University Press, 1998.

– *Morgante e lettere*. Edited by Domenico De Robertis. Florence: Sansoni, 1962.

– *Opere minori*. Edited by Paolo Orvieto. Milan: Mursia, 1986.

Pyle, Cynthia Munro. "Il tema di Orfeo, la musica e le favole mitologiche del tardo Quattrocento." In *Ecumenismo della cultura*, vol. 2, edited by Giovannangiola Tarugi, 121–39. Florence: L.S. Olschki, 1981.

Quintilian. *The Orator's Education*. Edited and translated by Donald A. Russell. 5 vols. Cambridge, MA: Harvard University Press, 2002.

Reeser, Todd W. *Setting Plato Straight: Translating Ancient Sexuality in the Renaissance*. Chicago: University of Chicago Press, 2016.

Reynolds, L.D., and Peter K. Marshall. *Texts and Transmission: A Survey of the Latin Classics*. Oxford: Clarendon Press, 1983.

Richardson, Brian. "Improvising Lyric Verse in the Renaissance: Contexts, Sources and Imitation." In *Cultural Reception, Translation and Transformation from Medieval to Modern Italy: Essays in Honour of Martin McLaughlin*, edited by Guido Bonsaver, Brian Richardson, and Giuseppe Stellardi, 97–116. Cambridge: Legenda, 2017.

– *Manuscript Culture in Renaissance Italy*. Cambridge: Cambridge University Press, 2009.

Rijksbaron, Albert. *Plato: Ion*. Amsterdam Studies in Classical Philology. Leiden: Brill, 2007.

Robichaud, Denis J.-J. "Angelo Poliziano's *Lamia*: Neoplatonic Commentaries and the Plotinian Dichotomy Between the Philologist and the Philosopher." In *Angelo Poliziano's Lamia: Text, Translation, and Introductory Studies*, edited by Christopher S. Celenza, 131–89. Leiden: Brill, 2010.

Romei, Danilo. "Dalla Toscana a Roma: Pietro Aretino 'erede' di Bernardo Accolti." In *Pietro Aretino nel cinquecentenario della nascita*, 179–95. Rome: Salerno, 1995.

Rospocher, Massimo, and Rosa Salzberg. "An Evanescent Public Sphere: Voices, Spaces, and Publics in Venice During the Italian Wars." In *Beyond the Public Sphere: Opinions, Publics, Spaces in Early Modern Europe*, edited by Massimo Rospocher, 93–114. Bologna: Il Mulino, 2012.

Rubenstein, Alice Levine. "The Notes to Poliziano's 'Iliad.'" *Italia medioevale e umanistica* 25 (1982): 205–39.

Salzberg, Rosa, and Massimo Rospocher. "Street Singers in Italian Renaissance Urban Culture and Communication." *Cultural and Social History* 9 (2015): 9–26.

Sarath, Ed. "A Consciousness-Based Look at Spontaneous Creativity." In *The Oxford Handbook of Critical Improvisation Studies*, edited by George E. Lewis and Benjamin Piekut, vol. 2, 132–52. Oxford: Oxford University Press, 2016.

Scavizzi, Giuseppe. "The Myth of Orpheus in Italian Renaissance Art, 1400–1600." In *Orpheus, the Metamorphoses of a Myth*, edited by John Warden, 111–61. Toronto: University of Toronto Press, 1982.

Shelley, Percy Bysshe. *Relics of Shelley*. Edited by Richard Garnett. London: Edward Moxon, 1862.

– *Selected Prose Works of Shelley*. London: Watts and Co., 1915.

Sipiora, Phillip, and James S. Baumlin. *Rhetoric and* Kairos: *Essays in History, Theory, and Praxis*. Albany: State University of New York Press, 2002.

Statius. *Silvae*. Translated by D.R. Shackleton Bailey. Cambridge, MA: Harvard University Press, 2003.

Stewart, A.F. "Lysippan Studies: 1. The Only Creator of Beauty." *American Journal of Archaeology* 82, no. 2 (1978): 163–71.

Strozzi, Beatrice Paolozzi, and Erkinger Schwarzenberg. "Un Kairos mediceo." *Mitteilungen des Kunsthistorischen Institutes in Florenz* 35, no. 2/3 (1991): 307–16.

Testa, Enrico. *Simulazione di parlato: Fenomeni dell'oralità nelle novelle del Quattro-Cinquecento*. Florence: Accademia della Crusca, 1991.

Tigerstedt, E.N. "Plato's Idea of Poetical Inspiration." *Commentationes Humanarum Litterarum (Societas Scientiarum Fennica)* 44, no. 2 (1969): 1–76.

– "The Poet as Creator: Origins of a Metaphor." *Comparative Literature Studies* 4 (1968): 455–88.

Tissoni Benvenuti, Antonia. *L'Orfeo del Poliziano: Con il testo critico dell'originale e delle successive forme teatrali*. Padua: Editrice Antenore, 1986.

– "La ricezione delle *Silvae* di Stazio e la poesia all'improvviso nel Rinascimento." In *Gli antichi e i moderni: Studi in onore di Roberto Cardini*, edited by L. Bertolini and Donatella Coppini, 1283–324. Florence: Polistampa, 2010.

Toppani, Innocente. "Poliziano e Omero." In *Studi triestini di antichità in onore di Luigia Achillea Stella*, 470–80. Trieste: Università degli studi di Trieste, 1975.

Tornabuoni de' Medici, Lucrezia. *La istoria della casta Susanna*. Edited by Paolo Orvieto. Bergamo: Moretti and Vitali, 1992.

– *Sacred Narratives*. Edited and translated by Jane Tylus. Chicago: University of Chicago Press, 2001.

Toscano, Giovanni Matteo. *Peplus Italiae*. Paris: Morelli, 1578.

Trinkaus, Charles. "The Unknown Quattrocento Poetics of Bartolommeo Della Fonte." *Studies in the Renaissance* 13 (1966): 40–95.

Tripodi, Claudia. "Guglielmo de' Pazzi." In *Dizionario Biografico degli Italiani*, vol. 82. Rome: Istituto della Enciclopedia Italiana, 2015.

Unglaub, Jonathan. "Bernardo Accolti, Raphael, and the Sistine Madonna: The Poetics of Desire and Pictorial Generation." In *Ut Pictura Amor: The Reflexive*

Imagery of Love in Artistic Theory and Practice, 1500–1700, edited by Walter S. Melion, Joanna Woodall, and Michael Zell, 612–45. Leiden: Brill, 2017.

– "Bernardo Accolti, Raphael's 'Parnassus' and a New Portrait by Andrea Del Sarto." *Burlington Magazine* 149, no. 1246 (2007): 14–22.

Valori, Niccolò. *Laurentii Medicei vita a Nicolao Valorio scripta ex cod. Mediceo Laurentiano nunc primum latine in lucem eruta.* Edited by Lorenzo Mehus. Florence: Giovannelli, 1749.

Ventrone, Paola. "'Civic Performance' in Renaissance Florence." In *Voices and Texts in Early Modern Italian Society*, edited by Stefano Dall'Aglio, Brian Richardson, and Massimo Rospocher, 153–69. New York: Routledge, 2017.

– *Gli araldi della commedia: Teatro a Firenze nel Rinascimento.* Pisa: Pacine, 1993.

Verde, Armando F., and Raffaella Maria Zaccaria. *Lo studio fiorentino, 1473–1503: Ricerche e documenti.* 8 vols. Florence: L.S. Olschki, 1973.

Verino, Ugolino. *Carlias: Ein Epos Des 15. Jahrhunderts.* Munich: Fink, 1995.

– *Flametta.* Edited by Luciano Mencaraglia. Florence: L.S. Olschki, 1940.

Versari, Pier Francesco. "Dialogo Pastorale." In *I giuochi olimpici celebrati in Arcadia nell'ingresso dell'olimpiade DCXXXIII: In onore degli Arcadi illustri defunti,* 47–51. Rome: Monaldini, 1754.

Vian, Francis. "Leodrisio Crivelli traducteur des Argonautiques orphiques." *Revue d'histoire des textes* 16, no. 1986 (1988): 63–82.

Villoresi, Marco. "Panoramica sui poeti performativi d'età laurenziana." *Rassegna europea di letteratura italiana* 34 (2009): 11–33.

– *La voce e le parole: Studi sulla letteratura del Medioevo e del Rinascimento.* Florence: Società editrice fiorentina, 2016.

– "Zanobi della Barba, canterino ed editore del Rinascimento." In *Il cantare italiano fra folklore e letteratura: Atti del Convegno internazionale di Zurigo (Landesmuseum, 23–25 giugno 2005)*, edited by Michelangelo Picone and Luisa Rubini, 461–73. Florence: Olschki, 2007.

Virgil. *Eclogues, Georgics, Aeneid 1–6.* Translated by H. Rushton Fairclough and G.P. Goold. Cambridge, MA: Harvard University Press, 1999.

Voss, Angela. "Orpheus redivivus: The Musical Magic of Marsilio Ficino." In *Marsilio Ficino: His Theology, His Philosophy, His Legacy*, edited by Michael J.B. Allen, Valery Rees, and Martin Davies, 227–41. Leiden: Brill, 2002.

Walker, D.P. *The Ancient Theology: Studies in Christian Platonism from the Fifteenth to the Eighteenth Century.* London: Duckworth, 1972.

– "Orpheus the Theologian and Renaissance Platonists." *Journal of the Warburg and Courtauld Institutes* 16 (1953): 100–20.

– *Spiritual and Demonic Magic: From Ficino to Campanella.* Notre Dame, IN: University of Notre Dame Press, 1975.

Walter, Ingeborg. *Lorenzo il Magnifico e il suo tempo.* Translated by Roberto Zapperi. Rome: Donzelli Editore, 2005.

Waquet, Françoise. *Rhétorique et poétique chrétiennes: Bernardino Perfetti et la poésie improvisée dans l'Italie du XVIIIe siècle.* Florence: L.S. Olschki, 1992.

Warden, John. "Orpheus and Ficino." In *Orpheus, the Metamorphoses of a Myth,* edited by John Warden, 85–110. Toronto: University of Toronto Press, 1982.

Welch, Anthony. *The Renaissance Epic and the Oral Past.* New Haven, CT: Yale University Press, 2012.

Whitehead, James. *Madness and the Romantic Poet: A Critical History.* Oxford: Oxford University Press, 2017.

Wilson, Blake. "The Cantastorie/Canterino/Cantimbanco as Musician." *Italian Studies* 71 (2016): 154–70.

– "*Canterino* and *Improvvisatore*: Oral Poetry and Performance." In *The Cambridge History of Fifteenth-Century Music,* edited by Anna Maria Busse Berger and Jesse Rodin, 292–310. Cambridge: Cambridge University Press, 2015.

– "Dominion of the Ear: Singing the Vernacular in Piazza San Martino." *I Tatti Studies in the Italian Renaissance* 16 (2013): 273–87.

– *Singing to the Lyre in Renaissance Italy: Memory, Performance, and Oral Poetry.* Cambridge: Cambridge University Press, 2019.

– "Sound Patrons: The Medici and Florentine Musical Life." In *The Medici: Citizens and Masters,* edited by Robert Black and John Law, 267–80. Cambridge, MA: Harvard University Press, 2015.

Wilson, N.G. *From Byzantium to Italy: Greek Studies in the Italian Renaissance.* London: Bloomsbury Academic, 2017.

Woods, Marjorie Curry. *Weeping for Dido: The Classics in the Medieval Classroom.* Princeton, NJ: Princeton University Press, 2019.

Zaccarello, Michelangelo. "The *Tenzone* Between Matteo Franco and Luigi Pulci in the Context of Renaissance *Vituperium*: Notes on Language and Intertextuality." In *Luigi Pulci in Renaissance Florence and Beyond,* edited by James K. Coleman and Andrea Moudarres, 51–72. Turnhout: Brepols, 2017.

Zannoni, Giovanni. "Strambotti inediti del cod. Vat. Urb. 729." *Rendiconti dell'Accademia Nazionale dei Lincei, Ser. 5* 1 (1892): 371–87, 626.

Zumthor, Paul. *Oral Poetry: An Introduction.* Translated by Kathryn Murphy-Judy. Minneapolis: University of Minnesota Press, 1990.

Index